A STOCKPORT TRILOGY

AN ACCOUNT IN THREE PARTS OF LIFE
IN THE FIRST HALF OF THE 20TH CENTURY

KENNETH GIBBONS

AuthorHouse™ UK
1663 Liberty Drive
Bloomington, IN 47403 USA
www.authorhouse.co.uk
Phone: 0800.197.4150

Published by AuthorHouse 10/14/2015

ISBN: 978-1-4817-6968-6 (sc)

Image on page 58, "Stainless Stephen," courtesy of Imperial Tabaco Company

Print information available on the last page.

authorHOUSE°

Why did I write this book?

About ten years ago, I came across a manuscript written by dad. I think it was as much for something to do rather than to exorcise any demons. Unfortunately, he died before it was published and was forgotten. After my older brother Terry died, my sisters Ann and Carol were clearing out his flat and disposing of his belongings only to discover a large battered brown suitcase containing about 300 letters written by our dad to mam. Carol took them home and after some time took on the unenviable task of collating them as best she could. Purely by chance, I was saying to Carol that dad's manuscript needed rewriting as it was as shame not to get it published. The problem was how to go about it? Then Carol told me about the letters. This revelation set the grey matter in motion. Here was a perfect opportunity to put something together incorporating dad's letters, eighty-year-old 'Box Brownie' photographs and many anecdotes. As I delved deeper into the subject, I had to include newspaper cuttings and quotes from Neville Chamberlain and Winston Churchill, entries from the school log, and a myriad of other sources.

The most arduous task was putting all these bits of information in some kind of readable order. I decided the best thing to do would be to start at the beginning. However, as I progressed, the book seemed to develop into a three part social history of the life and times of ordinary Stopfordians in the first half of the 20th century. With 113,095 words and 50 illustrations, I think I have done dad proud. I hope you find it interesting.

Kenneth Gibbons.

I would like to acknowledge the kind co-operation of the following people in no particular order.

Dad's sister Helena Lally nee Gibbons.

The Stockport Express.

The Stockport central Library

The Great Moor library.

Great Moor Junior School.

John/Tara at Mill cottages.

Mrs Edith McAndrew 43 Alldis Street.

Stockport County archives [gogocounty.org]

The Beamish Museum county Durham.

Tameside Heritage Museum Portland basin.

Stockport Heritage St Mary's Church Marketplace Stockport.

Vernon park Museum.

Llandudno Museum of WW11.

David Sankey Blueyonder.co.uk

Winton Community Forum

Frederic Robinson.

Brian Walton 16 Bredbury green.

The World Wide Web. And You Tube.

This book is not a work of fiction, all the characters, locations, photographs and stories are real. Because the wartime stories are real, there are a number swear words but that's the way things were. There are 50 illustration of one kind or another in this book. I could have included a couple of hundred but it would be too expensive. However, I think the individual reader can often paint better pictures in their own minds.

Kenneth Gibbons.

A STOCKPORT TRILOGY
BY KENNETH GIBBONS

This is the story of my early childhood inspired by hundreds of recently discovered wartime letters written by dad to our mam. Using passages from dad's manuscript for his book "I had an ordinary war" [never published]. Photographs, extracts from Greatmoor Council School's log, written almost daily from 1933 to the present day. There are full pages from the school log to match the entries in this book and can be seen at the back of the book along with many more pages to help you understand what school was really like during those very difficult times. However, I only refer to school log entries written during the war years. I have tried to include as many of my own childhood memories chronicling the enforced frugality of living a life of poverty and hardship, as was the lot of most people during that time.

TABLE OF CONTENTS

PART ONE

1925 SWEET 14

Mam and dad left school in 1925, mam in the summer, being about six months older than dad, and dad would have left at Christmas, both at the tender age of 14. As two poor naive innocent kids, with only a rudimentary education, they found themselves working in a rope making mill, known as 'The roperey' on Water street down at the bottom of Marsland Street Portwood smack bang in the middle of dirty mills, grime and poverty. Suddenly becoming grown up and enjoying their newfound freedom. As the weather became a little warmer, mam and her new pals would sit on the bank by the river Etherow and have a little picnic as it meandered behind the mill. Dad and his pals would have a kick-about and show off in front of the girls with a tatty leather football.

This new beginning offered all manner of new experiences, with the school discipline soon forgotten, particularly for dad as he went to a Catholic school, probably St Mary's on Dodge Hill just off Lancashire hill, and very strict it was too. Looking forward to their first pay packet on Friday afternoon and wanting to buy everything in the world, they soon came down to earth as they realised that this newfound freedom came at a price. As with most kids at that time, they were expected to give up the lion's share of their meagre wages to add to the family coffers. I can imagine them being so proud as they handed in their very first wage packet to their respective mams, but alas, the only thing that was bursting, was their chests with such pride. The wage packet was far from bursting, as two half-crowns and a few coppers did not make too much of a bulge. I think dad would have got a few coppers more, as equal pay was a long way in the future. Nevertheless, their pride was soon restored as they realised that they were making a real contribution for the good of the family in order to enjoy the occasional luxury. A joint of proper beef for Sunday dinner instead of brisket, tongue, or heart. New oilcloth in the front room or net curtains to show off to the neighbours. Mam received the grand sum of sixpence to spend for her week of toil in that dirty mill. Nevertheless, at fourteen, each in their own way were happy. They did not know each other before they went to work at the 'ropery'. Dad lived up Dodge hill, with two brothers Bert, and Charlie, and sister Lena, Helena on Sundays of course. Mam lived at 27 Marsland Street in Portwood, with her three sisters Frances, Ruth and Hilda. Mam, and probably her sisters went to the local school on Emperor street. They were just beginning to forget the hardships of the war to end all wars. Both being born in 1911, they, like me, Ann and Terry, had little recollection of *their* war. Mam's father was gassed and suffered shrapnel wounds to his stomach as he fought in the trenches of a foreign land with names now chiselled into history. Passchendaele, Ypres, the Somme. Dad's father too, did his duty for King and country; he served in the Royal Marines from 1904 until 1922, leaving with honours after eighteen years' service. One newfound freedom for mam and dad were the opposite sex! Each in their own way made their first shy glances as they passed each other on the ropewalk where the rope was twisted to form the rope. The memory of those shy glances through a tiny hatch in that dark dirty mill were to last forever. Mam lived round the corner and would dash home, or hang back, to avoid that lad seeing she lived in a little terraced house in that coal dusty back street. Just think, sweet fourteen, no money to speak of, lousy prospects, but not a care in the world. However, nothing stays the same. Those first fleeting glances and shy smiles at each other through that never to be forgotten hatch, were all to short lived. After a few months of dead end drudgery, and with the sun doing its best to shine through those grubby windows, dad wanted to find pastures new in an effort to better himself. He wanted to leave that dirty rope works, and get out into the fresh air. The only way to do that, much to mam's disappointment as she had really taken a shine to that tall slender fair-haired boy with no name. Moreover, I am sure dad too, took a shine to that slim shy girl with no name, just a happy smile. He grabbed the opportunity to be a plasterer's apprentice, even though the pay was only a little better he was determined to learn a trade and get out of the poverty trap and the feeling of suffocation in that dirty mill, day in and day out. After leaving the Ropery, and getting on with his apprenticeship throughout his teens, dad would sometimes think of that slender dark haired girl from the Ropery, and wondered if she still worked there. However, as the spring began to spring, and the trees in Vernon Park were beginning to blossom, mam too, was fed up with the dirt and grime of that horrible place and left soon after dad. What a mistake that was, her father was furious because she had not found another job to go to. He said if you were so fed-up with the place why didn't you get fixed up somewhere else first. Two days later, she started work at Meadow mill. Even though she made new friends there, she was very unhappy and felt very alone. Every morning as she passed Kershaw's Tannery and round the corner by the ropery to walk round to Meadow Mill she would hope against hope that that lad might be back at the Ropery, but it was no use. She missed that fair-haired boy so much she found it impossible to stay at Meadow mill. She tried what seemed like a cleaner job packing at the Cocoa works on Coronation Street just over Park Bridge near the gas works. She did not stay very long as all the girls had to stamp their feet every morning to scare away the rats that lived along the river banks below. However mam did not learn from experience as the rats were very fond of the chocolate in Faulder's mill just the same. The river Mersey was little better than an open sewer.

MOVING ON

Mam with her pals, and dad with his pals, by now a few years older and only a little wiser, wandered around Stockport town centre on Saturday afternoons, especially Prince's street. It used to be called Heaton Lane until it was renamed in honour of the Prince and Princess of Wales the (son of Edward VII.) on the occasion of their visit to open the Town Hall in 1908.

Mam and dad, each in their own little world would hang around Woollies, Nield and Hardy's, and Sheargolds record shops on Saturday afternoons. Those record shops were an irresistible magnet to young teenagers just as they are today. I am sure none of them could afford to buy any records, even at only a few pennies each, or even a record player to play them on. A price tag of 39/6^d for the cheapest model being about four to five weeks wages at that time was not something within their reach, but they had a lot of fun listening to the latest records of the day. With magical labels such as Brunswick and Victor, and singers, or crooners as was the modern parlance. The wonderful voice of the Great Caruso was always a treat for the girls to hear as well as Bing Crosby and many more. With little more than pennies in her pocket to spend, the market place was a popular meeting place. Mam and her lifelong friend 'Margaret' would wander round the market stalls and perhaps cadge an over-ripe apple from a friendly fruiterer. The only fast food in those days would be a bag of chips with a few scraps of batter that had fallen from the fish during frying, popularly known as "a penny lap up". Maybe a penny worth of black peas or hot chestnuts on a cold wintery day. Sarsaparilla or a penny lick of ice cream in the summer would be a real treat. They would save thrupence for the pictures during the week hoping to see a talking picture, but that could be as much as tuppence extra. It did not matter what was showing, it was the wonder of people actually talking to them from the silver screen. Laurel and hardy were a great favourite even though most of their films were silent at that time. The few coppers they had left had to last 'til next payday. This Saturday afternoon outing was known as 'the monkey run', I tried to find out why it was so called, but no one seems to know exactly why. I can only give you my version of how it came to be. It was, and still is, a kind of working class debutante's coming out parade, but with no real structure. When the weather was nice, the boys and girls would promenade up and down Prince's Street and the market place in their Sunday best, more in hope than expectation of seeing a boy or girl they liked. It was during these Saturday parades that mam and dad's paths would cross but shyness always prevailed between them as they were not ready for such adventures. Nevertheless, those brief encounters would soon become fewer and far between during their teenage years. It was about this time, early 1932 that dads father had a very nasty accident. It is quite ironic, as he served in the Royal Marines all over the world for years without a scratch, only to lose a leg whilst working on the construction of the Goyt valley reservoir.

A pile of logs, rolled down an embankment crushing both legs. Because of gangrene brought about by bad hospital practise, his right leg had to be amputated mid-thigh, his left leg, though badly damaged was saved but needed lots of treatment and physiotherapy followed by many months of rehabilitation and months off work. The prosthetic leg of the day was a padded cover for his stump, holding a crude imitation of a leg. It was made of Papier mashe and painted bright pink. Once on his feet, or should it be foot, he tried a succession of mind numbing jobs, made worse because he had been so active, and found it very frustrating and difficult to cope. With a family to support, he could see the few hundred pounds accident compensation dwindling with each passing week. He had little choice but to make his own way in the world. In late 1932, with the blessing of his family, he bought a little grocery/hardware shop on the corner of Lord Street and Norbury Street Portwood. The shop was big enough to accommodate all the family. There was a back parlour and four bedrooms so they all moved from Greenbank terrace to the shop. Dad was expected to help in the shop on odd weekends, unpaid of course until things started to pick up. Mam at that time knew nothing of the accident or the shop on Norbury Street. She began to think that that lad from the ropery had found someone else to be his girlfriend. However, all was not lost, when it rained Woolworth's and Nield and Hardy's record shop were amongst the few stores where the 'debutantes' could go to be out of the rain without actually buying anything. It made it more likely that the boys and girls would see each other. You see, love usually finds a way. Of course, they were all growing up by now. With their teens behind them, dad looked forward to Saturday afternoons and Stockport County's home matches. A shilling to get in and a penny for a programme. By this time dad had more or less completed his apprenticeship of something like five years. After all his hard work, he earned the title of 'Journeyman plasterer'. Luckily for mam, even though he could afford the 1/- entry fee, he could not always spare the time to go to many away matches as he had been trying to start his own plastering business. His beloved Stockport County had to take a back seat from time to time. However, if he saved enough money and had the time, maybe Rochdale or Oldham were within his budget. Even then he had to choose if he spent 1/9^d on train fare on top of his 1/- entry ticket and a penny for a programme. He wanted to save a few shillings for a pint with his mates in the evening. Sometimes County would put on a "sharra-bang" trip to an away match for about half a crown all in, depending on where they were playing. In the winter, he often had the time but not the money, added to that; he did not want to risk paying out his money just in case the weather caused the match to be postponed. However, their lives did not just revolve around Prince's Street and the market. Dad with his work during the week and football on Saturday afternoon, and a pint with his pals, often made it less likely that he would see that girl from the Ropery. Throughout her teens, mam had a number of factory jobs and made lots of friends. After all week in the stifling confines of a grimy airless mill, mam with her lifelong friend Margaret Cragg would go rambling during the summer months. Places like Buxton, Kinder Scout, New Mills and Edale. Not very exiting I know, but if all you wanted, was some clean air in your lungs, that was as good a place to be. They would, more often than not, stay home on Saturday night and hope the weather was nice on Sunday. With a jam butty and a bottle of water, sometimes pop as a special treat, they would walk many a mile if the weather was nice rather than spend it on bus or train fares. If they did not go to the pictures on Saturday and saved some money on bus or tram fare on Sunday, they could always go the Brinksway Pictorium or the Gem. "Now with sound." during the week for 3ᵈ or 4ᵈ. It was a treat to look forward to.

Dad had a few girlfriends during his teenage years but none could compare with that dark haired girl he used to see from time to time. One wet afternoon in Woollies, a fleeting glance, made him realise that that shy girl he first saw at the ropery all that time ago was still in his heart. The more he saw her the more he realised he was becoming more than smitten with that dark haired girl with no name. He found out from one of his mates her name was Mary, a name that pleased him no end. He decided to make more of an effort to get to know Mary. He would wander around Prince's Street and the market place with his mates, hoping to see her, by accident of course, and hoping to pluck up enough courage to ask her out. Mam said, after they were courting proper, even though she was teased mercilessly, said she would ask the men at work if County were playing at home or away. If they were playing at Blackpool or Chester, she felt sure he would not want to spend so much for one afternoon of football, and would most likely be around town. Likewise, dad too, would have a walk round the market, and promenade up and down Prince's Street. When mam and her pals, met dad and his pals there was the usual shy flirting. The boys would swank in front of the girls that they were going for a pint later that evening and wanted some of the girls to go with them. Dad was too shy to ask mam out on a proper date, you know, just the two of 'em. Mam and her sisters were brought up by a very strict Victorian father. Her mother was, as I imagine, just like any other matriarch at that time. Mam would be in big trouble if her dad knew she had been in a pub, particularly in and around Portwood and the market place with a bunch of lads. Most lads felt that they had not had a good night without punch-up somewhere. Eventually, dad did pluck up the courage to ask mam if she would like to go to the pictures. She jumped at the chance, a rare treat in the poverty of her sheltered life. Being a first proper date for both of them, dad now earning a bit more money each week, decided to take mam to the brand new pictures on Mersey square called the Plaza. One of nine new picture palaces built in and around Stockport during the 'thirties. The Plaza with its beautiful art deco design in heavy plaster and bold colours was always a special treat for them, particularly as dad was a skilled plasterer by this time. Of course, the Ritz, and Carlton, were equally grand, and were soon added to their list of favourites. Dad in his best suit, mam in her best frock, 7ᵈ in the best seats and a bag of chips on the way home and a goodnight kiss, marvellous! Mam's father, though very strict, was the kindest and most loving father anyone could ever wish to have. Nevertheless, one Saturday afternoon, he caught mam trying to rub a bit of red dye on her lips. A dye gleaned by rubbing a spit-upon finger on some cheap artificial red roses on the sideboard. He said why do you want to rub that muck on your face. She said she wanted to look her best for this lad. What lad, he bawled. She said he was a very respectable lad with a proper trade, and was starting his own business. Nevertheless, her dad was not very impressed so she had to stay home that day and help with the housework. Her dad was so Victorian; he 'whitewashed' all the mirrors around the house in case mam and her sisters Frances, Hilda, and Ruth were getting a little too vain. They too were beginning to look at boys and wanted to know all about mam's boyfriend, now with a name. Bill.

A SECOND CHANCE

The weather was often too cold to hang around town in the winter, but as spring began to spring, one morning in May 1933, dad did pluck up the courage to ask mam once again if she would like to go to the pictures. It had been quite a few months since the episode with the red dye on her lips; she thought that her dad would treat her a little more like the young woman she was growing into. She jumped at the chance, but not so obvious that it was noticeable. This was indeed a rare treat, little knowing that this second date was to be the beginning a love to last for over 50 years. Dad too, being happy to have a second chance, decided to take mam to the Plaza again. Dad in his Sunday suit, mam in her best frock, 7 ^{d} for the best seats, a bag of chips on the way home, their second goodnight kiss sealed their feelings for each other, as there was nothing more to do, but to fall in love. They could not see each other during the week unless they arranged things in advance, as neither of them had a 'phone. But they did manage now and again to go to the cheaper pictures, such as the Jem, the Star, the Kings, or the Brinksway, it was only 3^d or 4^d for a couple of hours cuddle on the back row. Mam, not being allowed to drink or even go in a public house meant that their outings were limited to the pictures, or a stroll on a warm Sunday afternoon along Carrington road and into Vernon park and sit by the band stand to listen to the Salvation army concerts. Now and again bands from neighbouring towns were invited to play in the park. When the bands finished playing, mam and dad would take the longer walk round by the Aviary and the flowerbeds, then into Woodbank for a stroll then back home in time for tea. The weather and finances often dictated when and where they saw each other. However, if dad had a job that was a good earner they could manage a trip or two to the seaside. Ainsdale was always a firm favourite, as you can see in the photograph of mam and dad taken in the summer of 1933.

Mam was not particularly religious, just a kind and loving person. On some Sunday mornings, they would go to St Joseph's Roman Catholic Church on St Petersgate, dad being a Catholic felt it was his duty, and as mam was falling in love, felt it was something she wanted to share with him. Mam's walks, or rambles, with her friend Margaret were all too infrequent as new opportunities and new directions presented themselves. However, when Mam's father heard about those new-fangled sunray lamps in the foyer of that posh picture 'ouse, he put a stop to what he called their shenanigans for a while. (The lamps were "Neron Vitalux." and were quite harmless.) He said that lad you are walking out with is a bad influence, and was trying to be like one of those bloody film stars, and that was that. Nevertheless, the lure of film stars such as Rudolph Valentino, Cary

Grant, Margaret Lockwood Anna Neagle, and not being able to see Bill, made mam's life a misery. Nevertheless, after tears and protestations, even her strict Victorian father could not keep them apart for very long as he realised what they meant to each other. In the late spring and summer of 1933, their friendship blossomed into a real love for each other, a love that lasted until the day mam died, and beyond.

After a suitable period of courting, dad managed to pluck up enough courage to say to mam, *"Shall we get married"*. Mam said, *"If you want to"*. (It really happened like that.) Everyone was thrilled to bits and like any bride to be, mam wanted a 'bottom draw', but incredible as it may seem, mam's spends at that time were 1/- a week, heaven knows how she managed. The only way to earn a bit more money was to apply for a job at the notoriously dirty but well paid wire works in Portwood. Dad too had to cut back on the number of County games he went to watch. The game against Halifax on January the 6ᵗʰ 1934 was indeed a real shame to miss. It was the match when County won by the biggest margin ever, 13-0.

With an extra half a crown a week, mam asked if she could keep a little extra money to buy a few bits and pieces for her 'bottom draw', and got the princely sum of 1/6 a week extra. This grand gesture brought her spends up to 2/6ᵈ a week; it seemed like a fortune at that time. She would walk around the market on Saturday afternoons in a 'girly group' with her friend Margaret and often one of her sisters looking for bargains and bits and pieces. Sam's stall was a mecca for the bargain hunters. One could buy a sixpenny or even a shillin' bundle of seconds, such as a tea towel, hand towel, and maybe a bed sheet, and few remnants to make up a dress.

It was about this time, only a few months into his dad's shop-keeping venture, because of failing business and not being able to get about as well as he had hoped, his dad decided to sell the shop. They moved into the mount, a house on Dodge Hill nearby. Even though they had lots of bills to pay, the sale of the shop put them back on the straight and narrow. There was still a bit of the compensation money left so they were able to help with the wedding expenses and even bought them a brown Rexine three-piece suite.

With a posh white silk wedding frock bought as a gift by her sisters, a bouquet of pink roses, and white gloves to cover her course hands because of working at the 'Wire works'. Dad in a 30/- suit from "Weaver to Wearer', *his* dad's white gloves that were once part of his Royal Marine dress uniform; They were married on 7ᵗʰ April 1934 at St Joseph's Roman Catholic Church on St. Petersgate Stockport.

The reception was at Crossley's cafe in the market place. They moved into five Mount Pleasant on Marple road just past Bean Leach Offerton.

A week following their wedding, the 'NEW PALADIUM' was showing a Laurel and Hardy comedy film, followed by the main feature "Hold your Man" with Jean Harlow and Clark Gable. It was described as 'A really gripping production, both intensely dramatic and romantic. A film for adults only. Little did they know that they were soon to be embroiled in a worldwide drama not just for adults, but children too? The 'gripping drama' that week was for six nights only. However, the drama of war, soon to be upon us was for 2,194 nights and days.

LIFE GOES ON

With few possessions and lots of hope for the future they began to build a new life for themselves. As they were both working, and mam could now keep *all* her wages, they could afford the few shillings a week to buy some furniture from shops such as Riding's, and New Day on Hillgate. A front room carpet for 1/6d a week, and luxury of all luxuries, a brand new double bed. As usual, friends and relations chipped in with gifts of a table, a couple of chairs, pots and pans, along with the bedding from mam's "bottom draw" and the usual bits and bobs, they got off to a pretty good start. Those first summer months must have been shear bliss, as they enjoyed life to the full in the fresh air of Offerton little knowing what hard times lay ahead. Dad's father found work hard to come by only having one leg. After a succession of menial sweeping up jobs, things were looking dire. However, not all was lost and things began to look up. Shortly after mam and dad's wedding his mam and dad with Lena, and the two boys, Charlie, and Herbert, he preferred 'Bert, moved into number 1 Mill cottages on Hampstead lane Great moor. It was a tied cottage in the grounds of the Hampstead cotton mill. The job that came with it was that of night watchman of the mill, and subsequently, though no one could foresee such a circumstance, he was fire watchman during the war. Quite how he persuaded the mill owners that he could cope with one leg I will never know, but he could certainly get about on his crutches by this time. It could well have been the

fact that he was in the Royal Marines for about eighteen years, and had an exemplary service record. Maybe the Navy had a hand in securing the job for him through some kind of benevolence scheme, but we will never know. As you can see in the photo' he was at ease with his disability.

As nice as the house was in Offerton, the isolation was a real bugbear. The trams that mam was so used to in and around Stockport were sorely missed as they didn't run along Offerton road, and the buses that did run, were few and far between. Added to that, mam was sure she saw a large brown rat in the garden, it was probably an Otter from the nearby river Etherow, but that was the last straw. With the difficulties of mam finding work, other than in Portwood, dad had a bike, but mam could not ride a bike and never did learn how. With no shops nearby, and being newly pregnant with Terry, they moved to 7 Heathland Terrace just off Shaw Heath. Soon, the inevitable happened, as two were to become three. As usual in the days before the National Health Service came into being, most babies were born at home. The midwife was the only option for most people. Luckily, for mam, the Midwife came highly recommended by the clinic, as she was very experienced. Everything went well and the patter of tiny feet as it were, lit up their lives and made them feel complete. Mam soon recovered from her ordeal. Terrence, 'Terry' weighing in at ten pounds, was born 16th February 1935. Mam said she felt a bit embarrassed being pregnant so soon after they were married, because people would know they have been having, you know, sex. It was only eleven months up to Terry being born. Nevertheless, family members told her not to be so silly, as that was the general idea of getting married. What seemed to be a bigger ordeal than giving birth, was the ritual of being 'churched' the following Sunday. It is not a service in the strict sense of the meaning; a visit to church and a simple blessing would be enough. It was something dad felt he should do. Being brought up in the Catholic faith he wanted to please his parents, and felt it would make them happy to see their first grandchild and daughter-in-law attending a service and being 'churched' before she could re-join society once more, and go out to the shops and visit friends and relatives. Of course, what was never mentioned was sex. I suppose they did not 'do it' so soon after giving birth and not until mam was duly 'churched' in any case. As they snuggled together on those cold winter nights by a crackling fire, they were so happy and looked forward to a cosy and happy future together. They soon settled down once more to a life of wedded bliss, and things were good. Mam looking after her first-born, a cleaning job on Great Moor to bring in a little extra money each week whilst gran, dad's mam, looked after their pride and joy, Terry.

The dark clouds of war made it more and more difficult for dad to secure the right kind of work; life was becoming a little more worrying as they began to settle into an uncertain routine. With dad's younger sister Lena always willing to baby-sit and grandma' always on standby, so mam and dad could go to the pictures now and again. The Don and Wellington were just round the corner. Sometimes they would have a treat and take Terry to Belle Vue Zoo in Longsite, just a short tram ride up the road towards Manchester, it was only 1/6d to get in and worth every penny just to see Terry's face light up at the sight of the lions and tigers. They could spend all afternoon there and while away a happy hour or two strolling round the gardens on a warm summer Sunday with an ice cream or a fruity drink.

BETTER DAYS ?

Dad's hard work as a plasterer, eventually paid off, but not in the way he wanted. He had to give up his ambition to be his own boss in favour of a regular wage coming in every week. He went to work for a builder named Mr West, or 'Westy' as he was known in the town. Dad started work on some new houses in lower Brinnington. After he had been working there for a few weeks, he made enquiries about how much the rent would be and wondered if they could afford to rent one of these lovely new houses. When he took mam to see them, she was very excited as dad said Mr West the builder gave them the opportunity to rent one of the bay windowed semi-detached ones. A few weeks later, they moved into a brand new house at 34 Sandyliegh Avenue at the lower end of Brinnington early in 1937. Mam was worried about the 12/6ᴾ a week rent, but dad, now on a regular wage said they would manage. This idyllic life of loving domesticity with a garden, inside toilet, bathroom, and hot water, life could not have been any better. As they set about making a home for their young family, few people had any idea of what was in store. Even as dark clouds were gathering over Europe, people hoped and prayed that Neville Chamberlain would be able to make peace with Heir Hitler.

Most people in those exiting days of the talkies with better picture quality and sound systems' were tempted to go to the pictures at least once a week, mam and dad were no exception. Mam liked the romantics with stars such as Googie Withers and Douglas Fairbanks Junior. Dad liked action films with John Wayne and James Cagney.

My sister and I came into the world in the morning of Saturday 21st May 1938 in our nice new house in Brinnington. As with Terry, it was not uncommon to use the services of a midwife for a straightforward home birth, instead of a doctor. Terry's birth was without problems, and mam was feeling quite well enough to have a home birth, and said she would like to use the same midwife that delivered Terry if she was available. Because of mams' size, numerous visits to the clinic to determine if twins were on the way were inconclusive. There was no such thing as ultrasonic scans in those days. It was down to the size of the bump and the weight of the mother now, and before conception, and then do the maths as they say. However, few people had bathrooms, let alone bathroom scales, so it was very much hit and miss as to whether she was having twins or not, sometimes two heartbeats could be heard, or was it three. It was difficult to be sure if it was two babies or if one of the heartbeats was mam's. Alternatively, it could be a very large baby like Terry was at 10 lbs. Nevertheless, they arranged for a home birth with the same midwife to attend as mam and dad had every confidence in her ability to cope. Mr West, dad's boss had signed dad on to the National Insurance Scheme. It did not cost very much, I think dad paid four pence a week; his boss paid three pence a week and the Government two pence. It was a great help in time of sickness or childbirth, but offered only the minimum of help for aftercare or time off work.

WOW WEE, TWINS!

In 1938.Gynaecology was not as advanced as it is today. Therefore, mam and the midwife were not as prepared as they would like to have been. Relatives, family, and neighbours alike thought mam was having a big baby at ten pounds as Terry was. The midwife, going off what she was told by the clinic felt sure it was another big baby and a lot of amniotic fluid. As the day dawned, mam was beginning to feel the first pangs of labour, but assured dad that she did not think she was going to have the baby until the afternoon. Dad said he will phone the midwife from the call box down on Brinnington road and let her know how things are just to be on the safe side, then get off to work nearby. As these events were so often unpredictable, and dad needing to go to work, a neighbour said she would look after Terry and pop in from time to time to see how mam was getting on. She could send someone to phone the midwife as soon as she felt that she was needed. I hope you will forgive me if you find this account a little short on detail, but suffice to say, Ann was born at about quarter to ten, dad was summoned home from his work nearby, just in time to hear the cry of tiny lungs taking their first breaths. After beaming smiles and congratulations all round, and dad pleased as punch with the arrival of a bouncing, not so little girl at ten pounds, mam and the midwife thought that it was all over, and just had to remove the placenta. Dad had to return to work, but as he was just about to put his coat on, the midwife called down stairs to him, wait a minute she said. At that moment, his mother and sister Lena turned up to see how things were going, but they were a bit late. Dad said Mary had had a little girl but could not understand why the midwife wanted him to wait downstairs before going up to see how thing were. Had something gone wrong he thought. As he was just about go up to see what was happening the midwife said, put the kettle on and make a cup of tea for us all. In those days, fathers were not welcome at the birth. His mother went up to see how thing were progressing. Still a little puzzled, dad and Lena made the tea, but did not have to wait long, about ten minutes; finally, the midwife called down stairs, 'you can come up now'. As they went into the bedroom, there, on each side of mam was one little girl, and one little boy, wow! Twins. My sister and I weighed in at a mind-numbing seventeen and a half pounds, but I nearly did not make it. Not so little me at seven and a half pounds saw the light of day some twenty minutes later. As I was the last out, and more to the point, not expected I must have been getting impatient and pulled my umbilical cord and got it wrapped around my neck. It was a good job the midwife knew her stuff; she earned every penny of her fee to bring us into the world, healthy, and with two of everything. Mam and dad were so caught up in the shock and excitement of the events of the day; they had forgotten that the father usually gave the midwife a little something for her services, a tip if you like. A shillin' was about the norm' even though she would receive a fee from the National Insurance Scheme, people where not yet used to the idea of not paying for such services. However, on this occasion dad felt that two bob would be the least he could offer, and the most he could afford. But what the hell! He felt great. I feel as though I came into the world with a price tag of one shillin' on my head. The arrival of twins came as quite a shock in many ways. Twins had not been planned for, so this situation as beset them was, to say the least, very difficult. They only had one of everything, one cot, one set of clothes, one set of feeding bottles, not enough nappies, and worst of all, a penny bun will now cost tuppence. However, in 1938 neighbours were much closer than they are today. Maybe it was the lack of a proper health service; People had to rally round in times of hardship, or illness. Sandyliegh Avenue was no exception being a young estate. Many young mothers rallied round when they heard the news that Mary and Bill at number 34 had had twins not just the one baby everyone was waiting for. There was never any shortage of offers of help. Someone lent them a cot, others gave nappies, or baby clothes, all manner of things they needed. Luckily, mam kept some of Terry's things so it was not too bad. One thing that was necessary was a twin pram. Fortunately dad read an advertisement in the Stockport Express, offering a Silver Cross twin pram for only 10/-. I believe he went on his bike to collect it, but had to walk back from Castle Street with his bike on the pram. Over the first weeks and months, after we were born there was always someone to turn to. Later in life, we were told our poor mam weighed little more than six and a half stone wet through after our birth. We came into a world on the brink of war for the second time in only just over twenty years, leading to such turmoil that would shape our lives forever. A war as never experienced before or thank God, since. With two more babies to provide for, a gift of Quaker Oates from the manufactures, welcome as they were did not help pay the 12/6^d a week rent. Life was getting very difficult as work in the building trade was drying up because of the very real threat of war. Mr West had to lay workers off. Dad was lucky as he was kept on until the winter set in.

As I said, a penny bun now costs tuppence. Investment in housing was drying up; the future was not looking at all good. We had to leave that nice new house in Brinnington for a much cheaper house down the road in Portwood, it must have been such a let-down as the only houses for the amount of rent that they could afford were in Portwood. They were so run down, it was heart breaking, but for 7/6^d a week what could one expect. I heard that mam was in tears at the thought of having to leave that nice new house in Brinnington, but at the same time it was difficult pushing a twin pram up Brinnington road with two babies and quite often with Terry sitting on top. After a walk round the market, mam would be exhausted. A succession of tumble-down houses little better than something from a Dickensian novel. A Dickensian Christmas just about sums up the dire situation they found themselves in. Mam told us she used to sit up all night to keep the cockroaches off us as we slept in our cots. Things must have been bleak indeed. All dad could do was to try to find any bits of labouring jobs to bring in a few bob and just hope that the spring would bring some plastering his way.

A NEW BEGINING

One day, dad's parents learned of a house for rent in Great Moor, only a stone's throw from mill cottages on Hampstead lane. The rent was 2/6ᵈ a week more than the hovel in Portwood. Nevertheless, even at 10/-a week, they had little choice, and moved into a two up two down terraced house at 55 Alldis Street Great Moor in early 1939 just in time for Terry to start school at the new Great Moor Council School, called locally, Southwood road. As with most terraced houses built around that time, a plaque on the wall across the street reads 'Alldis terrace 1907' even though the houses were only 30 years old they were sadly lacking what we now consider essentials, such as central heating, hot water, a bathroom and an inside toilet. At least it was cockroach free and a damn site cleaner, not only the house and surrounding streets, the air was fresher too. They soon had the place looking more like a home than a house.

By way of celebration, they went to see a new film called 'The Great Waltz' at the Davenport. A film featuring songs based on the works of Johann Strauss the first and second. In it, was a song called "One day when we were young". It became a very special song, their song. The title brought back memories of their first proper date "one morning in May 1933" I have written some of the lyrics at the end of this book, but because of difficulties with copy rights there are just the first four lines. There are several versions on the web.

FREE FROM GRIME

The gas works and mills in Portwood were very dirty places, the grit and dust was a constant companion in the streets and houses, no matter how people tried to keep them clean. Portwood seemed to have its very own Eco system too; the smoke and grime blocked out the sun for most of the day, and then when the cooling tower was built, steam would condense, and fall as rain even on cloudless days. In most industrial towns' washday was always on Mondays, because from Saturday noon, the mills closed for the weekend, and Marsland Street was a lot quieter as the Lorries did not trundle up and down all day long. By the time Monday morning dawned, the air was cleaner, so it was the best day to hang out the washing to dry. But now, mam could do the washing any day she wanted. They must have been very pleased to find a decent house they could afford. It was the one comfort they felt they could rely on, bricks and mortar surrounding their little world as the news on the wireless was evermore giving cause for concern. It was quite a substantially built house, the front being of red stock brick with a slate roof. The back door opened onto a garden with blue grey diamond patterned blocks forming a path down to a six feet high brick wall topped with copings the same blue grey as the path, a high gate, with a scrawny Lilac tree in the corner. There was a narrow strip of garden on each side of the path, one side soon to be taken up by an Anderson shelter. A cast iron wringer stood on a base of stone slabs and covered with a piece of tarpaulin.

The gate opened onto a cobbled passageway about ten feet wide. Even to this day, an uneven gutter runs down the middle, with constantly blocked grids; it ran all the way down the back of the terraces between Alldis Street and Lake Street. Number 1 passage ran at right angles across the bottom of the terraces. As we grew up, we found the smooth concrete was great for playing football on. Immediately to the left of the back door was the lavvy, with wooden seat and wooden cistern. A rusty chain to flush the pan, whitewashed walls and a choice of toilet paper, the Radio Times, or the Stockport Express. During the cold winter weather dad had to turn the water off to the cistern last thing at night then flush the toilet cistern to empty it and then place a night light at the back of the seat to stop the cistern mechanism freezing. He would wrap the cistern and pipes in swathes of hessian to help to keep the frost at bay. The coal shed and toilet butted up to next door's equally robust brick built toilet and coal shed with a gently sloping slate roof. The back room, or living room as we knew it, was fitted with a grey mottled cast iron gas cooker to the left of a shiny black cast iron kitchen range complete with bread oven. The hearth was a sheet of blue and white enamelled steel and wrapped around the whole grate was a three feet high wire mesh guard held in place by a spring twixt guard and grate. A brass edging round the top was as shiny as can be by constant use as a drying rail completed the ensemble. Tall brown painted cupboards atop three big drawers filled in the recess on the right. The bottom draw was the biggest, being about 10 inches deep. In it, dad kept all manner of tools from screwdrivers to hammers, bits and bobs that might just come in useful. The tall cupboards seem to have their own special smell. A smell of pine, and years of use for just about everything one could think of. Mam kept pots on the top shelves, too high up for tiny fingers to pull down. A piece of carpet served as a hearth rug over brown and beige 'cabbage rose' patterned oilcloth covering the floor served only to make the room easier to sweep or mop. A table with brown painted legs and pine top scrubbed within an inch of its life, a cutlery draw at the end nearest the window was the centrepiece of this little back room. A brown and beige stoneware sink about three feet wide and only four inches deep with a single cold tap would splash ice-cold water into a cream enamel bowl. The tall sash windows with curtains that did not reach from top to bottom were hung about ten inches down from the top, but they were more than wide enough. The curtains were on their fourth or fifth set of windows since Offerton. From a two up two down, to a semi-detached in Brinnington with bay windows, then back to yet another house with the little sash windows of a Portwood terrace, but, as I said, they were nowhere near long enough for the taller sash windows of a more modern terraced house in Great Moor. A clothes drying rack with four long poles slotted into two cast iron frames that looked a bit like coat hangers, hung from the ceiling on two pulleys that would squeak every time mam lowered it. A squeak that could be heard many a night as mam did some washing as we lay in our beds. The front room was about the same size, with the same cupboards both sides of a posh brown and beige mottled tiled fireplace. The cupboards on the left, had three drawers beneath, but the cupboards on the right by the window had two lower cupboards instead of drawers to accommodate the gas and electric metres. A solid front door opened onto a tiny front garden with a low brick wall topped by stone copings with cast iron railings set in lead filled holes.

To the left of the back door were the stairs leading to two equally sized bedrooms with tiny cast iron fireplaces. I remember them being lit on very cold evening to take the chill off the rooms. As far as I can remember, there were no cupboards upstairs of any kind but we did of course have the usual cupboard under the stairs. No one could have foreseen at the time that this little room at the back of a modest terraced house on Great Moor was soon to be mam's and our world for five long and difficult years.

DARK CLOUDS GETTING DARKER

One piece of news that must have been very worrying, on the 1st April 1939. Was when Chamberlain announces conscription into the armed forces, the first to be called up on July 1st. To make matters worse, on April 7th Italy invaded Albania. During the first few months of conscription, the war office called up men between the ages of 18 to 27 years old. Dad tried to assure mam that at 27, with three young children; he might not be called up for army service being at the top end of the age range. Nevertheless, in the back of his mind dad was very worried about what the future may hold. Mam and dad were soon to celebrate our first birthday with Terry, grandmas and granddads aunts and uncles. One piece of news that must have really put a damper on the celebrations, as the seriousness of the situation really hit home. Only about a month after the news of the call up, the council made it known that Anderson shelters and blackout curtain materials were soon to be issued free of charge to all householders earning less the £250 a year. Those on higher incomes had to pay £7.for a shelter and buy their own blackout materials, or A R P 'air raid precaution blinds'. They soon went on sale at places like Shaw's on Hillgate. To make them seem posher, because you had to pay for them, they were called "light-proof" curtains.

Mam and dad were earning nowhere near £250 a year, so dad applied for a shelter and a ration of blackout material. Over eight thousand families in and around Stockport applied for shelters during the first few weeks, about 2,500 were eventually delivered. As we were a family of three young children, we were issued an Anderson shelter within about three weeks. It was stated that it was intended for six to eight people, not just for personal use, it was intended for as many family members, or neighbours as we could fit in. Because of that directive, there was no shortage of neighbours to help, in the expectation that they, in turn would need help if they were to get a shelter. The council offered to help anyone who was unable "with good cause" to put up their shelter, as they all had to be erected by 11th of June. Dad being in the building trade at the time managed to borrow the necessary tools, and with help from neighbours, the required sized hole was soon taking shape to accommodate the base of the shelter. Our Cherry tree granddad did his best to help; he said it was for the sake of children in the forlorn hope, that we would never need it. The hole 6'x 6" by 4'x 6", and two feet deep was soon ready. The corrugated steel panels were pushed into the galvanized steel and wooden frame that formed the floor and bolted together as tight as can be. As dad and the neighbours were fixing the shelter, mam made up the blackout curtains for the four windows, and the back and front doors even though they did not have windows in them, mam thought it was better to be sure. Dad fixed the wires for them to be put up when they were needed. Over the next few weeks dad managed to scrounge some boards to form thicker floor to help keep it dry and warm.

During World War 1, when the zeppelins' floated over London to drop their bombs, the local electricity companies simply turned off the supply to their area. All those with the new-fangled electricity were plunged into darkness. The good thing about the blackout curtains during the air raids the second time around, meant that people indoors could keep their lights on. Those blackout curtains were the best curtains we ever had, being very close woven, it made the house much warmer during the coming winters. With lots of soil to cover the shelter, mam was soon planting flowers 'borrowed' from the gardens of mill cottage. Dad going to work, Terry going to school, mam looking after 'the twins' as we were usually called, trying to put the possibility of war to the back of their minds as best they could, but still wondered what the future may hold as they did their best to get on with their uncertain lives. Even the pictures of Chamberlain with his paper proclaiming 'peace in our time' did not help to allay the fear of the threat of war for very long. People soon realized that things were getting a lot worse when two neighbourhood shelters were built. One in Coombes street and one in Lake Street. As the winter and shorter days approached and the ever-present threat of war, these precautions began to take on a real sense of foreboding. However, the people of continental Europe were suffering terribly as Hitler began to get more and more demanding. After tea, dad would read the paper or listen to the wireless with mam. They would listen to the popular shows of the day such as Tommy Handley with his comedy show called I.T.M.A. "It's That Man Again." The title was a contemporary reference to Hitler, as he was mentioned on every news bulletin at the time. Rob Wilton, Arthur Askey, Victor Sylvester and his orchestra, and many more. Of course, they could not help but listen to the very worrying news about the war and wonder just how soon it would be upon us.

WAR DECLARED.

They did not have to long to wait. In the early hours of September 1st, the German army crossed the Polish frontier with over a million men, thousands of tanks and dive-bombers. This act of aggression by Germany was in direct breach of the agreement between Hitler and Chamberlain, remember, that famous "piece of paper", peace in our time. On Sunday the 3rd of September, at 11:15 am. Chamberlain said.

"I am speaking to you now from the cabinet room at 10 Downing Street. This morning the British Ambassador in Berlin handed the German Government a final note, stating that unless we heard from them by 11 o'clock that they were prepared at once to withdraw their troops from Poland, a state of war would exist between us. I have to tell you that no such undertaking has been received and that as a consequence this country is at war with Germany."

Mam and dad must have suffered the most worrying anguish on that fateful day, as did the whole country. That same evening must have been very frightening for everyone when the blackout was ordered. The new over zealous air raid wardens running around shouting the now familiar "put that light out". Millions of sandbags were stacked round government buildings and police stations; gas masks by the million had already been issued. Thousands of hospital beds were made available by discharging patients early.

Rationing was beginning to make a difference to daily life as petrol and foodstuffs were rationed within weeks after the declaration of war. I have just had a thought, even as little kids, we could have heard the voice of Neville Chamberlain on the wireless that Sunday afternoon, but we will never know.

I hoped to include copies of extracts from the Southwood road infant School log from September 4th 1939 to 5th July 1945. Unfortunately, it proved too problematic to do so plus the fact that they may be difficult to decipher on the printed pages. Therefore, I have transcribed the intended pages and placed them in the relevant parts of the book. I have copied them verbatim from the log in this account of school life during those war years to help to put them into context.

School log.

1939 Sept 4th School to be closed all week owing to outbreak of war with Germany.

11th School closed for a further week. Teachers are taking First Aid and Gas lectures.

The worst consequence of the war, as far as dad was concerned, was the suspension of the Football League programme. There followed seven seasons of regionalised football. Not wanting to be intimidated by the outbreak of war, dad was determined to keep things as normal as possible. He went to watch a friendly between County and Southport. It was a novel time for football fans as most of them took their gas masks with them. Players guesting for the Edgeley Park club ranged from 'stars' from other clubs, former County favourites and occasionally a spectator. Even my uncle Harry to be, played a few games in 1946. (see back pages) He married mam's sister Ruth after the war.

From the very outset of war being declared, a great German air assault had been expected. It was because of this fear that mothers and children were evacuated from the big cities. All schools were closed for a week. Then extended for a further week. The teachers could do little but to make sure that everything that needed to be done was done. Now we had the blackout enforced, gas masks and Anderson shelters distributed by the million, and thousands of beds held vacant in the hospitals. However, no 'knock-out- blow' from the air, or indeed any kind of blow at all. Nevertheless, all the teachers attended air raid and gas mask drill. There was an uncanny peace over the British Isles during the autumn and winter of 1939-40. The peace remained until well into spring. The probable reason why we did not bomb Germany was not to give them reason to bomb us. However, the real reason, was far more frightening. Quite simply we were nowhere near ready to defend ourselves if Hitler did decide to send over the Luftwaffe. Those five to six months respite gave us time to build up our forces, particularly our air force. Nevertheless, air raid sirens were tested; the blackouts were indeed very frightening at first, particularly for the children. Many newsreaders with strong regional dialects were hired by the B.B.C. to prevent imposters reading false news reports. The one that comes to mind was the very heavy Yorkshire accent of Wilfred Pickles.

School log.

18th Sept' School reopened Attendance 399 Roll 443.

Children admitted 13. Infants to attend only during the morning session.

Sept' 18th

Chairman visited school to inspect the air raid shelters .

Notified that Pauline Axon, age 5 1/2 yrs, class 9 was suffering from Diphtheria. All the material used by this child was burnt and the desk washed with disinfectant.

20th Nurse Smith visited school to examine the girls whose heads had been found dirty.

21st The Christmas concert was held in the Hall this afternoon.

22nd School closed for Christmas holidays.

1940

Jan 8th Re-opened school. Admissions 17 Roll 466 Present 377.

Alderman Patten called to view the air-raid shelter. Dr Rowell to view a modern school.

An epidemic of mumps is responsible for the poor attendance.

A number of milestones regarding rationing began. National registration day on 29th September 1939 every householder had to fill in a form giving details of the people who lived in the house. Soon after, every household was issued with ration books. Buff for mam and dad, blue for Terry, and green for Ann and me. Bacon was the first food item to be rationed in January 1940. Followed by all meat products except sausages. (There was very little meat in them anyway) In July, tea and margarine were next. Dad was most upset with the tea ration; he was a real "tea belly". Cheese, jam, eggs, even coal soon followed. Throughout 1941, more and more food and essentials were added to the ration books until the only thing not on ration were things in short supply in any case such as fish. Trawler-men did not want to risk their lives fishing for Cod with the threat of German submarines skulking around in the Atlantic waters off the north of Scotland and the Irish coast.

Air raid warnings demonstrated on the wireless every day making the fear of air raids even more real as we heard what kind of sounds to expect, be it a siren or police whistles. Only the police had authority to order the sirens to sound when they were needed. The siren we could hear was on top of the 'bandage works at the top of Store Street just 100 yards away. It was the most eerie sound imaginable, even to this day; it reminds a whole generation of those fearful air raids. The first sound of the siren started with a deep wailing sound then rising and falling in pitch. The all clear was a monotone high pitch that sounded for about two minutes. What a relief it was.

School log

1940

Jan 15th Attendance still poor this morning 78.5 % owing to Mumps.

The fathers or brothers of children attending this school, who are in the army, navy or air force have now all received a Christmas present of a box of cigarettes and a large packet of chocolate subscribed for by teachers and scholars. Wool is being bought with the money in hand to knit mufflers, pullovers etc for members of the forces.

This week a collection is being held aid of our Stockport clog fund.

26th The weather this month has been very cold. Many children away with colds and mumps. Attendance has fallen as low as 62%

29th Attendance very poor today owing to the severe snow storm. 42.9 %

School log

Feb 2nd Attendance for the week only 48% Conditions arctic.

Miss Ellis still absent with Influenza .

5th Miss Sheldon absent to day with cold. Attendance has improved to 71.2% no milk for the children all last week and none today.

6th Shrove Tuesday. School closed.

9th Dental inspection this morning. Percentage attendance this week 71.

12th Miss Jackson absent this morning with cold and cough. Miss Barker absent this afternoon. She had received a telegram to say her brother had had a stroke and was not expected to recover.

Dental inspection again this morning.

15th Alderman Patten visited school to see how the air raid shelters were progressing.

19th Miss Jackson and Miss Sheldon still absent with influenza.

20th Mrs Grossman, supply teacher came this morning.

School log

1940

June 28th Registers examined &found to be correct.

July 5th Miss Frost H.M.I. called this morning. She took particulars of children staying in our shelters etc and saw an air raid practice.

9th Nurse Smith called to examine the girls who had nits at the previous inspection.

15th A collection of aluminium articles made today.

16th Nurse Smith called to examine girls seen on the 9th

31st The chairman and director called at school this afternoon. They watched some of the items being taken in the hall as part of the 3 weeks' recreative and social activities instead of ordinary lessons during what would have been a holiday period but for the war.

As things became a bit more settled, some of the older kids would experiment with their gas masks in smoke filled sheds and outside lavvies' and generally lark about with them. If a warden or policeman caught anyone without their gas mask, they would get a ticking off. However, the girls would use them as hand bags to keep their bits and pieces in. A warden seeing their box would assume there was a gas mask in it. It was not long before the boys cottoned on and kept their catapult, conkers, bits of string, puppy dogs tails and other bits and pieces. Of course, Ann and I, at eighteen months old, could not know anything of those early years of the war, not even our little pink gas masks. I could not remember them at all until I went to the 'Imperial War Museum Northern' last year. As I picked up that little pink gas mask for the first time in about 70 years it all came flooding back to me. I did remember after all!

However, I have no recollection of actually wearing one for anything other than a plaything as their true need subsided. I remember blowing hard through the little rubber outlet to make a trumping sound like a Whoopi cushion much to everyone's amusement. As Alvar Lidell, Frank Philips and others read the news, reporting how the German army was like a monster trampling all over Europe. It seems that most of the civilian population were just waiting for the bombs and gas raining down on us almost the next day. It was only eighteen months (1937) since the bombing of Guernica during the Spanish civil war. A demonstration using Hitler's bombers flown by Italian air force pilots in an operation called 'Operation Rugen' to show the world what the Luftwaffe was capable of. With sixteen hundred killed or wounded in a matter of a few hours' it was indeed a very frightening prospect. The near total destruction of a small defenceless town with hundreds killed during two raids lasting a total of three hours on a small town not unlike Stockport. Mercifully, as I have said, the R A F did not bomb any part of Germany because of a fear of reprisals, coupled with the sorry state of our air force. We would have brought upon ourselves death and destruction in a way we never thought possible. In simple terms, we left each other alone. As Hitler was busy in eastern Europe we were spared the air raids for quite some time, even thou' most of England was within range of the Luftwaffe. What people called the "Phoney War" broke out. There was a peculiar eerie dreamlike quality about life during this period. Everyone knew that life would be different if it all began in earnest. However, nothing happened. There were no raids, no bombs, and no emergencies. We all thought the north of the country was reasonably safe in any case during the early months of the war. There were of course many warnings to 'Wear white at night' or carry something like a newspaper. It was even suggested that men should pull out their shirt lap during a blackout. All vehicles owners had to comply with strict lighting levels meaning a cowl over the headlights, and sidelights partially covered with black tape. Cycles had to conform to the light restriction too and to be sure to have a red rear light to prevent motorists running into them from behind. Many trees were painted with broad white rings round them as a guide for motor cars. Because of these light restrictions, the dim lights on cars and lorries, and the blackouts, the accident rate increased. Over four thousand people were killed during the winter of 1939/40. People began to realise that more were being killed because of the blackout than the air raids. Many decided that the war was not going to happen any time soon and stopped carrying their gas masks, but still had to adhere to the blackout restrictions. Some evacuees even went back home. Christmas 1939 came and passed with little realization of what the future had in store as we went into the new year of 1940. We began to realise there was nothing phoney about the war raging over Europe. The German "Blitzkrieg" using tanks and dive-bombers, was truly frightening as people listened and watched the unfolding of this terrible destruction and loss of life brought to us on the wireless, and cinema through the Pathe newsreels. Throughout those early months of the war, mam and dad tried to get on with their lives as best they could, dad off to work every morning, and Terry off to school. The war seemed to be a distant war, somewhere over in Europe.

However, on the 9th of April 1940. Germany attacks Denmark and Norway. On May 10th 1940, things started to get more serious as Germany invades Belgium and Holland. An event which at the time seemed something so unbelievable as to be almost unreal, and if not unreal then quite immeasurably catastrophic. To add to the difficulty, Neville Chamberlain resigned after losing a vote in the commons. Little did we know it was a blessing in disguise. Chamberlain asked Lord Halifax, the foreign secretary if he wanted to form a coalition government if the King approved. Even though Lord Halifax as foreign secretary enjoyed the support of Labour and Conservatives alike, had to decline the post. He said later. "As I rode my horse round my north Yorkshire estate, I felt the country needed a man far better qualified than me for such an enormous task, thinking it would be inappropriate for a peer to sit in the commons, who has only chased a fox or a rabbit, to serve in such circumstances. After three tortuous days of sickening worry by the whole country, the King, on advice from Chamberlain and Halifax, asked First Sea Lord, Winston Churchill to step in and form a coalition government.

BLOOD, TOIL, TEARS, AND SWEAT!

The country as a whole was not so sure if Churchill was the right man for the job; nevertheless, he formed a Government of national unity. One of his first tasks was to lift the country and try to instil some hope for the future. On the 13th of May 1940 in his first speech to the Commons, Churchill said he could offer no more than **"BLOOD, TOIL, TEARS, AND SWEAT"**. Within weeks, the "Emergency Powers Act" gave the Government control over persons and property. Many iron railings and gates were commandeered for the war effort. However, for some reason our railings were left intact, but the ones down the opposite side of the street were all cut off and taken away.

The news got worse day by day. The spectacular advance by the German forces through Belgium and Holland were very frightening. The British Expeditionary Force, B.E.F. along with many thousands of French troops and many of our allies had to be evacuated from the Dunkirk beaches. A wood and concrete breakwater known as the Mole with a road on top ran about a mile out to sea. It served as an unexpected saviour as thousands of men were able to board ships bound for England and comparative safety. The Luftwaffe constantly bombed the whole area. Operation Dynamo was the code name used during the evacuation of the B.E.F.

As Churchill showed us what he was made of, the whole country was amazed by such massive rescue of 330,000 troops of the B E F including thousands of allied forces.(Most of them French) Churchill won the respect and admiration of all the doubters within the first few weeks of his leadership. During those first few weeks, after the evacuation of Dunkirk we were all expecting Germany to invade us. With the fall of Holland and Belgium, France suing for peace, with the ever-growing threat of invasion Churchill gave his greatest speech of the war. He addressed the House of Commons, On June 4th 1940

Churchill >

"When I asked the house last week to fix this afternoon to make a statement, I feared it would be my hard lot to announce the greatest military disaster in the history of our country has ever known. We hoped twenty to thirty thousand might be saved as the enemy attacked us on all sides, the rest to be defeated on the battlefield or taken prisoner. But the Royal air force, and men on the ground fighting a rear action, the Royal navy and hundreds of smaller vessels, many of them manned by their owners was a testament of their courage, and a miracle of deliverance. But wars are not won by evacuation. Even though large tracts of Europe and many old and famous states have fallen or may fall into the grip of the Gestapo and all the odious apparatus of Nazi rule, we shall not flag or fail. We shall go on to the end. We shall fight in France, we shall fight on the seas and oceans, we shall fight with growing confidence and growing strength in the air, we shall defend our island, whatever the cost may be. We will fight on the beaches, we will fight on the landing grounds, we will fight in the fields and in the streets and in the hills, we shall never surrender, and if, which I do not for a moment believe, this island or a large part of it were subjugated and starving, then our Empire beyond the seas, armed and guarded by the British Navy, would carry on the struggle, until, in Gods good time, the New World, with all its power and might, steps forth to the rescue and liberation of the old."

ME>

I remember quite some time after the war, dad telling us that during the weeks after the evacuation from Dunkirk everyone felt that an invasion was only weeks away. However, Churchill's speech was the most uplifting moment of the entire war and a terrific boost to the moral of the whole country.

With the surrender of Denmark, Luxemburg, Holland, and the debacle of Dunkirk. Mussolini thought he might as well have a piece of the action. On June 10th Italy declares war on Britain and France. Churchill said we shall never surrender! Nevertheless, the French did. On June 11th, France declared Paris an open city. On the 17th of June1940. France capitulates. Churchill said, "Now the battle of France is ended, there must be a battle for Britain.

Only a few weeks later the Germans occupied the Channel Islands.

School log

Life goes on

16th July

Nurse Smith called to examine girls seen on the 9th

A FIGHT TO THE DEATH.

On the 1st of August, Hitler issues order number 17. A categorical order to the Luftwaffe to "crush the R.A.F. with all means possible". To begin on August the 8th. The R A F and the Luftwaffe literally fought to the death. The British fighters never gave the German fighters and bombers a moment's respite. Day in, day out. The Hurricanes targeting the bombers, the Spitfires fought the M e 109s, and both set upon anything else that flew. We did not realise it at the time, but because of the R A F's stubborn bloody mindedness and shear guts and courage in answering the call during those fourteen weeks in the summer of 1940, Goering had to admit that the Luftwaffe has not been able to crush the R.A.F. as he had promised Hitler. Because of the Luftwaffe's failure to "crush" the R.A.F., the window of opportunity for the invasion of Britain was closing fast as the weather and tides were changing, leading to the postponement of operation "Sealion" due to be launched on September 17th. Therefore, they [the Germans] changed tactics as the air raids on southeastern England took priority. On August 24th, the first bombs fall on North Weald, Hornchurch, and Central London. On September the 7th, the London blitz started in earnest. 300 German bombers, escorted by 600 fighters, drop 337 tons of bombs on London, the principal targets being Woolwich Arsenal and the docks area killing 306, and seriously injured 1,337. Huge fires were caused, as warehouse after warehouse caught fire. Many stored whisky, gin, timber, and many highly flammable materials making it the worst possible place to start a fire.

At 8.07pm. British GHQ issues the code-word "Cromwell" to Eastern and Southern commands, meaning, probable invasion of Great Britain within 24 hours. In retaliation to the raids on the docks, the R.A.F. bombed Berlin, soon to be followed by the first all night alert in London. Followed by air raids on several airfields in Kent, with the main target being Biggin Hill. Incendiary bombs by the thousand fall on factories and shipyards alike, and so it went on, and on, and on. The flickering black and white pictures on the silver screen were not films any more, it was for real, and people feared the worst. Fortunately, the population as a whole knew nothing of the code-word "Cromwell".

Dad being 28 years old by now, felt he might be too old to be called up, but as things got worse, and Germany seemingly invincible as they swept across France and occupied half the country including Paris. Dad felt he would be called before very long, and he was right. In August, he received the expected letter from the local recruitment office in Stockport, telling him to present himself at Great Ducie street in Manchester for a medical, you know, drop your trousers and cough, now touch your toes, o.k. you'll do, collect your expenses on your way out, we'll be in touch. Terry had just started school and was finding new friends and really coming out of himself. All mam and dad could do was to get on with life and hope for the best. Things seem to settle down into a quiet routine for a while. However, every time a letter dropped though the letterbox, dad would try to hide it from mam until he could see where it was from. They did not receive many letters in those days, as their world was so parochial. How do you prepare for war, with three little children and not knowing what the future may hold? Dad managed to put the possibility of being called up to the back of his mind, and hoped that things would settle down. The routine settled down for the rest of the summer with dad off to work every morning, Terry just getting used to going to school, Grandma' looking after us so mam could go out cleaning for those posh houses on Mile End lane and Davenport Park.

STONE SINK TO TIN BATH, HOW POSH.

Saturday night was bath night; this was always something of a ritual. Dad would lift the galvanised bath off the wall by the back door, mam would have the big cast iron kettle by the fire, and two or three pans on the stove. Ann and I, now we were getting a little bigger, graduated from the stone sink to the tin bath, posh ha! It was Ann and I in first followed by Terry, and off to bed so mam and dad could have some privacy, and make use of the still warm water left by us, topped up from the ever-simmering cast iron kettle on the kitchen range and pans from the stove. Sometimes after our bath, we would all have our hair washed in the stone sink using Derbac soap and rinsed in cold water. It was actually quite painful as the icy cold water poured over our heads, but that was our lot, we just had to put up with it. The soap was a kind of coal-tare soap with a very distinctive smell, yes smell, not perfume. It was medicated to keep knits out of our hair, the general feeling was that if a child had knits it meant that they had dirty hair but as we now know, knits are not fussy if hair is clean or dirty. If we were going somewhere special, like visiting an auntie or going to a wedding, mam would wash our hair as usual then rinse it with a splash of vinegar in the rinsing water. We would kick up such a fuss if any watery vinegar went in our eyes as it smarted like bilio, but it did make our hair very shiny, and mam very proud. The good thing about having our hair washed after our bath and not having a hair dryer meant that we could stay up a bit longer until our hair was dry. I distinctly remember combing mam's hair for ages to get it dry if she washed before our bedtime

Nevertheless, we did have a wireless, and mam and dad must have been very worried about the future and the rumblings of war and what kind of a life we could look forward to. To this day, when I see one of those big black ranges they bring back so many memories, so much so, I can almost hear the air-raid sirens wailing and mam calling us to get up quickly. In what was soon to become a way of life, nothing was ever wasted. Mam would save any potato peelings, cabbage leaves and tealeaves, in fact, waste of all kinds and wrap them up nice and tight in newspaper, and throw them onto the back of the fire to burn slowly for ages. Sometimes they would burn all night, sometimes they would smell quite appetising as left over peelings and bits of bacon rind would slowly cook through until next morning. This habit of burning most of our rubbish kept the back room nice and warm and was particularly welcome on cold winter mornings when dad got up to go to work. Nevertheless, this idyllic existence was soon to be shattered. Being twenty-eight years old by now, even with three young children he knew his medical in August was a prelude of things to come, and he would eventually be summoned for duty. Whilst waiting, he did his bit as a fire warden around the gas works in Portwood. It was a difficult time for him; going to work, scoffing his tea down as quickly as he could, then off to Portwood gas works on his bike two or three nights a week. Occasionally, he would be out all night. Wandering round and round in circles, often cold, sometimes wet, and certainly very dark, there were lighter sides to life even in those uncertain days. Whilst on fire watch duty round the gas works one very dark night, made even darker by the blackout, he heard the sound of deliberately quiet footsteps round the corner, unknown to my Dad; the other guard heard a similar noise round his corner. As they approached on tip toe and getting closer to their respective corners they both shouted as bravely and noisily as they could, "HALT, WHO GOES THERE!" Each in turn jumped out of their skin, and called each other a silly bugger, and had a good laugh about it in the guard hut the following night. No one knew what to expect during those first months. Dad, being the man he was, did his best to help the war effort and prepare his wife and young family for an uncertain future. He opened a post office saving account to try to save a few shillings just in case things got desperate. All he could say was that it will be over some day, and whatever happens, we must keep smiling, and just wait and hope for the best.

Up to now, I have only made a passing reference to the four most important people that were such a comfort during those difficult times. Our grandparents; My Man's dad was a small man in stature but not in heart. He was about five feet seven and little more than ten stone. As I said, he was wounded and gassed in the First World War, but he still managed to earn his daily bread thanks to retraining as a cobbler. He had been used to manual work, but found it too difficult to do a full day without stomach pains, but being a tough little man, a true old contemptible, he worked right up until he was in his seventies. Sadly, no photographs can be found of him or grandma. I remember Grandma as a kindly lady of about five feet four inches tall and seemed to be a little rotund, and always wore a 'crossover cotton pinny'. She was a typical gran with a typical name; 'Martha' and we loved her very much. Granddad was 'William' but of course, we called him granddad. As I said, they lived on Marsland Street in Portwood, before and throughout the war in one of five little two up two down terraced houses. There was a passage separating the terrace, with two houses on one side and three on the other being the only way round to the back of the houses. The grey granite cobbles polished by the rubber tyres and coal dust over many years as the lorries trundled to the nearby coal hoppers in the Portwood goods yard to fill up with coal, then trundle back to the gas works about half a mile away on Great Portwood street, then back to the hoppers once more. They would pass those little houses every half an hour or so during the day, but a lot less frequent during the night. The empty lorries made more noise as they rattled and banged about on the cobbles than when they were fully loaded. Mam said they got used to the noise and just didn't hear them half the time. Some drivers, with their fully loaded trucks would take the corner a bit quicker than they should in order to spill some of their precious cargo into the street as they came from the coal hoppers round the bottom of the street. Needless to say, it was soon put to good use by those tenants along Marsland Street. One lorry that did not or rather could not tip over to spill just a little of its mountain of coal was a steam driven lorry. When we heard the train-like hissing of the steam lorry coming up the street we would hurry to the front window to watch this monster trundling by. Hot ashes would spill from the front, black smoke through a funnel on top of the cab, and spitting steam through another pipe somewhere underneath. It really was a monster to any little kids as it trundled along on stiff springs and solid tyres preventing it leaning over more than a few degrees, thus preventing it from spilling any of its contents into the street. The steam lorry did not run during the night, as it was so noisy. As I look back to the times of those dirty noisy lorries, it must have been a dreadful job, especially as most houses did not have a proper bath, and I suspect that a bath in the coal yard was not something that was provided for the workers at that time. The back doors of the terraces opened onto a yard with cobbles that were just like up-turned eggs equally shiny and just as lethal in wet or frosty weather. A few green shoots of grass trying desperately to reach for a tiny share of sunlight as it cast it's warmth over lines of Monday's washing criss-crossing over that little yard.

There were three lavatories shared by the five families. (About 20 persons) Not unusual in those days, and strange as it may seem, it was not unhygienic, as you would think. Each woman of the house would go out of her way to keep the toilets as clean as can be. I remember the seats were always scrubbed white with Lanry bleach, and always smelt clean. However, one pest they could not get rid of was the regular appearance of earwigs. They always fascinated me as they scurried around my feet as I sat there. I always made sure I gave the paper a good shake to get rid of any unwanted company in my trousers. The reasoning behind all this cleanliness, was that each in turn did not want to be thought a dirty so and so by their neighbours.

I remember that little house in Marsland Street with great affection. The front door opened directly from the pavement into the front room. The fireplace was a kind of half-sized cast iron range not unlike the one at Alldis street but with a very small oven. The back room was of equal size with a tiny sash window and a flag floor same as the front room. All the rooms were lit by gas. The front room had just one mantle hanging from a simple frame. The area on the ceiling above the lamps was scorched brown by the heat. In the back scullery, there was just one mantle on the wall that was about as much use as a candle. A gas ring under a cast iron boiler heated water for the Monday morning wash. When mam took us to see grandma, we loved to play with the buffet that was kept in the corner of the tiny scullery. It had four legs a bit like a tall milking stool, by now the best part of a hundred years old. We used to push it up and down the flags under the watchful eye of mam or grandma. It was great fun. The sides of the legs and the stool top are worn square as can be seen in the picture below after many years of pushing it along the pavement up and down Marsland Street. If it were cold or raining, we could push it in turns round the stone floor in the tiny scullery.

There was no electricity in Marsland street till well after the war. In fact, it was still the greater part of ten years away. A stove with enough cast iron and steel in it to rebuild the Titanic stood in the corner. Next to it, beneath the tiny window was a stone sink complete with cold tap. A curtain hung in front to hide the buckets and bits and pieces of cleaning materials. I do not remember ever going upstairs, but guess it would be just two cramped impoverished rooms. So there you have it. Marsland Street, Portwood. A dirty, coal dusty street, noisy lorries, trains pulling coal waggons over the grey brick railway bridge every hour of the day but mercifully fewer at night. Three lavatories between five families. Not a lot to fight for, but a lot to lose.

Most youngsters call their grandparents by their first name, like Grandma Martha, and granddad William or Bill. However, as they lived in Portwood, we called them our Portwood grandma and granddad, maybe it was said one day, and just stuck.

Dad had two brothers and a sister, but his Mother, my grandma' actually gave birth to six children in all, but lost two babies Ronnie and Kenneth to Diphtheria in a period of just eight days. To make it more of a tragedy, as they were attending Ronnie's funeral, Kenneth died that very same day. I was given the name Kenneth in his memory. Such tragic circumstances were all too common in the nineteenth and early part of the twentieth century. Mercifully, all this happened before dad was born. Some of my early memories begin with number1and number 3 Mill Cottages built about 1880. They were, in the strict sense a pair of semi-detached houses rather than the stereotypical cottage but we always said 'Mill cottage'. Grandma and granddad lived at number 1. I can remember as I grew up, the back door opening into quite a large kitchen. The bottom third of the walls were painted dark green, the top two thirds was painted a rich creamy colour, a thick black line formed a kind of border between top and bottom. It had a red and blue/grey square quarry tiled floor and lots of cupboards. The usual stone sink under the window had a curtain across just below the sink to hide the buckets, and cleaning things such as donkey stones for the doorsteps and black lead for the range. The miracle of two taps, one with hot, and one with cold water was wonderful to us. The living room had the usual cast iron range with bread oven, cupboards on top of the usual three draws filled the recesses on each side. A five armed gas chandelier or, 'gasalier' to give it its proper name hung over the large square table covered with a beautiful brown and dark blue chenille tablecloth. I used to love stroking it as if it was a soft furry pussycat. Gaslights gave off a warm glow accompanied by a feint hiss of the gas flame. It would take a few minutes to warm up then cast its soft glow over the room, unlike Portwood grandma's poor excuse of a single light it was quite bright if turned up to its full power. The front room or parlour was reserved for visitors such as the rent man, the insurance man or the doctor. From the front door was the hallway leading to the stairs, at the top was the bathroom. A separate room with a bath was quite a novelty to us at the time. In the somewhat wild gardens was an abundance of Rhododendron bushes and Lupins. As you can see in the picture, we had a great time all around the garden as it was a great place to play.

When we got a bit older and bigger we used to collect the dead leaves from around the base of the Rhododendrons when they were dry and curled up. We would try to find the right sizes to fit on our fingers to make us look like witches with long fingernails. We would chase each other round and round the garden and have lots of fun. Living just off Cherry tree lane, grandma and granddad were called Cherry tree grandma and granddad. As with Portwood grandma and granddad.

Like any little kids at that time, we had no idea about what was going on, or what the future may hold. With the country in one hell of a state, war raging, the constant fear of invasion, the shortages, and the blackouts. Those first few months must have been dreadful, for the grown-ups made worse by the never-ending stream of bad news about the war from home and aboard. The first air raids on Manchester were in August 1940. A sickening realisation that the Germans were getting closer and very frightening it was too.

School log.

1940 continued.

16th Closed school this afternoon for summer holiday which is to be a fortnight this year.

Attendance has been down this week because some parents who have been on holiday have kept their children from school.

September 2nd Reopened school. 33 children admitted. Roll 462 present 409

4th . Air raid warning this morning. Children assembled in shelters. Two warnings this afternoon. After the all clear for the second raid which was at 3.40 pm the children were taken to their classrooms and dismissed for the day.

5th Only 143 present at 9 am this morning owing to the extremely long air raid last night.

9th Alderman Patten visited school this pm and enquired about the air raid precautions.

12th Air raid alarm at 10 45 this morning.

16th Air raid alarm at 8.50 this morning. The few

Page 76

Children who had arrived at school went immediately into the school shelters.

17th Air raid alarm at 10 35 this morning. All clear about 11.20.

19th A cheque for £21-14/- was forwarded to the Mayor of Stockport for his fund to buy a Spitfire Aeroplane.

26th Exhibition of films by Cadbury Bros this morning in the Hall. 'A' life of a Gannet. 'B' West coast of Africa. 'C' Bourneville- work and recreation, & Micky mouse. Closed school for Friday and Monday holiday.

October 1st Re-opened school. Miss Brown absent through illness.

3rd Miss Brown returned to duty. A R P Practice assembly in cloakrooms and passages in case bombs fall near school before siren is sounded.

8th Air raid warning as we had assembled in the Hall at 9-0 am for the morning service. Children sent to shelters. All clear at 9.30 am. Air raid warning at 2.pm. All clear at 2.20 pm.

In those early days of the war, the sounds of sirens were heard almost every day. Mercifully, there were few bombs falling on Stockport. However, Liverpool and Manchester were more obvious targets of course, and were on the receiving end of many air raids. Terry would dash home to tell mam about the sirens, then retold dad the same story when he came home from work and how they all went into the shelters and put on their gas masks. You may wonder how those teachers coped with frightened little children whilst at the same time trying to teach a rudimentary curriculum. Truth be known, most of the older kids thought it was great fun and a good excuse to get out of lessons.

Dad expecting to be called up to do his duty, leaving mam alone with three little kids, not knowing what the future had in store. It was the same for many thousands of woman and kids at the time. At least we were all together, as millions of children were evacuated in those early dark days and months of the war. Mam had to get on with life in a room where she washed our clothes, a room with the distinctive smell of Lanry bleach, a room where she cooked our meagre wartime rations, a room where she kept us clean and warm, a room where we laughed and cried, a room where mam would write to dad in the never-ending belief that he would, one day, return home safe and well. Trying to be brave, but fearing the worst, what a hell of a way to spend Christmas. With three little kids, mam did her best for our sake in those very uncertain times. How do you explain to a five year old and two toddlers why daddy was going away? Even in the worst of times, children see life very differently than one would expect. Terry was quite excited that his dad might be a soldier with a gun and a helmet.

This book did not begin as a story about the war; it was to be a story about a boy and a girl leaving school, in 1925 starting work, falling in love and raising a family during difficult times throughout the first half of the 20th Century. However, I could not write about our time as children growing up during the war without including a large part of dad's memoirs. With three quarters of the world's population caught up in this war, 55 million people killed and millions displaced. The material costs incalculable. It was a major part of all our lives at that time and cannot be anything other than a significant part of this book.

KODAK FILM

is in the Shipyards

ensuring faultless construction

Detecting unseen flaws in steel construction work, revealing vibration stresses, and in many other critical ways, 'Kodak' Film helps war-time shipbuilding. The variable pitch principle of Rotol aircraft propellers has now been adapted to marine use, with the aid of vibration analyses recorded on 'Kodak' Film. Such vital work must come first—that's why you can't always get film.

PONTINGS
"CELANESE"
RAYON LOCKNIT
UNDERWEAR

41/M18. KNICKERS in Directoire style with long double gusset at back, also in wearing parts between legs. Shades to match petticoat 41/M17 on left.
W. size. **4'8**
Post 3½d.
2 Coupons.

WX 5/1½ OS 5/11
Extra Outsize in Peach, Turquoise, Beige or Black 6/4½.
Post 3½d.
2 Coupons.

AND IT DOESN'T HELP THE WAR A BIT

FOOD GERMANS CANNOT TAKE
From Our Special Correspondent
STOCKHOLM, Sunday.

Large stocks of Danish dairy produce are lying in Denmark's refrigerating plants, I am informed by Free Danish circles here. It is earmarked for Germany.

Germany's war-strained transport cannot handle it, so that much-needed food must remain in Denmark.

Missing Hubby

MY dear, since you went away
My house is tidy, I must say;
No ash scattered o'er the floor,
No garments hanging on the door,
No muddy footprints to be seen;
Yes, my house is very clean.

But I find the clock won't go,
Willie's boots need mending so,
The radio is mute and still;
I must confess to you, dear Bill,
My house, though very spick and span,
Needs you back soon—untidy man!

NO INCREASE IN MILK YET

Though Cheese Cut

An increase in the weekly milk allowance was promised to follow the cheese cut from 3oz. to 2oz. which begins to-morrow, but it has still to materialise.

There was an increase on March 14 last year, but there has been a heavy demand from the forces for condensed milk this year.

Canned meat and fish supplies have been increased so that the extra four points available in the new four-weekly period can be expended on these to replace the cheese protein loss.

There is no change in the personal points available for chocolate and sweets.

ASTORIAS
The **most popular American type cigarette** *can be sent*
DUTY FREE
TO
PRISONERS OF WAR 200 *for* 4/-
H.M. NAVY (SEAGOING SHIPS) (IN COMMISSION) 200 *for* 4/6
H.M. FORCES OVERSEAS

Apply for full particulars and order from your tobacconist or from—
THE HOUSE OF STATE EXPRESS
Dept. V
210 PICCADILLY, LONDON, W.1.

ASTORIAS *Easy to Smoke*

WOT, NO EGGS?

Davenport
Great Moor 3524.
Cafe Restaurant. Free Car Park

This Week-end—
MARGARET LOCKWOOD, TOM WALLS and STEWART GRANGER in
"LOVE STORY."

Monday, May 14, for 6 Days—
BETTE DAVIS and MIRIAM HOPKINS in
OLD ACQUAINTANCE

Monday to Friday continuous from 5-45. Saturday evening two houses at 6 and 8-15. Matinees each day at 2-30.

BLACK-OUT TO-NIGHT		
	p.m.	a.m.
LONDON	9.35	to 6.22
BELFAST	10.06	„ 6.40
BIRMINGHAM	9.45	„ 6.27
EDINBURGH	9.59	„ 6.23
LEEDS	9.46	„ 6.25
LIVERPOOL	9.51	„ 6.29
MANCHESTER	9.48	„ 6.28
NEWCASTLE	9.49	„ 6.19

This gay suede shoe is gusseted,
Resilient, snug, and trim.
Its polished wooden sole is hinged,
With two-toned fluted rim.

Clarks

WOODLAND GUSSET

W. Gibbons,
PLASTERER Etc.

7 GREEN BANK TERRACE,
OLD ROAD, HEATON NORRIS,
STOCKPORT.

School log.

1940 continued.

Oct' 11th The chairman of the Education Committee, Alderman Patten, and the Medical Officer of Health Dr Yule visited school and inspected the air raid shelters.

21st Enemy plane over this morning. Kept in shelters from 10.30 am until 12 am.

Another short alarm this afternoon. In the shelters about half an hour. Miss Cookson absent from duty with Lumbago.

In the afternoon, we had a puppet show by Mr Bruno Tublin, an Austrian refugee from Vienna. Visitors present were the Chairman of the Education Committee, ALDERMAN Patten and Mrs Paten. The Director of Education, Mr Holgate, Alderman Shepherdson, Councillor Ellis, Mr Lee H.M.I. Miss Frost H.M.I.& Miss Wakefield H.M.I. The children were most interested in the performance.

OCT' 30th Short air raid alarm this afternoon.

November 8th Short air raid warning this morning.

11th Armistice day. No service this year owing to the war. Flag flown half-mast.

15th Air raid alarm this afternoon lasting about half an hour.

25th Morning session begins at 9.30.am and ends 12. am. Afternoon session begins at 115pm and ends 3.15 infants and 3 30 juniors. This will continue until the end of February.

26th The head teacher absent this afternoon through illness.

29th Beryl Powell a child in class 3 died this morning from diphtheria the staff and

Continued. from page 78.

Children propose to show their sympathy by sending a wreath.

4th December. Short air raid warning 1.30 till 1. 45

5th Air raid warnings 1.10-1.40 All children used shelters 1 and 2. Register closed at 2 pm.

9th Miss Barker returned . Mrs Hoyle retained to assist during Medical Inspection.

10th Medical Inspection began

11th All day medical Inspection.

12th All day medical Inspection

November 29th 1940

Beryl Powel a child in class 3. Died this morning from Diphtheria. The staff and

School log

children propose to show their sympathy by sending a wreath.

December 10TH

Medical Inspection begins.

11TH All day Medical Inspection,

12TH All day medical inspection.

The second part of this account of life during the war is based on extracts taken from dad's memoirs. I have condensed, and rewritten many passages to try to do justice to dads' hard work.

PART TWO

I HAD AN ORDIARY WAR

BY WILLIAM GIBBONS

Generals, Politicians, and other notables have written about their war. This is an attempt by a nonentity, both as a civilian and very much so as a soldier, in an effort to correct the balance on behalf of the thousands who like me had an ordinary war.

Dad >

"As I waited for the expected brown envelope to drop through the letterbox, I tried to reassure Mary that all would turn out for the best in the end. On Friday, December 6th, 1940 my 29th birthday, the summons came. I didn't look at the envelope, I just tore it open. A postal order fluttered to the floor. I picked it up, and saw that it was made out for the sum of one shilling. Granny had not forgotten my birthday after all I thought, but it was not from my ageing grandmother. Some ageing gentleman had decided that they could no longer pursue the war without my help and they wanted me for the 12th of December. The one-shilling postal order was for refreshments the other paper was a travel warrant to take me to Marske by the Sea, near Redcar north Yorkshire and instructions what to do and where to go. No please or thank you, just be there on Thursday, 12 December".

"With just five days to wrap the kids Christmas presents, say goodbye to the neighbours as we had a last drink together in the Dog and Partridge on Buxton road. Some of the lads there were waiting for their call up papers. Of course, friends and family said Mary could call on them if she needed any help. How could I prepare for what could be the last time I would see Mary and the kids for a very long time. The night before I was due to leave, I had a talk to Terry, trying to reassure him that daddy would soon be back home, and as he's a big boy now, at nearly six, he must look after his mam, and help to look after his little brother and sister. I need not have worried too much; he was so excited that daddy was going to be a soldier. A few doors down the street was a typical corner shop of the time, run by a Mrs Rogerson, a tiny lady with thin lips and seemingly no teeth. It was the kind of shop that sold almost everything, from groceries to firelighters, sarsaparilla, milk, hairclips, and bread. That little shop was a lifeline for many neighbours. Even though Terry was only five, sorry, five and three quarters, he was a little trooper. Mary, having to keep an eye on 'the twins'. Terry could run to Mrs Rogerson's with a note for a few bits and pieces, Mary could watch both him and the twins as he ran the fifty *yards down the street and back in no time. The night before my departure, the children stayed at my mother's round at Mill cottage rather than having to cope with three little kiddies at six o'clock in the morning as their dad left them behind. Along with five or six other men with wives, girlfriends, and mothers saying their goodbyes, we hugged and kissed one last time on that cold, damp morning on the 12ᵗʰ December 1940."*

School log

December 12th 1940

Air raid warning 2:45-3:10. A number of parents who were hear for the Medical Inspection were accommodated in the Junior's shelters.

ME.>

The departure of dad coincided with the Sheffield air raids. Mam must have been worried sick when she heard about the terrible loss of life only forty miles away. The Sheffield raids, or 'blitz' as they were called, were on the 12ᵗʰ-15ᵗʰ Dec'1940. The air raids this far north were far too close for comfort with hundreds killed as bombs rained down on the city trying to smash the steel works. But alas, the civilian population suffered more than most during those air raids on towns and cities alike. The Marples hotel in that Sheffield raid suffered a direct hit with an estimated 70 deaths, and that was only the beginning.

Dad >

"I did not feel too bad, as I had decided to make the most of it. However, on reflection, we realised how our wives must have felt. They had to return to a house without a man, and then take on the burden of all the responsibilities of running the home and bringing up the children. They must have felt utterly desolate. Even though Redcar is only 135 miles away, we did not arrive there until six o'clock. By that time, it was pitch black, and still raining. As we got off the train, we lined up for a roll call. I did not realise that there were so many of us on the train. It seems that dozens of lads swelling our number to about forty joined us at various points on our journey. As we stood shivering on that cold wet deserted station, no one knowing what to do, a sergeant came round the corner and balled at us to stand by the trucks, and get move on! When we were all accounted for, we were told to board the trucks and

hold on tight, and away we went. No one knew where we were going; all we could do was wait and see. After about half an hour of the most uncomfortable ride imaginable, we turned into a lane then through the gates to an army camp. We saw a badge three feet high painted in green and gold as the truck's headlights illuminated it as we swept through the gates and stopped by a guard hut with two soldiers manning a check point, one lad shouted bloody hell were in the Royal

Artillery, the nine mile snipers, but no one knew exactly what he meant. All we knew was that we were in a regular Army camp used by the Royal Artillery"

"As we persuaded our cramped up limbs into action we were shepherded into a large First World War Nissen hut where comfort was conspicuous by its absence. Even though it was bitter cold the two pop-bellied stoves were just warm. The hut was painted a sickly shade of yellow at about the time of World War One. A row of about twenty beds down each side made this hut so heart breaking as we had all left our cosy little homes just twelve hours ago. NOW! said the Sergeant, when you have all made claim to your beds, I'll take you to the cookhouse for something to eat. This was the best news we had had all day, we were, to a man, starving. He said, as you haven't any eating irons, I'll get you some. After a few minutes, he came back with a box full of cutlery, for some inexplicable reason he unceremoniously dumped them with a clatter on the concrete floor. Get a move on he balled as we scrambled about on our haunches for a set of knife fork and spoon. I think this method of silver service was to see if any kind of pecking order was beginning to evolve. Something to eat was a good description, rather than a meal. It consisted of meat, cabbage, and spuds slapped on a plate with little thought to whether it was on the plate or in your hand. Nevertheless, as we were all starving, no one complained and no one left a scrap. By now, it was well after nine o'clock and we were all knackered. After our supper, we were marched to the quartermaster's stores and were issued four of the roughest blankets I have ever felt, let alone to sleep under. When we got back to our hut there was a ration of coke and a few bits of wood. We decided to shove just the minimum amount on the stoves in case we needed some coke later. Watching people undress was a real revelation. Some stood and stripped off quite openly, others shyly pretended they were not embarrassed because they wore pyjamas, others because they didn't, and there were those who couldn't have cared less whether they wore them or not, truly a cross section of British manhood. A deep silence fell over the hut as the lights were turned off just after ten o'clock. Amid groans, you could hear a mile away, one lad said "I should be in the taproom at the King's Head with my mates having a game of crib and a nice cool pint of Robbie's bitter". Although our army service was little more than four hours each, I think most of us were fed up to the back teeth already. Then there came to our rescue one of the reasons why we won the war; the great British sense of humour. Joke followed joke followed story followed a good night's sleep".

MY FIRST OF 1,857 DAYS

"Our first visit to the ablutions was quite a steep learning curve as was most of the next few weeks. Our first pay parade was a real revelation and quite a laugh. This was the first time that we had come face to face with a real live officer, apart from the M.O. and the Chaplain. Some men were a bit jittery as you will read here. The variations on that simple piece of drill were worthy of any pantomime. Some men halted too far away from the table, remembered to salute, extended the left hand and found that they could not reach their pay being offered to them. Having made this mistake, some took another step forward, then did not know whether to give another salute or not; some did, some did not; others tried to do an invisible shuffle forward. Some forgot to step back and salute and were brought back to do it properly, others just got everything wrong, even taking the pay in their right hand and trying to salute with their left hand. Realising their mistake, they would try to pass the pay packet to their left hand and try again. Sometimes we were there for over an hour. One lad was overheard complaining about the delay when the sergeant said what's your name son? Phillips sir, Why aren't you with the F^s you silly bugger."

"Our first lecture was a history of the Royal Artillery. This turned out to be far more interesting than we imagined. The guns in the Royal Artillery are the regiment's colours. We did not have flags leading us into battle. The guns are protected and retained at all costs. If they had to be left behind, they had to be destroyed. The gun on our cap badge is an 1871 muzzleloader. The motto "Fras et Gloria Ducunt, "Where right and glory lead us" The army chaplain came to introduce himself officially then after a few words about how he could help anyone who felt the need of a friend, he lead us in the Royal Artillery prayer".

O Lord Jesus Christ,

Who dost everywhere lead thy people in the way of righteousness, Vouchsafe so as to lead the Royal Regiment of Artillery, that wherever we serve, on land or sea or air, we may win the glory of doing thy will.

Amen.

We were to say this prayer many times on Church parade, often with a great deal more fervor as the war progressed.

ON A CHARGE FOR LAUGHING

"We were told, or ordered to read the inside front cover of our 'Pay Book' as follows".

ALL RANKS.

"Remember- Never discuss military, naval or air matters in public or with any stranger, no matter to what nationality he or she may belong. The enemy wants information about you, your unit, your destination. He will do his utmost to discover it. Keep him in the dark. Gossip on military subjects is highly dangerous to the country, whereas secrecy leads to success. BE ON YOUR GUARD and report any suspicious individual"

"Some of the lads said it was no use asking them anything as they knew bugger all. Overhearing this remark and the laughter that followed, the sergeant put them both on a charge for insubordination".

Me >

As I was far too young to remember those early years of the war, I can only piece together things I was told, and tiny fragments of my early memories with photos and extracts from letters. Many letters must have been lost. However, fortunately, dad's very first letter written in December 1940 has survived these 73 years. Though still intact, dad's first letter has suffered the ravages of time so I have transcribed it verbatim.

Dear Mary.

We have just had the usual meat and cabbage spuds. We did not arrive till nearly six, I picked up with a lad from Reddish and was wondering if that Plasterer that I was examined with was going. I looked for him on the train when we got to Marske. I seen him just getting on the lorry he was pleased to see someone as he was all alone but he was put in another battery. The chaps here are very decent lads seem to want to help, there was about 50 in our batch. The Srg M came in and put us wise about different things and he is very genial and one of the other soldiers told us he is the best man in camp. They don't seem to be badly done to but I will tell you better after I been here a bit. Well no more just now as I won't get the post as he is waiting. Your Loving Bill *xxx KEEP SMILING.*

Dad>

"After a few days, we were fully kitted out and looked more like proper soldiers. As well as all the items on our kit list, we were issued with a ground sheet that doubled up as a cape. We also received a gas cape that was more suitable as a raincoat. However, it could only be worn in the event of a gas attack. Some lads were very confused, and asked, can we wear our gas cape as a rain coat. If we have both gas and rain which one do we wear... Sir. They were taking the piss of course. There were a number of

mystery items to make up this ensemble. A sort of mini scarf, called a cap comforter, a length of course brown string called a Lanyard, used to pull the firing pin on the gun. As it was deemed too scruffy to wear with our uniform, we had to buy our own white plaited Lanyard from the N A F F I with our own money of course. One night, I was having a shave when some bright spark decided to sound the air-raid sirens. As we were plunged into darkness, I shaved off part of my moustache, and had to shave the other side off later to even it up. The annoying thing was, it was just an exercise. One of the lads dared me to leave it as it was, as there are no rules regarding half moustaches, but I'm sure they would find something."

"As hair was kept short in those days, one would imagine that those not requiring a haircut would get the best deal, however, logic was not the army's strong point. Weather through frustration at not having enough hair to attack, or whether the barber had instructions to remove as much hair as possible, I will never know. Maybe he was only dreaming of getting back to his peacetime occupation as a sheep shearer."

TOO CLOSE FOR COMFORT

ME >

On December 23rd and 24th 1940, Manchester suffered one of the many air raids on and around the cities of Salford and Manchester. Christmas must have been a sorry time for mam even though grandmas' and granddads' were on hand to try to make the best of a very difficult time for our mam, and think of all the thousands of families throughout the country in a similar situation. In one sense, we were fortunate to be the only grandchildren at the time. The weeks soon turned into months as the war, with the ever-increasing shortages and worrying about the future. Rationing became more and more widespread. Dad finding his way round the mystifying world of army life, mam doing her best to get on with life as a single mother, grandmas' granddads' helping out, Terry off to school, things seem to settle into a routine. Nevertheless, the air raids on Manchester, Salford, Liverpool, and Sheffield, were just the beginning. As we move into1941with the New Year well behind us, a constant flow of news about the war on all fronts was forever on the wireless and on the newsreels at the pictures. As Hitler's shadow lengthened over Europe, many children were evacuated away from the danger of increased air raids. Seventy two thousand Children from the Manchester area in the early days following the outbreak of war were evacuated.

Dad >

"Christmas was soon upon us, but few of us were bothered, or even cared. Even as a Catholic I was becoming very disillusioned with the whole meaning of Christmas but I never told Mary. She wrote and told me that Mrs Rogerson managed to get a few nice Christmas cards for her regular customers and sent one to the children telling them it was from their daddy. With the presents we managed to get ready before I was called up. I felt content in the knowledge that both sets of grandparents would do their very best to make Christmas a happy time for Mary and the children. I could not find anything special to send home for Mary. The only thing I could send was my love in the words of my letters. I did not tell Mary in so many words, but I thought I would put Christmas on hold and hope that God is on our side. Next came our medical inspection, yes, inspection, not examination as you would expect. As far as I could see it was only meant to prove three things; first, that a man could walk, second, that he was in the right branch of the service, not the women's branch, and thirdly that he could cough".

BACK TO SCHOOL

"There then followed ten weeks of lectures, courses, jabs' route marches, snow shifting, fall in fall out and shake it all about. Cleaning our allotted gun to within an inch of its life after every training scheme whether we fired the gun or not was a real pain in the arse. Having been in the building trade in Civvy Street and a spell in the home guard, the physical side of army life was easy for me to handle. We had some basic training on First World War Howitzers at Marske, and a number of films on safety and how they worked. The most boring job particularly as it was so cold up there on the north Yorkshire coast was keeping the bloody things clean and in good order whatever the weather was like. Reading this today makes these guns seem old, but they were only a little over twenty years old at that time. One seemingly silly throw back to the First World War was a duty known as "stand to"; this I gathered, was a remnant of the times when all attacks took place at dawn. At dawn, one unfortunate was issued with a rifle, no bullets; that would be far too dangerous. He had to walk out of the camp across a field to an isolated headland. There, he would stand staring out to sea for an hour then return to camp to report no enemy ships sir, then go back to bed for an hour. No one told us what we were supposed to be looking for, or what we should do if we saw anything that we thought looked like even a tiny bit like a German seagull. The few times I spent on that headland, I would take a moment to think how Mary and the children were getting on. I would wonder if they were suffering any air raids and if the shelter was ok. One morning I spent half an hour releasing a sheep that was caught up in some barbed wire, so at least I had the satisfaction that my time was not entirely wasted. As we were nearing the end of our three months basic training, we knew we would be moving out soon and dispersed far and wide. I thought a farewell get together just for our hut, would be a good idea. The main obstacle was a lack of funds, so with the help of the girls from the N A A F I, we acquired some raffle ticket. A couple of us managed to sell a few round our part of the camp at a tanner each. The prize being a ten shilling note. A soldier's pay scale was a total mystery. We had to pay a kit allowance of 5ᵈ per week (for blanco, soap, razor blades, tooth paste, metal polish, and 6ᵈ a month for the regimental barber whether you used him or not. Laundry was free, but limited to only seven items a week; of course, there was nothing to stop any of us doing our own washing now and again. There is always at least one silly bugger to ask if a pair of socks is one or two items. However it was worked out I got ten bob a week. Mary, with my allowance to her, and Government grant made Mary's total about £2 /18 shillings week. After I got my ten bob back, the draw netted three pounds two shillings and six pence. Enough to buy a couple of pints and a pie each. Not exactly a banquet, but we enjoyed ourselves and had a good laugh about some of the antics we got up to. Having completed our basic training, we had a passing out parade in front of the Major, and very smart we looked and felt more like proper soldiers by now. The army moved us a few miles inland to another camp for some rifle drill and target practice, to make room for the next intake at Marske."

"We had target practice with rifles that had been converted to fire a ·22 bullet. I think it was less dangerous for beginners. As you can imagine some were hopeless and some were good. I was amongst the latter. Shortly after arriving at this new camp I was promoted acting unpaid lance bombardier, unpaid being the operative word. It is thought to be the first step to that Field Marshal's baton that is supposed to lurk at the bottom of every soldier's kit bag along with my lanyard and cap comforter. I got my promotion so quick because a German plane made an emergency landing a few miles away on top of the wind swept moors of north Yorkshire. As guard commander, I was detailed to take six gunners to perform guard duty round the crashed aircraft. When we left the camp on that nice sunny Sunday afternoon shortly after two o'clock the weather was fine, but as we went higher and higher the wind was bitterly cold. There were plenty of bombardiers and sergeants at this camp, but as it was Sunday afternoon, I can only assume that they were out of camp or could not be roused from their kip. Hence my unexpected promotion. Because we were in such a hurry to get out of camp and see something different, we were quite unprepared and suffered the consequences of not getting adequately dressed. By that, I mean we should have taken our ground sheets and an extra jersey, and our gas capes". With the pilot off to hospital, we were to mount the guard to keep sightseers and looters away until some regular soldiers could be found. We had a tent in our truck, but in such strong gusting winds, it was near impossible to put it up in a way to stay up, so three of us huddled on the sheltered side of the truck in sight of the plane, the rest of us got our heads down in the back. We learned our lesson the hard way. It did not happen again"

"Even on such a bitter cold hillside there were still people scrounging around for souvenirs or anything to make a few bob. We were not relieved until well after six o'clock and did not get back to camp until turned seven to be met by an orderly in the canteen with what was left of our evening meal of stew and mash. I thought if being a Lance bombardier means more of the same duties, they could stick it. We were not alone in the silliness steaks. When we were called up we all took our civilian gas masks with us. It was a good job too; there was a shortage of service respirators so we carried our civilian ones for the time being. No one seemed to be bothered if they had one or not. However, when we were issued with our proper military respirators we saw that they were much more robust than our civvy ones. We had to wear them at regular times of the day until we got used to them. This is where things started to get silly. We were given instructions on the best way to carry them and put them on in less than a minute. They were extremely uncomfortable but we had to persevere. One idea was to have half the men wear them all morning and the other half in the afternoon. However, if a soldier was not wearing his, he would say he was in the afternoon group and vice versa. This was by no means satisfactory, so we all had to wear them at the same time, something like an hour at a time. We seemed to be getting on with these confounded contraptions until it was our turn for a shower. Because we had to keep them on for an hour, we took it literally. Close your eyes and try to imagine a dozen or so men, stark naked except for their steamed up respirators trying to have a shower. That directive to wear the said item was soon forgotten."

ANYTHING FOR A CHANGE

"A war weapons week was to be held in a town a few miles down the road. A national event to persuade people to give or lone money for the purpose of buying weapons for the Armed Forces, these displays were held all over the country, particularly by the army. As we were nearly real soldiers, we were to take part in the local display for a day at an industrial town a few miles away. Having made ourselves all spic and span, away we went with our guns and support vehicles to demonstrate just how quickly we could leap into action. Arriving at our allotted station, a large square in the centre of the town, crowds packed a dozen deep all around the square waiting for our arrival. With official photographers on hand to record this momentous event, and feeling very important we made ready our guns and started our well-rehearsed drill with great smartness and efficiency. Unfortunately, "Jerry" decided to send a plane over at that precise moment, the air raid sirens sounded and sent our audience dashing for cover. I think it was the first time they had heard the sirens for real and at first hand as it were. Leaving us to demonstrate to a rather battered statue of a man on horseback. By the time the 'all clear' sounded, we were on our way back to camp, feeling decidedly deflated. Still, some photographs were sent along to us later, and I must say, we looked quite good."

"At the end of our three month spell in north Yorkshire, we were all assembled to be told what we already knew, that we were going to be posted to new units. Some of us were going onto super heavy guns and only men of 5ft 8"or over were required. Being 5ft 11", I was one of the 40 or so chosen. Before we were posted to our new camps, we were given ten days leave. I left with fond memories of all the men I met, and wondered how many I would see at the next camp. Whilst I was on leave, I recall that although it was early spring, and by no means warm, I had difficulty breathing indoors for the first couple of days, and had to sit by the back door from time to time for comfort. After ten glorious days, during which time we managed a little celebratory drink in the Dog and Partridge for our seventh wedding anniversary, playing with the twins and Terry, and enjoying the love of my wife was wonderful. Seeing my mam and dad, and sister Lena, round at Mill cottages, taking great delight having a ride on the top deck of the tram with the kiddies to Portwood to see Mary's mam and dad, it was a real treat. Other family members and friends called on us at Alldis street, wanting to know how thing were, and when will I be home for good. It may sound silly, but we went for a walk round Princes Street, the market place, and Mersey Square on the Saturday morning before I went to catch the train, yes, 'the monkey run'. But on this occasion, things were very different as we relived the sights and sounds of yesteryear and wondered what the future may have in store for us as we strolled around our old haunts. We walked down princess street towards Nield and Hardy's record shop. We could here Bing Crosby singing "Let me call you sweetheart", we paused a while, but had to leave such pleasures until we were together again. Trying hard to hold back the tears we kissed goodbye as the train was about to leave, but this time it was quite a nice sunny day, not the blacked out miserable morning of last December. Those ten days were the shortest ever. When the time came to leave my young family, I

was heartbroken, but I knew it would be equally upsetting for Mary if she knew how I felt, so I had to put on a brave face for Mary and our three little children. Being the way of the Army, I had to return to Marske-by-the-sea. We were in a state of limbo, living in tents, taking the micky out of the new intake and generally having an easy time."

School log;

(30th April 1941)

"202 eggs and £3-16s-6d in cash sent to Stockport Infirmary as school contribution to the annual egg appeal"

"After about a week, a dozen or so lads and I were posted to Catterick camp, slap bang in the middle of north Yorkshire. Before leaving my previous camp, you know, the one where the German plane came down, I asked if I would be keeping my stripe. I was advised to keep it until I was told to remove it. Being so far away from the fresh sea breezes of Marske it was a bit of let-down. Nevertheless, as I settled in, I gained some benefit by keeping my stripe. No standing about for hours on guard, and no fatigues, it was great. Then some little shit of a sergeant said those of us that were only acting Lance Bombardiers should have our stripe taken away, because it was thought that we had an unfair advantage over the rest and as we were at a new camp, we all had to start from square one. A stupid and petty suggestion but I had to give up my stripe. 'It took me three and a half years to get it back'. We started training on 12" railway guns that could fire a 600lb shell more than 15 miles. When we did eventually fire those guns down on the south coast, the power was awesome. We did not actually fire any shells while we were at Catterick; it is a lot more than fifteen miles to the open sea. These guns too, dated from the First World War. The ultimate aim was for us to operate them for coastal defence, but never did."

ARMY FORM BLANK

"*In between gun drill, cleaning, and route marches, we had some very amusing lectures about sanitation and personal hygiene. An officer explained why the toilet paper, or 'Army form blank' to give it its army name, was rough on one side and smooth on the other. It seems it was rough on both sides until the women complained. So it was made smooth on both sides, till the men in turn complained, the Army in its wisdom made it one side smooth and t'other side rough. This arrangement, after endless discussions did the trick and everyone was happy. As you can guess, everything in the Army is on ration and that includes toilet paper. The sergeant said, in deadly earnest, your ration is four sheets per man per day, this is sufficient for one up, one down, one across, and one polish. Unbelievably one man was put on a charge for laughing. Insubordination was on the charge sheet. We had to collect our ration of army form blank from the Q M stores, but few bothered to collect their ration. We dubbed it as a chit for a shit. The practice was soon dropped as most of us kept any bits of tissue paper or thin wrapping paper we could find. The ration of toilet paper was soon rescinded in favour of a number of toilet rolls per hut per week. We could buy toilet paper from the N A F F I but we all felt that the army were being a bit mean. I was quite happy at Catterick, the food and conditions were very good. However, the main bugbear, silly as it seems, was that there were so many soldiers, we hardly saw a civilian.*"

A PINT IN THE DOG AND PARTRIDGE?

"If we had no guard duties, or could swap with someone, we were entirely free from Saturday dinner, until Monday morning, a couple of lads decided to chance it and try to get home for a few hours. As we all lived in Stockport, they said if you want to see the wife and kids for a few hours, get your leg over and have pint of Robbies best mild, come with us. To cut a long story short, we were all caught by the military police a few miles down the road, and shunted right back that same afternoon and had to face the music after parade on Monday morning. Three days confined to barracks, not so bad, I suppose. Some of the lads said we could lose three days Royal Warrant, meaning no pay. That turned out to be just the lads taking the piss. That episode put an end to my wanderings. While we were at this camp, we heard about Germany's invasion of Russia. It was June 22nd 1941. It caused scarcely a ripple; most of the lads were more interested in what they were having for their next meal."

It was about this time; July 1941 that Churchill initiated the 'V for Victory' campaign during the early stages of the war. The BBC used the opening notes of Beethoven's Fifth Symphony, which matched the dot-dot-dot-dash Morse code for the letter V, playing it before news bulletins on the wireless. Churchill announced, "The V sign is the symbol of the unconquerable will of the occupied territories. So long as people continue to refuse all collaboration with the invader it is sure that, his cause will perish and that Europe will be liberated. What this article dose not tell you is that the musical notes were taken from a recording by the Berlin symphony orchestra.

"The time was drawing near for us to take up the duties for which we were being trained. Our new commanding officer, made his appearance wearing a very fine silk cravat instead of the regular khaki collar and tie. This created the impression that he was not a "bullshitter" who insisted on petty rules and restrictions. He said, "We are all going to do a job together, and there would be no unnecessary discipline". He turned out to be one of the most supercilious of men we served under throughout the war, as we were on the receiving end of his whims. He even gave a soldier seven days C. B. for having dirty soap. Moving out day came, we occupied several railway carriages, but before you think how nice, they were not, I think these too, predated the First World War. Most carriages were third class with hard wooden seats that were very shiny after many bottoms polishing them day in day out; second class had leather seats, they too were shinny making it impossible to sit on them without bracing ones legs against the seat opposite to stop yourself sliding off. The officers had 'First Class' as one would expect. With two guns positioned in the middle of the train, four men were detailed to sit on the guns, two at the front and two at the rear as guards, and off we went. At first, we thought they had landed bad deal; however, it was not long before some of us would have swapped places with them. On the few occasions, when we travelled during daylight enemy aircraft would shoot at anything that moved on the railways including our train. The carriages were nowhere near bullet or bombproof. However, the lads sitting on the guns could dive under the heaviest part of the gun to take cover if it was getting a bit hot. Those of us inside had to scramble under the seats until we realised that the chances of being hit by

cannon fire or a bomb was quite slim. The journey took five days. We had to wait for clear lines, give way to goods traffic, and plan a route to avoid low bridges and electric cables. Sometimes we waited a whole day in a siding in the middle of nowhere. We travelled part of the way by night, but despite all these delays, the lads travelling on the guns were only relieved for meals and toilet. On one occasion, we thought it was raining, until one lad stuck his arm through the window only to realize it was one of the guards having a pee. You dirty bastard he shouted amid little sympathy. When we stopped all night, a patrolling guard, along with more home guards than you could shake a stick at would take over. By the time we reached our destination the lads on the guns had imprints of rivets on their arses, and were very happy to show them off to anyone with a mind more curious than was good for them. Our destination turned out to be Hailsham in Sussex. A small town on the south coast, about four miles inland. We pulled into the station sidings, which were surprisingly large for such a small town. We had a total compliment of between 80-90 officers and men, divided into 'A' and 'B' troop. I was in 'A' troop. Each troop was responsible for one gun. There were 14 gunners, augmented by drivers, signallers, cooks, mechanics, and all manner of odds, and sods made up the rest. We spent the first week settling in and getting our bearings. The villages were very helpful and accustomed to soldiers who had come from other camps. We were told never to tell anyone where we came from, or what you have been doing. Our predecessors were posted to a new position just before we arrived. In the picture of the regiment, my new friend Curly is 6ᵗʰ and I am 7ᵗʰ from the right on the bottom row".

"When we arrived in this idyllic little town in the height of summer, we were all quite pleased with what we saw. Until we were all shunted into a very large barn with a palliasse bag each, directed towards a pile of straw, and told to make ourselves comfortable. I have never heard such a load of whingers in my life. Why, I have no idea. The weather was beautiful; we were in a new camp with lots of new things to discover, and we were to fire some real guns. The First World War railway guns weighed in at 70 tons each and were built on a massive framework of steel girders. After two days of swearing and lots of muffled laughter, we managed to get the guns in position. The early days were spent doing lots of gun drill, not firing of course, that would be far too dangerous even though we were only a few miles from the channel. The guns were inspected on Saturday morning, covered up

until Monday morning, and then the whole routine would start all over again. One day, presumably to give us something to keep us occupied, the Major thought it would be a good idea to move a pile of shells from one compound to another. As each gun weighed 70 tons, it had shells to match at 600 lbs. each. There was a purpose- made wheeled contraption to help do the job. A couple of lads went to collect the 'shell transporter' from the Q. M. stores. The quartermaster had no idea what he was looking for. The lads knew it would be far too big to be on a shelf, and went into the yard to look for it. They soon found a large frame on two heavy iron wheels about 24" in diameter, this contraption could only be used for one purpose, to move heavy shells. After numerous attempts to get to grips with what was a simple device made unbelievably difficult by an inept sergeant. After many trials and near misses of trapped fingers, he wanted to try carrying a shell on a heavy steel wheelbarrow. Just how he got his stripes, I will never know! During the fiasco with the wheelbarrow, I kept my distance, in the certain knowledge that someone was going to get hurt. This method seemed to be working until the shell suddenly started slipping forward as the barrow was lifted. Realising that hands were in danger of becoming trapped I ran to help. Unfortunately, everybody decided to take their hands away just at that precise moment, and mine were the ones to be trapped. How ironic, after my warnings, I was the one to get hurt. I was taken to the medic's station for treatment. After waiting for ages, I went in to see the M. O. After a cursory glance by the Medical Officer, he demanded, "What the hell are you doing here with a couple of scratches like them? How do you think you are going to go on when in action and really wounded? See the orderly." Seething, I went to the orderly, he said "Blimey, they're in a right mess, I'll soon fix you up." After bandaging my fingers, he put my arm in a sling, and gave me some sulphonamide stuff, and then I returned to my billet on light duties for a week. At first everything was ok, but I soon got frustrated not being able to sweep up and make my bed properly and threw the brush to the far end in the billet. Fortunately, being right handed, I could wipe my bottom and shave o k but most importantly I could write to Mary but I did not tell her about my injury because she would only worry about me."

"A week or so after this episode, we moved into billets in the village. Troop, 'A', my troop, moved into an empty three storey shop, while 'B' troop moved into a semi-detached house. The officers had their own billets down in the village. I, and a couple of mates from Marske, shared a large first floor bedroom, and even had a bathroom and soon got ourselves organised. We scrubbed the floor, and one of the lads was named Jack, but because he had a very short back and sides was soon nicknamed 'curly' managed to scrounged three pieces of carpet, one each, making it clean and comfortable. We did not ask, or expect any credit for this, but I must say that although we occupied that room for nearly a year, never once did any officer comment on our efforts. There were the usual gun inspections, and kit inspections, you would not think there was a war on. Mary was pleased that we were known as part of the 'Home Army' I suppose it would not do to send every soldier abroad in case Hitler did decide to invade us. Some of the lads went to a gunnery range near Lewes about ten miles away for a different kind of firing drill. We all said it was a pity that we were not firing at the f.kin' Germans"

"Once we were established into our daily routine, I had a word with the major to see if there were any restrictions regarding my wife and children coming down to stay for a while. He said, even though our

position is relatively safe from enemy action I must caution you that there is always a possibility of a stray enemy aircraft. He went on to say there are many occasions when men are stationed near to where they live and see their families on a regular basis. He said you would be expected to take full responsibility for them in such matters as lodgings, ration books, register on a doctor's panel, and education as necessary. In addition, of course, under no circumstances do anything to embarrass the Regiment. As I was in such a hurry to see Mary and the children I could only find digs for Mary and just one of the children. Ann and Terry stayed with my mother round at mill cottage. Ken, being a bit run down, was the lucky one to stay for a week's holiday with his mam, just to see how things worked out"

"There was an E.N.S.A. concert one evening during the week, a rare treat for us. Of course, I fell for guard duty at the last minute, but I did manage to slip in to see the last half hour and enjoyed it very much. I was so frustrated not to be able to walk Mary back to her lodgings and enjoy each other's love for just one night. I applied for a sleeping out pass while my wife was so close by, but my request was turned down because it would not be fair to the other men. I pointed out that the other men did not want to sleep with my wife sir. This attempt at humour fell on stony ground. Mary, and Ken enjoyed their all to brief holiday so much I thought if I could find a place cheap enough for Mary and the three children, they could stay for the rest of the summer. I tried to arrange for them to stay at the same house as before. But the lady said that she would have to charge extra for the two extra kiddies, but in any case, as much as she would love to have Mary and Ken to stay, three children were a little too much of a responsibility, even for a short stay. However, she very kindly arranged for them all to stay with an elderly lady down the road".

HOW LUCKY

"Miss Sally Butler lived alone in a bungalow with a big garden that would be ideal for the children to play in. Nevertheless, I could not see how it could work. How could an elderly lady accept the presence of another woman and three children? They were bound to disrupt her way of life. There were a number of imponderables to sort out first. How much rent would she want? Where is the nearest school and shops? When I went to see her, she said her way of life had already been disrupted by the war and would be more than happy to have them stay as long as they like, as her guests and went on to say she would love the company. We like to think our children are very well behaved, but they were children after all, but she would have none of it. We came to an agreement that in exchange for a peppercorn rent, Mary would look after the children of course, and keep the house clean, a plus point was that Mary loved gardening and would be such a good help. She would take all the ration books and medical information and with the help of Miss Butler would sign up with all the appropriate shops and the local doctor. A couple of weeks later Mary and I had managed to reassure family and friends that everything would be ok, and promising to write every week. I went to meet them at the station on a cool sunless afternoon, the children were very excited to see their daddy, and clambered round my legs as I embraced Mary, she too had been looking forward to this moment. The walk from the station took just a few minutes, I introduced Mary to Miss Butler then I had to leave her and the children to settle in and went back to camp. Later that evening I went to see how they were getting on. During a quiet moment as we strolled round the garden on that cool August evening in 1941, Mary told me there was a fire in the sitting room that would not keep a cat warm. But soon after we arrived the old lady threw some coal on the fire, and got an ancient pair of bellows working, saying as she did so. "We can't have the little children getting cold can we."

Me >

It is obviously very frustrating that there are no letters during this period as there was no need for any. I can only piece together how I remember things during the time we spent that summer of 1941 until spring 1942 in Hailsham. By now, Terry would be seven years old, and probably remembered a lot more that Ann or I do. But alas, Terry died in 2003 and took many memories with him. I can remember a very large garden with a greenhouse; I believe we called it a glass shed. Soon we discovered new tastes, colours, and smells a wonder to behold. Apple trees and what can only have been plumbs, strawberries, blackberries, and raspberries, never having seen such things before we were very curious what they tasted like. Being a keen gardener, the old lady now 'Aunt Sally' to us, had rather neglected the house, but mam soon got it spic and span.

As little kids, we did not know very much about what was going on in the world, but me Ann and Terry loved our new "Aunt Sally" and the big garden to play in. We thought it was great that there were no stairs and so many rooms and a big garden to play in, we were in our element. As you can see in the picture, we are most likely trying new tastes such as raspberries or strawberries.

"*Mary soon arranged for Terry to attend the local infant school in a proper grown up class, and the Twins in the nursery class, and soon settled in her new home. One day when Mary was helping in the garden, Sally told her that she had a younger sister who had died at the age of twelve, and although it was so long ago, she still missed her. It was because of the sad loss of her sister, that Sally took a real shine to Ann, and always called her Rosie in memory her sister. She even asked Mary if she could adopt her, but it could never be. From time to time, I manage to get a weekend pass. When we went to bed, we would sink out of sight, in a deep feather filled palliasse, fabulous! I had my Sunday tea there regularly when I was not on duty, but when I was on guard, Mary, would often come and have a chat for half an hour*".

School log

"September 16th 1941.

The children went up to the main road at 10.0 o'clock this morning to see the tanks go by."

See photo' on back pages

September 30th

Dr Moir visited school in reference to the question of diphtheria immunisation

October 7th

Dr Kippen visited school for diphtheria immunisation. Twenty six children were treated.

October 28th

Dr Kippen visited school to give the second diphtheria immunisation treatment

FLIPPIN' KIDS

"The old lady, having few friends, would open up to Mary during quiet moments in the garden. She told her that she was pure, as no man had ever touched her. Mary did not know where to look, and could only offer a sympathetic ear. Even though we were at war, there is always an innocent child without a care in the world to embarrass you. I remember an occasion, when Curly and Bob came to Sunday tea. Ken, even at only three and a half years old, suddenly said for no apparent reason. "Ann hasn't got a robin, has she" Be quiet and eat your tea, Mary said hastily, blushing scarlet. After a few minutes silence, "I have a robin haven't I" No one made any comment and I breathed again. Then after a few minutes silence, the little monkey, innocent as he was, suddenly said to his new Aunt Sally, "But my dad's got a big one" enough said. During this most embarrassing episode Ann and Terry said nothing the whole time, but I could see that Terry was somewhat amused by the whole thing."

Me>

As I said earlier, there are no letters during this period of our stay in Hailsham, and nothing in dad's memoirs about Christmas 1941. Being little more than three and a half years old we have very little recall of the time we spent down in Hailsham. Nevertheless, it is amazing how the brain can retain the tiniest embers of memory from all those years ago. Mam told us how she would walk us down to the local junior school at the bottom of the road. Terry to one classroom, me and Ann to the nursery classroom. It must have been quite daunting for Terry leaving his new found friends at Southwood road school back in Stockport. Moving to another school far far away where the kids talked funny, living in a house with no stairs, I can only guess how he must have felt. However Ann and me at least had one another, one thing I do remember about the nursery school was the practise of having a nap in the afternoon. I can remember it as if it was last week; I have a picture in my mind that the classroom seemed to be full, maybe about twenty kids. The teaching lady, as we called her, when it was time for our nap said we had to cross our arms and place them on the desk and lay our heads on them and close our eyes, and be as quiet as a little mouse. Other times I remember at aunt Sally's, was when we had a saucer of tiny new potatoes with a knob of butter, or was it margarine. We would sit on the back doorstep on a summer evening eating fresh strawberries and cream from the local farm. As I said it is a shame, but I have no recollection and no pictures of that kindly lady, who shared her home with mam and three little children during the summer of 1941 and into spring of 1942.

School log

January 15th 1942. 17 cwt 94 lbs waste paper to Cleansing Department.

January 26 th £293-4-10 paid into school bank this month.

School log

February 17th 1942 Shrove Tuesday school closed.

25th February. "Stainless Stephen" Comedian visited school this afternoon in connection with the salvage of paper. Alderman Patten was also present.

Stainless Steven was a comedian from Sheffield, hence the name. His real name was Arthur Clifford Baynes. He served in the army during WW1. However, he was to old serve in WW II but did a lot of good, helping the schools collecting valuable waste for recycling.

Dad cont. >

"This seemingly cushy time with Mary and children, the lovely walks round the lanes of the Sussex countryside made me feel a bit embarrassed to call myself a soldier, and frustrated because we were not doing what we have been training for. I had the usual quota of leave but did not take them as I had all I wanted right here in Hailsham. But as a special treat for Mary and the kids I made a supreme effort to save enough to pay the train fare and a bit of spending money so we could all to go and visit my gran' and granddad in Sidcup Kent for a few days. She was so pleased to see the children, particularly the twins for the first time."

"It was all very nice, but I wanted to see some action, and get the war over with, and get on with life once more. There wasn't much anyone could do, but be ready when the call came. One or two enemy aircraft had been attacking a seaside town about seven miles away, and the odd aircraft flew over the village. The powers that be, decided that the fire piquet would mount a Bren gun next time an enemy plane approached. We were all itching to 'have a go' at Jerry, but it was considered too dangerous to allow a permanent gun position or issue us with any ammunition until we needed some. The drill was for the Bren gun to be in the guardroom. When anyone heard an enemy plane the fire piquet would collect the gun from the guardroom, take it into the station yard, a distance of about 50 yds. The duty officer would hurry from the officer's mess, about 100 yards in the opposite direction, to issue a chitty for ammo' then someone else would run back the 100 yards with the ammunition. This fiasco didn't last very long as enemy planes were very infrequent, on one occasion when one did pass over it was probably safely back home by the time we had mounted the gun and received the ammo. Although we were stationed in that village for over a year, we saw hardly any enemy action, but the week after we left, three bombs dropped on a nearby village, fortunately, no one was killed or injured. Saturday morning became a ritual. Clean the gun for a couple of hours, back to our billets for kit inspection, and then back to the gun for inspection by the Major. In the mess hall hung a chart smartly drawn

by somebody in B H Q showing how kit should be laid out. Our two tin plates were depicted as two circles, but it was impossible to tell whether the plates were face up or face down. One day the Major said I see that your plates are face down, and some of the others have them face up. What does the chart show? The sergeant said, I will have a look sir, and off he went like little lap dog to the mess hall. However, the chart was inconclusive as it showed the two circles as we told the Major, so it was decided to place them face down to keep the dust off them. This silly episode illustrates the awe in which some officers held their superiors. One lad, being told to display everything he had been issued with, placed his false teeth on the bed. When challenged he said he was only obeying orders, as the army had issued them. He was taking the piss of course, knowing he could not be put on a charge for obeying orders. I must say though, when we did finally go into action we were under the command of a different class of officer altogether".

"As the danger of invasion had now receded, it was decided to hold an athletics meeting with several coastal batteries taking part. We heard by chance that one of the batteries had some athletes from Thames Valley Athletic club on its strength, so we did not expect much success; it was the sport that we enjoyed more than winning. With little time to prepare ourselves by way of a few trial runs round the camp, those of us taking part in the athletics meeting missed breakfast, contenting ourselves with a few cups of sweet tea. Being in the army, our sergeant told us to stop whinging and get on with it; you should be fit enough by now in any case. We boarded the trucks along with as many supporters as possible that were not on duty or taking part. The arena was some fifteen miles away. However, the Major arranged a few trucks to take as many spectators as possible including Mary and the children. Even though I was more than happy to spend a day away from camp, I would have loved a proper game of football, as we were very good. In the photo' I am second from the right back row."

POOR LAD

"There is sadness in all walks of life. At one stage, for various reasons, there was a shortage of men for guard duty, so a dozen or so were drafted in from B.H.Q. Even though there was little sign of enemy aircraft, we were on 24 hr. guard duty at this particular time. One of the new lads was a quiet, retiring type with dry sense of humour. One day he was on guard, having already done two shifts. After breakfast he went out to do his third duty; eight until ten o'clock in the morning. His post was down at the far gun. After nine o'clock parade some of us would go down to the far gun for a fag where we could not be seen then back to our own gun to carry out the usual cleaning and maintenance, on that particular morning we did not go as the sergeant was knocking about. When the ten o'clock relief went down, the lad on guard was dead, shot in the head. The news got round quickly and we were paraded at two o'clock to be told officially by the Major. Why no one heard the shot is a mystery to this day. After an enquiry, the Major informed us that a verdict of suicide had been recorded, because of that, there would not be a military funeral, adding that as his family lived only a few miles away they were calling to collect him at noon tomorrow for his internment. If anyone wished to pay their respects when his family arrived, they were at liberty to do so. A soldier's dislike of dress parades made it even more heart-warming to see every man who was not on duty, on the parade ground slowly marching behind the coffin. We all felt if he was not caught up in the war he would not have the inclination or the means to kill himself. I was proud, and at the same time sad to be one of the bearers. We all saluted as the coffin was loaded into the hurse as it left the parade ground followed by his parents and family members. There was no last post or twenty-one gun salute, just a quiet dignified farewell. I felt he did get a sort of unofficial military send off and felt sure his mother and father were very proud of him. A few days later, the Major was on parade and read to us a letter from the lad's mother thanking us all for such a dignified farewell."

"Another tragic peace on news to go round the hut was about a lad who lived in Liverpool. He went on leave last Friday. No sooner had he settled in when a policeman came to the house to say his mother had been knocked down and killed by a tram just an hour before he got home, adding to the tragedy of his father being killed in an air raid only a few weeks previously as you can read here".

rotten piece of news today, Paddy Reilly went on leave last Friday and on the first day he was home soft his mother got knocked down and killed, and as you know his father was killed in an air raid on Liverpool

"One day it was decided that one of the guns should actually fire a real live shell. As the guns had not been fired for quite some time. Elaborate preparations were made. A dugout, surrounded by a 6ft high wall of sand bags with a corrugated iron roof built some thirty yards from the gun was more than adequate for the purpose. There were a lot of visiting officers, though not all Artillerymen, we had to get it right. Apart from lowering the gun onto the track, there were other things to be done to prevent it toppling over from the recoil. It took two days to execute, but it is far too complicated to enlarge upon. At last, after much checking, all was ready. By now, the whole village was waiting for the bang. The order was given and away went the shell. Few of us had heard a 600lb shell fired from a gun weighing 70 tons, some 15 miles out to sea. Believe me; even with our hands covering our ears, it was the loudest bang I have ever heard in my life. We all heard the explosion, but no one saw the shell leave the barrel. I think we all had our eyes shut tight anyway. About half a minute later, a dull thundering sound seemed to whoosh over our heads as the shell exploded ten miles or so out in the English Channel. Two elderly ladies who lived in a large detached house about two hundred yards away wisely decided to go and stay with friends for the day. It was a good job they did. All the doors and windows were opened to prevent blast damage, but when the gun was eventually fired, it blew all the tiles off the front of the roof. The first round having proved a success, a second round was to be fired as soon as we were ready. The Sergeant was once again in a splutter and tearing round like a blue arse flee. After about an hour, we were ready to demonstrate just how good we are. When everyone was ready away went the 600lbs shell towards the open sea. That was the last time we fired those enormous guns, thank God. The tiles were replaced on the roof and no one got hurt. This was indeed an exciting week."

Even though the weather was cold and wet well into the spring, Mary was looking forward to getting in the garden."

School log

May 1st 1942

Twenty three children received diphtheria immunisation treatment this morning.

School log.

 May 22nd Dr Moir came to school this morning to give the children who are having the Diphtheria immunisation treatment their second injection.

BACK HOME

"Sadly, Mary and the children had to return home to Alldis Street as the authorities were looking for accommodation to requisition to let to refugees. Ma' wrote to me telling me about the ministry of housing checking on empty properties. She also read in the paper that many refugees were coming north. Some of them from the Channel Islands. I had to tell Mary about the bad news from ma. As I would expect, she was very understanding and said that we had had a very good time these past few months and even though she was reluctant to go back to Stockport, it was the only thing to do. How anyone knew that Mary was away I am not sure, but we could not grumble, as we were glad that the visit had lasted far longer than we could ever have wished for. I tried to get a pass to take Mary and the children home. But the best I could do was a pass to London. Mary having to leave at such short notice was a real blow; not just for Mary and the children, but me too.

School log

June 4th 1942 The silver cup for collecting most waste paper during Feb' March & April, was again presented to the children this afternoon together with an illuminated certificate.

School log

July 10th Miss Brown left school at 2:30 pm. To attend a meeting to consider the school sports to be held during Wakes week.

"Aunt Sally was very upset and begged us to leave 'Rosie' for a bit longer, but we decided that it would only make things harder for Ann and Mrs Butler when she did have to say goodbye for good. As it happened, the twins were due to start school at Southwood road infant school at the end of the summer. I managed to adjust to army life without Mary and the kids once more, made easier by my visits to Sally Butler's every now and again. The garden was looking very sad as autumn closed in and the days were getting shorter."

Me >

Terry had been attending Southwood road school since August 1939 with the gap in between in Hailsham. Ann and I began to attend at the end August 1942. Like Terry, we were about four and a half years old when we started school. I cannot imagine how mam must have felt on that fateful Monday morning. Terry already at school, now Ann and I off to school leaving mam once more in an empty house. Maybe she was glad of a bit of freedom. She could look round the shops in Stockport and see her mam in Portwood without too much hassle.

School log

September 18th 1942 Received N.U.T. Cup won by the school at the sports during Wakes Week.

School log.

October 5th 1942

Received cheque for 12s/2d from English Sewing Cotton Co for cotton reels collected by the children.

"Now that the weather was getting cold and the nights closing in, it was hard to adjust to empty evenings. A couple of my mates and I joined a woodwork class at the local school, it had kindly been put at our disposal along with quite an array of tools. By now, it was nearing Christmas 1942. Along with a couple of lads, Nick and Bob, we set too and made some toys for the children. Bits of wood gleaned from the stores, packing cases, the joiner's workshop, and any bits and pieces we could put to good use were spirited away. We were by no means Chippendale or Sheraton, but we managed to come up with our own unique masterpieces. A sewing box for Mary and a doll's house for Ann. I managed to make Ann's doll's house just small enough to fit inside the sewing box so was able to send them home in time for Christmas. Terry and Ken did not miss out but it was a long time ago. My mates in their own way, managed to enjoy a certain satisfaction with their primitive masterpieces. Even though Curly did not have any kids, he made a few bits and pieces just for the sake of it. He was very good at scrounging for us. He even scrounged some gold, green, and black paint and a couple of little paint brushes. Christmas eve, I lay on my bed and thought about the children being so excited, and Mary hoping this would be our last Christmas apart.

Christmas in the army is something of a mixed bag. If you were a Christian, you were expected to attend Church parade from time to time. If the Major was likely to attend, we were encouraged to put in an appearance. We thought it better to keep on the right side of the Major and God in that order just in case. Most of us were glad we went if only to put a bit of perspective on the meaning of Christmas. Other denominations had their own way of doing things."

London. 1st December 1942. Sydney Silverman, MP. reports that more than 2,000,000 Jews have been exterminated by the Nazis up to the end of September

School log

January 4th 1943.

Reopened school. Nine children admitted. Roll 452 Present 354. There are many cases of Whooping cough and Chicken Pox amongst the infants.

School log

February 16th 1943 "Richard Shore, a pupil in class 7 died rather suddenly. He was a refugee from Guernsey. The children subscribed for a wreath and there was £3 over which was given to Mrs Shore who was in poor circumstances.

A WELCOME CHANGE

"Our newfound hobbies didn't last very long into the new year. As the war progressed, and the need for coastal defence had greatly diminished, we guessed that we would soon be on the move again. About twenty blokes went on a scheme, but we were not told a thing. Whilst realising that during wartime many things have to be kept secret, we were never told anything even when the information would have posed no risk at all. General Montgomery held that whenever possible, even the lowest ranks should be informed of what was happening; but we must have been even lower than that because even when in action we were told hardly anything. That is why there are few locations mentioned later on in this book, only events. Most of the time when we were abroad we did not have a clue where we were."

"When we finally moved out of Hailsham, there were some tearful goodbyes from the local girls with whom some of the lads had formed relationships. A couple of the lads actually returned to marry their girlfriends; others were just relieved to get away. Most of us welcomed a change because although this had been an easy period, we were getting bored. We were posted to Tonbridge, a town some forty miles inland, not to be confused with (Royal Tunbridge Wells). We took up residence about a mile and a half outside the town in the grounds of a large country house. The house itself was requisitioned for use as the R.H.Q. 'Regimental headquarters' We met up again with most of the lads from Marske and spent many an evening reminiscing about the times we had in those seemingly far off days."

School log

May 10th 1943 Started school dinners today. 118 children paid for dinners and there were 4children on the free list.

School log.

May 14th 1943

The dinners have been good all week. The children have enjoyed them and nine more children have paid for next weeks' dinners.

"We were allowed to go out in the evenings, but we had to walk or cadge a lift to town and had to be back in our billets by 10.30 pm. It was impossible to go to the pictures, and then call for pint before making our way back to camp. It was very easy to get a late pass until midnight, so why the 10.30 pm curfew in the first place. God and the army work in mysterious ways. The Saturday dances were always enjoyable until the Americans moved in. Your average American serviceman could not do ballroom dancing, just their 'jitter bugging', and bebop; and were not very popular with the British servicemen. For one thing, they were always flashing their money about, so attracting the girls. Their 'jitter bugging' prevented our own lads dancing in the 'old fashioned' way. A typical English compromise was worked out, with Wednesday and Saturday evenings, being jitterbug free. A few weeks after we arrived at our *new camp. We started training on some Howitzer 25-pounders. Even though they were spotless, we spent hour after hour cleaning them, learning the basics, attending lectures and film shows on safety and maintenance. Becoming more and more familiar with the guns, we went out on one-day schemes, one-night schemes, day and night schemes. Of course, there is always some moaning Minnie saying I wish they would make their bloody minds up. An officer heard about these moans and groans and gave us all a right bollocking saying Jerry is not going to wait until daylight just to please you lazy lot! We are here to get used to deployment and simulated field conditions whether you like it or not! This is equally important for the officers as well as the men. Actually, we should have been thankful as it gave us much more freedom than we had with those bloody awful railway guns down in Hailsham. Many things went wrong, and were often very frustrating. The most annoying of all, was nothing to do with the guns but the random meal times. Sometimes we had field rations, other times, the Royal Army Service Corps (R A S C catering) was on hand but this lot were only just getting to grips with alfresco cooking. A six o'clock breakfast, on the road for seven or seven thirty, reaching our destination mid-morning, sometimes later, dinner sometime between one and three o'clock, our evening meal when we got back to camp. The only thing we could count on was regular mugs of tea, often going cold, but we supped it anyway. Quite often, we could sneak a brew when things went a bit quiet. On some schemes, having deployed our guns, we lay in the sun waiting for orders. On days when we had field rations most of us ate them long before dinnertime as we were so bored. The worst thing that could happen was running short of smokes and having to spend time sneaking round searching for a few fag ends to roll up. Eventually, we did get some firing orders without actually loading a shell. Some of us would shout BANG! when we got the order to fire. One day we got another bollocking for shouting BANG! then laughing. The sergeant said we could not fire live shells to suit you lot, we have to save them for Jerry! We realised he was right and knuckled down and stuck to the task in hand. The days often dragged on and by two o'clock, we were all getting ravenous and expecting some grub soon. However, one day everything went very quiet, we wondered if everyone had gone back to camp without us.Orders did eventually come for us to stand down, and away we went. We did not get a 'mid-day' meal; we had to wait until we got back to camp about four thirty. We had our evening meal about seven o'clock. What a bloody cock up. No explanation was given. We went on dozens of schemes during our time in Tonbridge. Each one seemingly more frantic than the one before. Sometimes we moved three or four times a day round the countryside of the South Downs. Some days it was beautiful weather, some days we got wet through. We were beginning to think we were being pushed harder in our training because we might soon be going into battle. It is a good job the army did such a thorough job, as you will see. We had a number of lectures and film shows on safety because we would be firing live rounds very soon on some new schemes out in the wilds but no one gave any hint as to where that might be. On one wet miserable day in the middle of nowhere, waiting for hours for the order to fire, we were surprised to get the order to move out. We were puzzled by the sudden move, and just thought it was part of the training. We got back to camp early in the afternoon, and thought, great! Until we had to clean the bloody gun before we could eat. Sometime later, we heard on the grapevine that two of the guns were pointing in the wrong direction. You may think that it did not matter, as we were firing dummy shells, but we cannot afford to make mistakes of that seriousness, we could well fire on our own men if* we were in real action. The 'brass' had tried to cover it up by moving out so quickly. You may laugh, but in the middle of nowhere pouring with rain, it is an easy mistake to make, hence the intensive training. After we had been at the camp for a few months, getting a bit blasé I managed to find some digs for Mary, a place near camp with a couple in their early fifties but there was only enough room for one of the children in the little terrace. Mary thought that Ken would get more benefit seeing his dad and getting some fresh air even though he was the lucky one last time in Hailsham.

"When I called to take Mary for a walk, the lady of the house was delighted to look after Ken. I said to Mary that I noticed that her husband always wore a cap, even indoors. It transpired that he had a cyst right in the middle of his head the size of half an egg. You can guess what was about happen. I was invited to tea one evening, and knowing that Ken would not let it go unnoticed, and would want to tell me about it, we told him that dad knew the master had a poorly head, and must not say anything. As we sat down, we held our breath, as our host, being a gentleman, removed his cap as we sat at the table. Our little boy was so busy eating his tea of 'Prem butties' about five minutes passed before he glanced up and saw this magnificent shiny lump. With eyes wide open, a look of amazement spread across his little face as the lump was lit up like a beacon. We had drilled him well; he did not say a word. It would have been far better if he had, the agony of the silence was just as bad as saying something and would have been easier to deal with. As it was, he stared intently at that shiny lump for the rest of the meal despite our gentle prodding to finish his tea. We were glad to finish our tea without any embarrassing comments. Ken never ever mentioned the lump at any time. It was a time when silence was not so golden. As you can imagine, that was, once again, a very short week. As I escorted Mary to the train station Ken was more interested in the train journey than what it meant to us."

The only letter written my mam to survive these 70 odd years is sadly very faded. I have transcribed it verbatim, as it is difficult to read.

The taxi were 2/9d

cheap

Dear Bill,

Well we got home alright but it was 7-30, Well when you left us we got along O.K. and then the train did go slow, when I got to Victoria at just 1-0 and you can tell I had to rush I asked a train man if he could take us to Euston he said he could just do it so I could get that train at 1-15 I had to dash and the ticket man said if I were you I wouldn't go on that one it's packed and those kiddys I said I'll have to he said well can't you catch the other so he told me then that there......

I am a little puzzled how mam got from Victoria to Euston in 15 minutes

"We carried on with some dummy shell schemes, more often than not; we did not know exactly where we were or even what day it was. On many occasions, no sooner were we back at our barracks, we were off again, sometimes with only half an hour warning. Not all schemes were bad; some were even *enjoyable, especially in the better weather. They say never volunteer for anything in the army, but there were times to volunteer and times to shuffle your feet and whistle. One such time to volunteer was after our evening meal, often still hungry; I said we would be willing to help the cookhouse orderlies to wash up. My mates were somewhat puzzled by this, but joined me anyway. The logic was, that there could well be some spuds and gravy left, or a dollop of rice puddin', and there usually was. The only drawback with this master plan was, that we had to eat our 'freebies' first before it went cold. Then we had to wash up, but more often than not, it was worth it. One real bane in our lives was the camouflage nets. These were about twenty five feet square, with strips of green and brown hessian to tie it down. We were expected to form a canopy, but had nothing to achieve the required effect as we could not get high enough to cover the 'horns' of the gun, and was proving extremely difficult, and caused a lot of aggravation. Someone complained that we did not have anything to tie it down with. The sergeant blew his top shouting as loud as he could. Would you like me to ask one of the girls in the N A F F I to find you some ribbon or knicker elastic! Bloody well get on with it. As usual, we improvised, and cut some branches off a nearby scrawny tree and formed the camouflage net into the desired effect. However, when the gun was fired, the recoil caused some of the netting to collapse over us like something in a Tarzan film. We soon dropped that idea, and came up with a more modest arrangement that served us well for the time being. They were even more of a nuisance when we went into action."*

BACK TO CAMP LIFE

"The Major decided we should have our very own camp cobbler. Jack, we called him "Curly" because of his very short back and sides, volunteered for the job. After a short course, he was issued with a bench and the tools he needed and installed in a small hut in his new official capacity as "camp cobbler". He got the grand sum of 1/9ᵈ a week, but no stripe. He said they can keep their stripe I am quite happy with the extra money. Some of the lads teased him about being 'Curly the Kamp cobbler', and asked him if he could mend handbags. His popularity reached new heights when he refused to repair an officer's boots saying he was there for lower ranks only. As the weather was getting colder, Jack was afforded the luxury of a stove and a regular issue of coke. Me and a couple of lads decided to make a few wooden toys like we did last year as it was coming up to Christmas. We could easily scrounge the small pieces of wood as we did when we were at Hailsham. We were better off now that 'curly' let us have some little brass tacks and glue, but where to obtain the tools? All we had was one screwdriver, two small hammers and a penknife. We took our problem to the chap who ran the Toc. h. A Christian movement founded in 1915. They are to be found in most theatres of war to this day providing rest and recreation, and if you feel the need, spiritual guidance too. He very kindly fixed us up with the loan of the few tools we needed. I sent home for some bits and pieces that I thought might come in useful. We could work in the corner of Curly's hut in the evenings, and enlisted the help of our roommate Bob. It was his skill as a sign writer that transformed our efforts into a professional looking job. Of course, we could only find Royal Artillery colours amongst the bits of paint we could scrounge, but as they were predominantly green, gold, and black, it was better than anyone ever expected. He got a lovely dark green gloss finish on our first effort of a railway engine, with gold lines running round it applied with a chewed matchstick. It looked a bit like an American train. We could only find four jam jar tops for the wheels, two back and front, but it looked very good".

"We made quite a few toys between us and were not doing it for profit; not, that is, until Curly suggested we make a real effort and come up with an extra special toy, to raffle on Christmas Eve for some beer money. Now that we had the hang of things, we made another engine just like the first. It was about two feet long, and looked great. Our sign writer friend found a colour photo of a nice looking American train, and studied it for details of livery to copy".

"We sent some toys home, and one or two lads who were going home on leave wanted some bits and pieces for their kids. When I look back, I cannot for the *life of me understand why I made two toy 'Tommy guns' one each for Terry and Ken. I 'found' two lengths of floorboard and thought they were just the thing. I cut and carved them in a way to resemble two stylised tommy guns. After painting them brown, I scrounged some brass tacks off curly, and tacked out the names* TERRY *and* KEN *on the butt*

> I will fix up whatever wants mending when I get home. I have got some wood for two tommy guns and a table for ann I will get cracking as soon as week end is over

of each gun. What was I thinking about, with the world in such turmoil, making 'Tommy guns' for my two boys? I never saw my children at home on Christmas morning all the time I was in the army. I was called up in early December 1940. The next time I was home at Christmas with my children, was 1946. Even when Mary and the children were down in Hailsham, I somehow missed out at the crucial moment, being on guard duty all night. It was very frustrating to make toys for the little ones, only to be deprived of the greatest pleasure of all. To see their little faces light up on Christmas morning as they opened their presents" Mary was very apologetic as she said she tried to keep the actual day of Christmas and the present a secret, but you know what kids are".

"As toys were hard to come by, we had no misgivings as we set out on Christmas Eve to sell a few raffle tickets. We decided to start in a club that had a mostly civilian clientele, we thought we could sell more tickets than in the little pubs, and it worked, until Jack, a real joker, was having a laugh and joke with some of the customers. We were half way round the room when the steward was alerted by the buzz of activity and laughter at the far end of the lounge. He asked Jack what the hell do you think you are doing, and chucked us out. A few minutes later, we were all down the road laughing fit to burst. What about the money I said, we cannot go back in. Well it's not our fault, said Jack. Deciding it would be too awkward to refund all the money, I said RUN! Well what else could we do? We were undecided what to do with the engine, no one disagreed when Jack said, give it away to some poor bugger. To cut a long story short, we went into a large pub in town and sold a few more tickets for some beer money, and drew a ticket when we had a few bob. Unknown to us Jack with some sleight of hand, arranged the winner to be a woman with a ten-year grandson, and that was that. When we divvied up, we had enough for a Christmas drink or two, the woman had an unexpected toy, and everybody was happy. Another Christmas away from the children, another year of wondering what the future had in store for us. On the stroke of midnight, we had a toast to friends and families, and not forgetting our troops overseas."

THINGS ARE BEGINNING TO HAPPEN NOW

"About a week into1944, we were knee deep in bullshit. I have never seen such a commotion. We all thought Churchill or Monty, or even the King himself was paying us a visit. However, we were in for a surprise. One day the whole regiment was on parade to take delivery of eight brand new guns. This was an entirely new set up; we were to be part of the newly reinstated British Second Army with brand new guns, and a brand new emblem. The new emblem was a blue cross minus corpus Christy, therefore not a crucifix. It was on a white background surmounted by a sword. As you can imagine some of the lads were all fingers and thumbs when it came to sewing them onto their Battle Dress. Many cigarettes changed hands between the girls in the N A F F I in exchange for a bit of fancy needlework so we were all properly turned out on Monday morning parade".

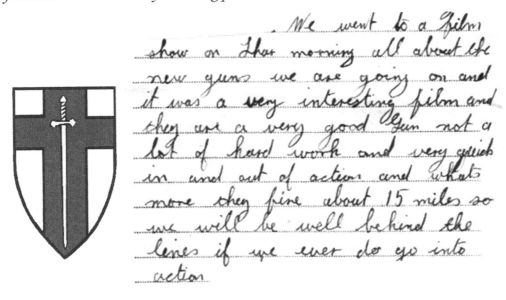

We went to a Film show on that morning all about the new guns we are going on and it was a very interesting film and they are a very good Gun not a lot of hard work and very quick in and out of action and whats more they fire about 15 miles so we will be well behind the lines if we ever do go into action

"These new guns were 4.5inch Howitzers modified to fire the heavier 5.5 shells. At 100. Lbs they were for offensive combat meaning only one thing to us, we were soon to be on our way. After the gun artificers checked them over we made the mistake of thinking they would be like a new car all spic and span. (Not that any of us knew what a new car would look like.) How wrong could we be? They were covered in grease that attracted every speck of dust and dirt from a radius of about ten miles. It took us days to get them looking like something the regiment could be proud of. We had weeks of lectures, polishing our gun, more lectures followed by more cleaning. Apart from cleaning every morning, there came a time when we had a couple of easy weeks attending films on how to deploy the guns in double quick time while the N.C.O s learnt the new drill in the afternoons. Spring began to spring, and as I had no duties on such a beautiful Sunday afternoon I had a wander around the grounds of the big house where we were billeted even though the gardens were out of bounds to the lower ranks; I came across a large greenhouse and a gardener tending some flowers. He asked me in and showed me some flowers I had never seen before. He said they were Camellias. I said I did not know that such delicate

flowers would begin to bloom so beautifully at this time of year. As long as I can keep the hard frost off them, they are fine. There are actually trees, the same family from which we pick camomile tea. You live and learn every day I thought. As I showed an interest, he said he would let me have some the next time I go on leave. He had been given permission to carry on tending to them and sent some to London regularly and gave some away for weddings. I thought wouldn't it be nice if I could take some home for my sister Lena's wedding in a few week time. I had a word with the sergeant to see if I could take my leave in time to go to my sister's wedding on April 8th.1944. Exactly ten years and a day since Mary and me were married. I was in luck; the sergeant was quite sympathetic and said he would see what he could do. A couple of weeks later with a box made up of two shoeboxes tied with garden twine, I had a dozen lovely deep pink camellias wrapped in damp grass and leaves. Mary was thrilled to bits with such a rare treat."

"I was able to swap my leave with one of the lads. Better still, I would be able to leave camp on Friday afternoon so I would be home in plenty of time for Lena and Gordon's wedding on Saturday. Ever the generous one, with no prompting from me, Mary said she would love to give some to Lena and Gordon on their wedding day. My mother, who had spent her early life in the country, recognised what they were right away and was very pleased with them. Lena and Gordon were married on a lovely April day in 1944 at Our lady's Roman Catholic Church on Shaw heath, with the reception at Crossley's café in the market place. They had to book a wedding car weeks in advance so petrol coupons could be saved up. The same company hired out cars for funerals so was able to get a little extra petrol for the business. Some of those lovely flowers were still looking quite fresh by the time I was about to return to camp. Mary could not throw them away without a little sadness. She asked Lena for one or two of the best ones and tried to press them in a book, but without success. Even the holocaust of war cannot erase some of the little inconsequential things of life. I had only been back from leave for ten days, when one of the guns had to go away for some adjustments, a very rare event. It was the only occasions I remember any gun breaking down, apart from when were in action abroad. For some reason or other, I was chosen to go with the gun, as someone had to represent the army and keep an eye on things. Once the gun was hitched to the waggon, the driver said he knew where the depot was but did not let on that he knew, so we could take our time and enjoy the ride. The driver, his mate and I had a leisurely afternoon trip through the Kent and Hampshire countryside. As we approached the depot just outside Aldershot though I did not know at the time, being a distinct lack of signposts. I thought we were in a street of terraced houses. We drove in through the double doors that had a striking resemblance to a brick wall. We realised that we were in the shell of about ten terraced houses all held up by steel trusses. I had been detailed for sleeping eating, and nothing else. I reported in, and the driver unhitched the gun then took the truck back to camp. For the next couple of days I lead the life of Riley, no parades, no roll calls, my only duties were eating and sleeping. The cooks were very good, plus the fact that we had big portions and real meat. After breakfast I would stroll down to where the gun was being repaired and wander in, only to be told to come back tomorrow, we have not even looked at it yet. There was a strange atmosphere about the place, no one was saying very much. The place was packed with howitzers all with tarpaulins tied down tight and more than the usual number of guards on duty. With a bit of fancy footwork I wangled a forty-eight hour pass, in such a way that I could get away early on Saturday morning. As I sipped my tea by the fire, the twins

on my lap, Mary was thrilled to bits. Terry was playing in the street but did not need calling twice. He too, was thrilled to bits to see his daddy, if only for a few hours. His first words were, can you mend my football dad."

"*I felt so frustrated not being able to make a proper repair for him as the stitching was ripped open. All I could do was to stuff it with some of Mary's peg-rug bits of wool and stitch it up with some string. I managed to pacify him by telling him that I will soon be home for good and I will buy him a brand new football. I told Mary how I had wangled my 48-hour pass then had another cup of tea. The next day we made a flying visit to my ma' and pa' then a quick dash to Mary's mam and dad with the children. But alas the hours at home were never enough, but we can't grumble. Because of the delay waiting for our gun to be repaired, we did not get the gun back to camp until after all the others had left to go on a scheme. Why we couldn't catch them up, I'm not sure, but I think it was because we would need a military or police escort. A gun being towed behind a truck, followed by support vehicles could cause havoc on those country lanes around Tonbridge. An added bonus was the fact that our very own cook had been added to our strength. Having only a few men to cater for, he cooked beyond the call of duty. We had meat pie chips and peas. He even found some jam for our rice puddin'. What more could a man ask for.*"

"*I had only been back from my mini leave for a week, when we had a real shock to the system. We went to a regular army firing range in the Brecon Beacons in South Wales. It took us all day to get there, set claim to our beds in one of about fifty Nissen huts under a conglomeration of trees, and camouflage netting. It was the wildest, bleakest, and most miserable place I had ever seen in my life. It was bitter cold, even in April. It only stopped raining for little more than a few minutes at a time during the first few days we were there. It was so isolated that I am sure if we fired our guns facing north, south, east, and west, we would not have done any damage. There were no sheep, or wild life, not even birds; all the noise and explosions must have frightened them off. One lad said he felt sure he saw a polar bear. The scheme lasted fifteen miserable days, even when it was not raining we got wet feet and ankles. Our socks soaked up the rain even through our gaiters as we walked through sodden grass and scrub of one kind or another. As I said, we were billeted in a camp specially built for the purpose, with gun and vehicle parks scattered about nearby. Arriving back at our gun enclosure often after dark, we were cold, wet, and hungry; we could spend as much as thirty to forty minutes getting all the guns and vehicles in a straight line. With the Sgt Major on his knees in the pouring rain, saying, "Forward a bit, no, back an inch." Then to be covered with camouflage netting. We asked why we needed to camouflage the guns when it was pitch dark; we just got a grunt and told, do as you are ordered. No wonder those of us with the slightest scrap of intelligence became so exasperated, and contemptuous of such nonsense."*

"On one such scheme without tents; I do not know whether there were none available or whether it was to toughen us up. Eight of us could sleep in the back of our truck; the rest had to sleep under the stars or under the truck if it was raining. We had our ground sheets to lie on, but the issue of three blankets per man, hardly kept us warm. Our winter issue of a fourth blanket ended in March. We could do with them now, especially when there was an early morning mist. At the far end of the field, I saw a rough dry-stone shelter that was for grazing animals to shelter in in quieter times I suppose. I went to investigate, and found a horse-blanket with a few holes and badly burnt at one corner, it was draped over a rail just inside the door. As it was dry and reasonably clean, I decided it would be better keeping me warm than the rail. I only intended to keep it for the duration of the scheme, but as it was so warm and very unlikely that anyone would claim it, I kept it with me right through the war. We could not sleep in the shelter, even if we were allowed to because it stunk to high heaven. We were always being told, look after your rifle, as it a soldier's best friend. Wrong, my best friend without a doubt was my horse blanket once I had washed it back at camp."

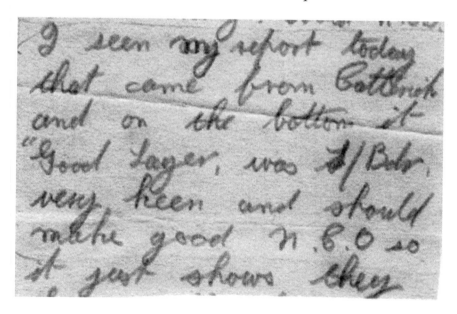

"General Montgomery, or Monty as he was known, was back in England in the new year to take command of the army in Britain. Although we did not know at the time, he was not just here to oversee the British army, but to oversee the build-up of the invasion forces. (Though we could only guess) On one occasion, a large number of men were taken to meet him, including our battery. We lined up in a small non-league football stadium. He just wandered amongst us, talking about the job we had to do. We all knew that the invasion of Europe was not too far away, if anyone asked about it, we were told

to keep your trap shut and just get on with whatever we were doing. There was no saluting, no bowing and scraping, except by one or two brown-nosed officers, it was all quite informal. Even though we did not all go into raptures, Monty' created a good impression. The following day a Sgt Major came to stay with us while the Battery Sgt was at H.Q. He billeted with us for a week, though hitherto we had little contact with him. We heard he was going to stay with other troops as well in order to get to know his men better. From the little we knew about him we formed the opinion that he was strict but reasonable. This new officer, plus the rumours confirmed by some of the drivers as they ferried people around, that thousands of tanks, guns, trucks were just visible through the trees and camouflage nets all over the place. This new officer had only been with us for two weeks when my name appeared on orders to the effect that I was promoted to Lance-Bombardier with a pay rise of 9ᵈ a day. I had long since become resigned to remaining a gunner, and was really floored by it. That stripe was a big help for Mary too, inasmuch I could send her a bit more money.5/3ᵈ a week to be exact. She was thrilled to bits, but did wonder if I might be in more danger. I knew it was more than likely as we would soon be posted abroad, and they wanted a few more N.C.O.s, but I did not tell Mary what I thought. Sensing that the invasion of Europe was getting closer, we were ordered to prepare for moving out and to take everything we owned, right down to our last piece of 'army form blank' as the army still called it. That confirmed all our suspicions; we were finally off to fight Jerry. We travelled (in the wrong direction) in two convoys, of four guns and towing vehicles along with a dozen or so ancillary transports. Sometimes we were separated from our sister battery so we could be accommodated easier in a school or church hall. We were not in any particular hurry so we had many stops on the way, spending one night on Doncaster racecourse, another night near our first training camp at Marske. However, even these landmarks and other snippets of information didn't help; we had little idea where we were, or where we were going. To be honest, I don't think the army knew either. We crossed the border into Scotland for a few days, one comedian said well; at least we can say we have been abroad. We spent three days wandering around the borders area of England and Scotland. We slept at some of the most unlikely places. Such as schools, a farm in the middle of nowhere. We shared a big barn with some chickens, and as dawn broke, the loudest ruddy cockerel in the country. T.A. drill halls were the best, as the young lads were so pleased that they were doing something positive for the war effort. They were mesmerized by the size and obvious power of the guns with trucks and various other support vehicles, and stared in amazement; some of them wanted to come with us to Germany. Round the back of the drill hall under the trees, were three petrol tankers. A dozen or so home guard personnel filled every truck's fuel tank to the brim and as many two-gallon petrol cans as we could find as a couple of regular army officers kept an eye on things. A group of the T.A. lads, and their mams turned out to help our cooks with the grub and helped to wash up and store the equipment afterwards. Breakfast was a bit of a problem for the locals but did their best with toast and margarine to augment our rations. We even had some jam and tins of cakes and few a biscuits to take with us. Our sister battery was usually on the other side of town, camp, or racecourse. Some men were lucky, if we stopped any length of time near their respective homes they could snatch a few unexpected hours leave. Some would happen upon an unexpected lodger; others were frustrated when we passed through or near their town or village but did not stop. As it happened, I was never near enough my home to be tempted, besides I could have lost my stripe and the extra money. One or two did take a chance and jumped ship as it were, but still managed to get back in time. The reason we were sent so far north was to make more room for the massing of over two million troops, thousands of guns, tanks, trucks, and thousands of tons of equipment including food, medical supplies, spares and tools to fix and mend just about anything and everything ready for the invasion of Europe"

INVASION OF EUROPE

"We had not been north for very long when we heard the news that the Invasion of Europe was underway. 'D Day'. The biggest invasion the world has ever seen. We were so far away from the south coast we had no idea what was going on or what our role would be. Rumours began to circulate as we neared Hull that we might be going to another part of Europe, but we soon found ourselves travelling south again. Now making up the whole Regiment of sixteen big guns, people cheered and waved to us in a sort of invasion frenzy. As we passed through towns and villages with our trucks full of equally cheering men leaning over the side to enjoy all the good wishes as apples and yet more cakes were thrown into the open arms of the men. I suppose a whole regiment of big guns going to fight the enemy would make an impressive sight. Travelling through London for the first time, we were given a bigger and an even more rousing reception. We felt it was payback time for Jerry for all the bomb damage and destruction we saw as we trundled through London's battered streets. We arrived at a holding camp a few miles south of the river; Thousands of troops had already left for Europe. Many thousands were still leaving from docks all along the Thames and the south coast."

DOOGLE-BUGS

"The 13ᵗʰ June 1944. At about six o'clock in the morning, rumours began to spread about a flying bomb. We had no idea what it was, other than a bomb that flies without a pilot. The newspaper headlines gave the impression that they were a complete surprise, but Fighter command, along with Bomber command was already making plans to counteract their threat. The R A F was bombing a place somewhere in Holland. We heard later that of the ten V1s launched on that first day at about 3.30am only four reached British soil, and only one lands on London where it killed six people. Hundreds of Anti-aircraft guns were in place all over Kent and Sussex. However, they soon realized that if one of these flying bombs or "Doogle-bugs" were shot down over the approaches to London the damage was done anyway. Therefore, there was a mad dash to get as many 'anti-aircraft' guns as possible in place all along the south coast to try to shoot them down over the Chanel. Fortunately, the flying bombs had their inevitable teething troubles and were grounded for a few days giving the R.A.F. time to find some fighter planes from somewhere to destroy the ones that got through the antiaircraft batteries. Some brave pilots would tilt the wing of a flying bomb and quite often sent it off out to sea. Over eight thousand were aimed at London from June to September until the launch sites were finally destroyed by the British and American air forces. The next generation of death and destruction was only a few weeks away, the V2 rockets being launched from mobile sites proving much were more difficult to destroy, but they were in the end."

"As we watched and listened for the ones that got through our defences, everyone under the flight path, would look skywards, listen to the splutter of the engine, and wait for it to cut out, sending it plummeting to the ground for twenty seconds of total silence, hopefully landing in a field somewhere, or in the Thames. When it did hit the ground, the explosion was deafening, as you would expect. One actually turned round in a semi-circle and disappeared out to sea and we all cheered and shouted go back to bloody Hitler. Soon the bombs were coming over day and night, but none in our vicinity. I was born in Sidcup and moved up to Stockport when I was seven years old. I had a grandmother in Sidcup, the one who used to send me the birthday postal orders. I thought I might get the chance to see other family members too. Being only a few miles outside London, I decided to try for a twenty-four hour pass. Apart from the pleasure of seeing gran', I was looking forward to a good night's sleep in a proper bed. As expected, a pass was out of the question. However, my stripes seem to help me for the first time since my promotion. I told the sergeant my grandmother was in her eighties and I might not get the chance to see her again. He was a decent chap and asked me when I was on guard duty next, 0.800 hours sir. He said he would give me a sleeping out pass from 1900 hours until 0.700. Adding, if you are late even by a minute you will be on a charge, and do not boast about this privilege, because that is exactly what it is, a privilege. Once again, a seemingly good idea was not so good after all. Gran's house was right in the middle of what became known as 'bomb alley', later 'flying bomb alley'.

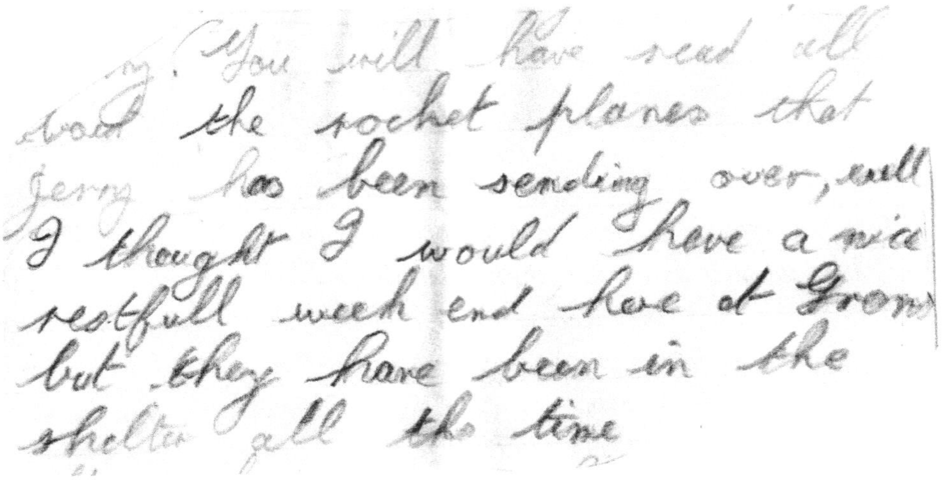
my. You will have read all about the rocket planes that Jerry has been sending over, well I thought I would have a nice restfull week end here at Grans but they have been in the shelter all the time

"Gran spent nearly all night under her Morrison shelter, a sort of steel reinforced table. I thought sod it and went to bed upstairs until a bomb dropped a bit too close for comfort in the next street, as granny swore at bloody Hitler; I somehow managed to squeeze under the stairs. As I lay there, my mind wondered back to the times Mary and I had to shelter in the shelter with the children, often with a dread of what was to become of us. So long as we were together I felt that we would get through this nightmare before too long and just hoped that everything would soon be back to normal. Nevertheless, these bloody flying bombs turned out to be very frightening. Once again, that trip to my Gran's was all too brief, I got back to my unit in plenty of time to do my guard duty, but felt cheated as I didn't even get a sniff at the bar maids apron. We lost one lad by this time; he was so fed up of waiting to get at 'em he volunteered for the infantry. He was a most untidy soldier, but he was a tough, genuine kind of lad, just the type one would want beside you in a scrap with Jerry. I often wonder how he went on. We were now on standby and moved to London's docklands. We had no idea when we would be on our way, a situation that did not put us at ease one bit. Most of our time was spent listening to briefings on how to look out for each other as we are all in this war together. I never understood, of all the lectures we had throughout our training, only the medical corps actually had any training in all things medical. During questions after one such briefing, a lad said could we catch German measles sir. Amid the uproar of laughter the sergeant said are you pregnant? no sir, well, you will be ok. I felt that a simple first aid course could help in times of action and may even save a life. One morning Jack received word that his younger brother had died of Peritonitis. He was stunned. His opinion of Army medics sank to new depths. To be killed in action is one thing, but to die of an illness seems even worse. He was refused compassionate leave as we were nearing our embarkation time but he went home just the same. Fortunately returning just in time to catch up with what was going on. The fact that he had absented himself without permission was overlooked. The call for all the drivers to report for duty set the rumourmongers in a spin, and though the army frowned upon it, there was always an amateur bookie on hand to make a few bob. When the drivers came back they said they had loaded our trucks on to a troop ship, along with tons and tons of equipment going with us. When he said "with us", it really struck home that we were about to get up close and personal with the enemy".

"We got the order to fall in with our kit and marched a mile or so to a big customs shed. After a while, we all marched back again. It transpired that a flying bomb had dropped on the quayside near our

ship during the night, and, although the ship suffered no damage, our guns were loosened from the cables holding them secure. Later, we were marched back yet again, and once more lined up in the customs shed. We heard the sound of a flying bomb for the first time chugging away overhead. No one took much notice of it until the engine stopped. Never before or since, have I ever seen such a concerted movement. One minute we were all standing smartly to attention, the next we were all flat on the floor with a tremendous clattering of rifles and helmets. For fifteen to twenty seconds you could hear a pin drop; then it exploded. We thought it had dropped in the next street judging by the noise, but were surprised to learn it was about a quarter of a mile away"

ON OUR WAY AT LAST

"About ten days after D day, we were actually on our way at long last. Boarding one of the dozens of Liberty ships bound for France. We could only speculate where we were actually going, but we were sure it was somewhere along the Normandy coast. By now, we felt that we really were part of the British second army. Before this, we were just a rag tag and bobtail of the royal artillery. To a man, we were very proud to be a part of this bigger picture. It took us nearly all day to get everyone in their right place. As we were checked for rank name and number we were told to "find somewhere to get your head down and don't wander about". We all felt excited, anxious, and afraid of what we will face in the days and months to come. Not one of us knew what it was really like to fire a bloody great gun at someone only a few miles away with the intention of actually killing some poor soldier on the other end. As we sailed down the Thames into the unknown, we passed a number of large factories with loud speakers booming out songs by Vera Lynne, Ann Shelton, even George Formby. The Tannoy speakers along the shore rang out messages from all the workers, expressing their thanks, good wishes and hope for our success".

> 4
>
> we were in London Docks waiting to come across, while they were dropping flying bombs one fell very near to where we was. We sailed down the Thames and Fords motor works had a big load speaker set up and they read a message to all the ship as we passed saying all the workers wished us good luck and a speedy return and a lot more things it did seem nice, and as we went through London all the people were cheering us and giving us things. I am telling you all this because I could not tell you before but you understand.

"This unexpected send-off was very moving; it made us realise that we were not alone, and that many people were with us in spirit. One lad that lived in the east end of London for a spell in the early part of the war showed us where the very first air raids started on the docks at Woolwich. We could go below if we wished, but most of us wanted to watch the last little bit of England disappear in the sunset as *we sailed between Shoebury Ness and Sheerness towards Margate and out to sea. After we had some corned beef wads and some rice puddin' followed by a mug of tea we hoped to catch a glimpse of the shore line on the south coast, but it was going dark so we could only just make out a few building on the shore. We were told to get some sleep if we could, but after a lot of swearing, and cursing Nelson and bloody Drake, those that persevered managed to get the hang of sleeping in a hammock. Some of the less determined gave up and slept on the floor. A few cheeky buggers scrambled under the tarpaulins covering the lifeboats. No sooner had we settled down when someone came up with the disturbing news that 2 a.m. would be the most dangerous time, as we would be in range of the German coastal batteries on the French coast as well as skirting round the edge of the minefields. That information prompted quite a number of the lads to go on deck, saying they at least wanted to see whom we were fighting before we are sunk. The next morning was a beautiful sunny day, with the sea like a millpond; the war could have been a thousand miles away. The only sight on the horizon was what appeared to be a huge drum being rolled on the choppy waves. We found out that it was the laying of 'P.L.O.T.O.' Pipeline under the Ocean to pump oil and petrol across the channel from the Isle of white to the Normandy coast. We also saw some massive concrete blocks being towed by at least six powerful tugs to each one. These turned out to be caissons for the 'Mulberry Harbours'."*

"It was the 19th of June. The weather was so lovely it came as quite a surprise when the ship dropped anchor in the late afternoon, seemingly miles from the shore, if there is a shore out there somewhere. One or two of us had a look through some powerful binoculars borrowed from a crewmember. We were a bit disappointed not to see some kind of battle going on, 'silly really'. We could hardly make out where the land was. All we could see were plumes of smoke blowing inland by the strong offshore winds. We were told that there had been a sudden spate of bad weather during the last 48 hours and things had been held up on the landing beaches. But we had our own thoughts as to why. We were thinking that the German resistance was much tougher than had been expected, leaving many casualties and damaged vehicles strewn all over the beach. We heard a few days later that we were not far wrong about the casualties, and there really was some very bad weather at that time. Of course, some grumbled that the bloody war would be over by the time we got ashore, others hoped it would. To take our minds off what we were about to face, a few very friendly boxing matches were organised. Some of the lower ranks couldn't wait to have a go at the senior officers, without a court martial. But as I said, it was all just a bit of fun. Setting off again we sighted land again early the next morning and dropped anchor about a half a mile off shore. We had crossed the channel on a Liberty ship, built for us by the Americans and Canadians to offset our losses. It took one ship to transport our battery of eight guns, and their four wheel drive ACE Matador towing vehicles. 30 cwt Bedford's were packed with reserve ammo', and numerous other vehicles, and of course, the best part of one thousand men and all their own equipment completed the load. Landing crafts by the thousand had come across under their own steam, and hundreds were towed or carried by anything that was available at the time."

WELL, HEAR GOES.

"*The heavy guns, towing vehicles, and gun crew went on the same landing crafts first, closely followed all the miscellaneous kit and personnel. Scrambling down the nets into the landing craft was the one thing we had not been able rehearse on dry land. Even though the sea seemed to be calm, the swell up and down between the two ships was about six to eight feet. This was as nothing to a regular sailor, but we were landlubbers to a man. Following the guidance of the sailors, so we would not slip we had to land on a pile sand bags as the two craft were as near to level as we could tell, then jump. We all made it in one piece with no broken legs thanks to the sand bags, and no loss of equipment. Our troop, troop "A" were the first to cast off. The sea looked quite calm as we set off but we were in for a rough ride. As we approached the beech, we saw to our left, row after row of bombed out houses and a badly damaged detached house at the far end of the beach and dozens of wrecked landing craft, some still smouldering. From behind a concrete gun position blackened with soot, a bearded Frenchman immerged to guide us in, probably a fisherman as he seemed to know what he was doing. As the ramp dropped with an almighty splash, we could see he was wearing long waders up to his waist, and fastened with some makeshift braces. He was standing on some concrete ramps making sure the trucks kept to the right track and did not sink into the sand. These ramps were soon nicknamed chocolate concrete. (Look on Google earth) All the trucks had been treated with a plasticine-like substance to make the electrics waterproof. The drivers had strict instructions to be ready to go like hell the minute the ramp dropped regardless of what was happening around them, and not to deviate from the ramps or the tracks marked with white tapes up the beach and onto the road. The plasticine had to be removed as soon as possible after clearing the beach landing areas. As the ramp dropped with a splash, our driver took off so fast we thought he was going all the way to Berlin there and then. We were all hanging on for dear life and at the same time straining to see where we were going. I felt nervous for the drivers, even though they were well briefed. Having been warned that Jerry had laid thousands of mines, one wrong turn could have spelt disaster. We cleared the beach in double quick time. Strangely enough, we saw few signs of the battle that was part the "D Day" landings. One lad said what did you expect, bodies all over the beach. We learnt later that day, that we had in fact landed on Juno beach. That piece of information was meaningless at the time, but we soon began to appreciate the cost in men and machines on that terrible day. Not only British, but many Canadians too. It seems that our delayed landing really was down to the weather, not some kind of excuse to move dead and wounded even though there were quite a lot of casualties. The medics and Royal engineers needed time to move the field hospitals a bit further inland and wait for the damaged trucks to be towed away and the damaged landing craft floated off the beaches. Most of us could not wait to have a go at Jerry. We drove inland at break neck speed for about a half a mile and stopped to enable the driver and his mate to remove the waterproof compound, the exhaust extension can wait he shouted as he jumped in to carry on to Berlin. We saw make shift boards with the skull and cross bones and a warning saying. 'MINES' ROADS ONLY CLEARED'. We had already been warned to not to stray from the vehicles in case there were any land mines still lying about.*

That was one order that we didn't need to be reminded of. One lad got down on his knees as if to prey to Mecca, we could hear him almost kissing the ground and saying, "land, land, bloody dry land, thank God. It's amazing how people can have a fear of things, but in times of need, overcome them without a word to anyone. He admitted that he was terrified of water and that crossing was agony. The first evidence of casualties were three rifles stuck in the sand high up on the beach behind some makeshift screens surmounted by British steel helmets, an all to graphic reminder of why we are here. We all had our own little problems, but I really felt sorry for one poor lad, he had had most of his teeth extracted two days before we sailed. How he managed, I shudder to think. After our driver had completed his checks, we were off. As in England, and particularly along the south coast, all the road signs were taken down. France was no different. Nevertheless, one lad managed a glimpse of a sign that had been daubed on the gable end of a house, Caen. Where ever that is! The driver was, by now a little calmer as we rolled along at about twenty miles an hour. We moved about two miles inland, and holed up in a sandy hollow, near some trees, we were joined by three other troops and remained in that sandy area for a couple of days while the rest of the Regiment were unloading. After our sea voyage, and a couple of days in the summer sunshine we were soon wondering where the fighting was, until someone said you will find out soon enough. So we made the best of our mini break."

Our gun in the picture doesn't look very powerful, but if you look at the breach block through a magnifying glass you will see just how powerful it really is. I am third from the left back row.

"It turned out we were only a few miles from the battlefront, yet everything seemed almost too peaceful in that lovely June sunshine. One of the lads showed us how to make a quick brew without a fire as such. He dug a hole about the size of an eight inch plant pot, then with a stick he raked the bottom to loosen the soil or sand, 'sand was best', pour in some petrol and stir it up a bit, then throw a match in to set it alight and place a billy can of water on it. When the flames died down it was a simple matter to stir the soil and ha' presto! it would burst into life once more. Apart from the British sense of humour, the things that contributed to the moral of the troops was the regular mail from home. We took plenty of cigarettes, Oxo cubes, and powdered milk with us. Coupled with the ingenuity of the lads to make a brew anywhere, anytime, made our time here just a little more tolerable for the time being. For most of us, it was our first time in a foreign country. When any villagers approached us, we were just as curious about them as they were about us. Some gave us wine, some gave us fruit, but the one thing we welcomed most of all was a few fresh eggs."

O. A. S. ON ACTIVE SERVICE

"*Letters home were postmarked 'France' and stamped O. A. S. (on active service). That same afternoon, the Major paid us a visit to see how we were getting on; he asked me how I liked being abroad. I thought to myself, what a stupid question but replied that I had never been out of England sir, but under the circumstances, I had no complaints so long as it didn't get any worse, but of course, we knew it would get much worse. In fact, that very same night, under cover of darkness, we set off for our first taste of action. We travelled for nearly an hour, but felt we hadn't covered more than a few miles. The driver said, the truck's milometers were not reliable, but he was sure we passed the same farmhouse at least twice. Finally arriving at our position, I thought to myself, I'm glad we had those bloody awful schemes in those God forsaken Welsh hills, but this time it's for real. At least the weather was nice. We not only had to dig a gun pit, but a pit for the shells, a pit for the fuses, another one for the charges, and last but not least a pit for us. While all this digging was going on, an R.A.S.C. truck rolled up with yet another load of shells, so we had to dig another trench. Jack (curly) remarked with a comical grimace, "I thought we had come to liberate France, not bloody cultivate it"*

REAL ACTION AND RED HOT BARRELS

"Our sister battery was only a hundred yards away to our right, and other batteries were spread out along a line and disappeared somewhere in the distance. Having no idea of what to expect once we went into real action, it felt as though we were more or less deployed as if we were on a scheme back in England, and wondered how the other batteries fitted in. We assumed that this would be the pattern for the future. But how wrong we were! We were briefed on all aspects of what to expect once we went into action. If it was to give us a bit more confidence or just to pass the time, I am not sure. We soon realised that no amount lectures or simulated firing schemes on the Brecon beacons in the middle of nowhere even came close to what we were about to experience. After three days of waiting and wondering, we were off on our first taste of real action. It was indeed a baptism of fire. All Day and all night, we were firing shells as fast as we could. When in action like this, we needed to stop every few rounds, reposition the gun and pour water over and down the barrel; and stand back as the water spit out scalding hot in all directions. When it got dark, we could see from time to time parts of the barrels glowing red-hot. If any of the guns developed faults and went out of action, we had our own gun artificers; minor faults were soon put right. Guns with major faults were towed away to a field workshop, to be swapped or returned in an amazingly short time. Sometimes as quickly as an hour. Snatching our grub when we could, with only a few minutes respite, unloading shells brought in by the R.A.S.C. Then after preparing them, keeping a constant supply of shells ready for firing, with a pool of at least 20 shells near the gun at any one time in reserve. We were all getting really knackered, but of course, there is always one comedian to keep spirits up, as a lad shouted, "tell Jerry to hang on a minute while I have a shit". To our alarm, we began to realise what was going on up front by the distance we were firing. Our maximum range is 15,000 yards, but it varied around 6, to 8 thousand yards. Once, to our alarm, the range came down to 2,000 yds. I had a horrible thought for a minute that 2,000 yards is only as far from Alldis street to the Wellington pictures. Thankfully, by daybreak, the range steadily increased back up to 6,000 yds. Apparently, there had been a protracted battle for a small village. We passed through what was left of that village a few days later. We were astonished by what we saw. A pile of rubble was all that was left, not a village as we so naively expected to see. I could not help but think we must have killed many a soldier and, unfortunately many civilians alike with our barrage of shells. After a few days of relative calm, we had our first site of the enemy. A plane came zooming in very low; as it passed overhead, we saw the German markings under the wings. One of the lads suddenly realising that it was the enemy, pointed at the makings but was so dumbstruck he could not get a word out he just pointed at the plane and stuttered, "It's a fffu**in' Jerry!! Later that same evening, the Germans bombed a nearby wooded area where some 7.2-inch guns (the biggest in the Royal Artillery) were in action. At dawn, two of our officers went to see what the damage was. As they were helping a lad who was trapped in a collapsed slit trench, one of our officers was hit by a piece shrapnel from an exploding shell and was killed outright, the other officer had a big gash on his arm. He was relieved of duty and sent back to the lines for the rest of the day. There was no need for our officers to have gone; it was a humane act by two brave men, unfortunately one of them never came back"

"Remember all the palaver back in England, trying to get our camouflage nets to look right. We were glad we did get them right after seeing the damage done by the enemy to those guns in the woods. Quite often, from that moment on, our gun looked more like a tree than a gun. Shortly afterwards we suffered two more casualties, but I have no idea what happened to them. Two men went out on *a target spotting patrol in a Bren carrier. Both men and the Bren carrier vanished without trace. As I was a lance-bombardier, I was in charge of a detail to take three men to prepare our next position. Most of the other batteries were doing the same. We were taken in a truck with tools, and side packs, and of course our rifles. Arriving in the late evening, even though we were ready for a brew and a kip, we made a start by a hard sandy track that ran through a field obviously made by the passing of many cattle and carts. After an hour, we had a brew and something to eat and got our heads down for a bit of kip. Two men have to be on guard duty for a two-hour stint, but as we were all knackered, I suggested one hour on and one hour off in turns. The toss of a coin put me on the first duty roster. As dawn brought a new sunny day we could see in the distance a little covered truck making its way towards the gateway next to where we were digging. It was travelling quite slowly so we stopped digging to watch them pass. As it neared us, we could see the Red Cross and R.A.M.C. (Royal Army Medical Corps) on the side. As it passed, our driver and I crossed ourselves in respect for the dead as we could just see army boots sticking out from the ends of the bundles in the back of this make shift ambulance, not just any boots, but British army boots. This was our first real close up and personal encounter with death. Unfortunately, it was not our last."*

"As the sun came up over the trees, a lone aircraft circled overhead, we were speculating if it was one of ours or one of theirs. Then suddenly, I was overwhelmed by a sense of black despair, a feeling of sheer terror, how could I get away, where could I go? The enemy overhead, the sea was one way, the Germans the other, the dead bodies, the feeling of helplessness, what was I to do. I just had to deal with it the only way I knew how, think of Mary and the children and get on with it. As I lay there, I thought if this bloody war were to last fifty years, I would still find my way home. After what had happened I felt that that feeling of panic was brought on by a combination of exhaustion, lack of sleep, and lack of food added to the fact that I was miles from home".

"We were still digging the trenches at dinnertime, when yet another single German aircraft started to circle overhead. All of us tried to get into the same trench at the same time. As we crouched to watch him fly round in a circle he dived down and opened fire, the noise was incredible, but fortunately, he was well off target. I reasoned that the fighter's guns were on a fixed trajectory, so I stood up to watch the plane making a second run. I told the lads that if he was not in line with us we would be ok to watch. SOD OFF! they shouted and told me I might just be unlucky, so I jumped in the trench with the rest of them. It seems we can all get over our feelings of panic the second time around, and I was not that stupid. The next morning we were ordered to fill in what we have just spent a day and a half digging out and wait for a truck to take you back to your gun position. During what turned out to be the final phase of the Normandy landings, though we did not know it at the time, we were soon on the move again to a new gun position on a slight rise a few miles north west of Caen".

"*Caen was meant to be liberated on the first day of the Normandy landings, but was proving much harder to take than was anticipated and put the whole invasion weeks behind schedule. Things were a bit quieter in our new position, but not for long. We were told to make sure to get some grub, and a brew, and be ready for a hard time. After about an hour all hell was let loose as we got our orders to take post. Our firing rate was increased to an almost impossible number of shells a minute, the angle of fire varied no more than a few degrees, this meant that we were about nine or ten miles from our target. Remember us being called the nine-mile snipers, well, that lad at Marske was right. The barrel was red hot, and the water supply was some distance away, there was no respite for more than half an hour at a time, even then, it was only to let the gun cool down a bit. All in all, about 90% of our guns were in action at any one time. Shell after shell, the warm barmy weather, no time for a brake or a proper brew, or even a pee. We were just about getting knackered, when the Tannoy belted out "cease-fire"! The sun was just beginning to rise, and thinking we had done our stint, we were very much mistaken. When we ceased firing, we could still hear the ringing in our ears. We were provided with earplugs but they were a nuisance at times, as we could not always hear the commands. I suppose we should have had sun glasses as well, the flash as the gun blasted the shell at a thousand miles an hour was as bright as the sun and louder than a thunder clap. Not only our gun, but hundreds more along the line. It was a good job that our natural reflex is to shut our eyes, and cover our ears, if only for a split second. We only got about an hour for a brew and a breather after the order to cease-fire as we all collapsed in a heap. With guns to the left, guns to the right, firing a barrage of shells all night, the whole regiment was deployed along a front several miles wide. With our sixteen heavy guns, and thousands of shells, charges, and fuses, ferried by the R.A.S.C. were just a small part of the whole barrage; it was like the jaws of hell. After cease-fire, we had to spend the time we had getting everything sorted for our next barrage. As we stopped in turn, there was no end to the noise, the shouting, the R A S C up and down the lines all day and all night, it was Bedlam. We threw our camouflage netting over the gun. Why, I don't know, the whole area was lit up like Blackpool illuminations. While some of the men prepared shells for firing, the catering corps kept a brew on the go, and then set about making us something to eat. All they could do was to favour the men actually in action. By seeing to us first. Piles of scrambled powdered egg, slices of corned dog and some beans seemed like feast. We did not ask too many questions about who was getting what to eat; we just wolfed it down with a very welcome mug of tea. Day and night, sending high explosives shells down on Caen and surrounding area for over a week. We did eventually get the order to cease fire at about 5 o'clock in the morning of the umpteenth day. As I said, the noise of our guns was deafening. We found out after it was all over, that there were about 700 artillery pieces involved one way or another throughout the Normandy bridgehead, no wonder it was so bloody loud.*"

"*We were told for the first time in just over four years in the army, what was actually happening. We were part of the first phase of operation Epson and there was to be a 600-bomber raid on Caen later that day. That was the first definite indication as to where we had been shelling, but we had guessed as much. I think we were given this information to help us understand why we were being pushed so hard over these past few weeks. This news did not ease our aching backs or quench our parched throats but we felt that we really were part of the liberation force. After all the schemes, gun drills, yes sir, no* sir, and three bags full sir we were glad we did it. Until one lad from Stockport uttered those immortal words, "I could murder a pint of Robbies best mild! "We all threw clumps of soil at him and told to him shut up. We were not quite in the 'thick of it', but we did experience for the first time in our lives what real action was all about. Now we had a feeling that we were to witness a truly awesome spectacle. Before we started our bombardment, we were all given yellow markers to mark our gun positions, we put ours under the truck covered with grass and bushes so the German spotter planes could not see us. We all sat around enjoying a brew and the very welcome sunshine. Then we heard the dull distant drone of hundreds of R. A. F. bombers approaching us from the northeast and on towards Caen in the distance. We had a grandstand view of the whole spectacle; they must have dropped hundreds of tons of bombs in that first wave. Even though we were quite a few miles away, we could see the bombs falling from the bellies of the aircraft leaving the town and surrounding villages and farms, smouldering ruins spread out below. Hundreds killed, burning crops and no doubt lots of dead livestock."

"As soon as we heard the aircraft we knew the raid was underway and we uncovered the yellow markers and hoped that our spotter plains could see us as friendly. Wave after wave flew over the town, dropped their bombs, then disappeared out of site as they turned round and headed for home. How nice it would be to cadge a lift in one of them. A week later, we passed through what was left of the City of Caen after the bulldozers had cleared a way through; it felt like it was not of this world with the unforgettable smell of death. We were amazed at the ruin brought about by the air raids, the thousands of shells, and the street fighting. One bizarre site sticks in my mind, an ambulance, seemingly undamaged, had been blown about thirty feet up in the air and landed in a massive oak tree".

"The battle of Towton field north Yorkshire in 1461 was the bloodiest battle ever fought on English soil. More than 50,000 men perished by the sword in one day. 1916. Nearly 22,000 British and French soldiers were killed on the Somme in one day. On D-day 1944, even though estimates vary widely, the

allies suffered thousands of casualties and many deaths on the Normandy beaches. However, war has now become a war of machines against machines. Tens of millions of tons of tanks, guns, vehicles, ships, explosives, iron, steel, bricks, mortar, concrete, all blown to smithereens. As we moved inland, we saw what real war was all about. Bridges, railways, factories, whole towns, reduced to rubble, now we had a war of total destruction followed by the bulldozers to clear a path so we could fight on. Is this really what victory means"?

"After this episode, we were on the move again, a day here an hour or two there, with no idea where we were half the time. It was about this time that some German prisoners told us that the war will be over very soon, but of course, no one thought anything of it at the time. (After the war, I was reading about one of the many attempts *on Hitler's life, I realised that it was about that time in France that those German prisoners words were so nearly prophetic. As an attempt was made to kill Hitler at Rastenburg on July 20th 1944. It makes you wonder.) There were many signs saying, 'drive slowly dust kills', so we did. The Americans later dubbed this as 'the battle of the hedges' Each side would be alerted by the rising dust of enemy activity, therefore asking for trouble".*

SO MUCH FOR CAEN, WHERE NEXT?

"Our next deployment was Carpiquet, a badly damaged airfield about ten miles west of Caen, As we pulled into our gun positions, we found a lot of British and Canadian equipment lying about as well as lots of German stuff. The place was full of bomb and shell craters. As we looked round at all the battered aircraft hangers we suddenly realized the Germans had their own nine-mile snipers firing back at us".

"That was a real wakeup call. Once we were all sorted out, and had some grub inside us, one of the lads said he has started to notice just how often the number thirteen keeps cropping up. How many shells are fused? 13. How many are there still to fuse? 13. How many left in the ammunition trench? 13. The number 13 cropped up so many times we all began to think of other times this happened. The number of our Regiment is 13. The combined number on our truck was 13. The combined numbers of the ship we crossed the channel in, added to 13. We were 10 crew, plus a driver and mate, and we often carried an officer's batman, totalling 13. Even today, after all these years, I sometimes count 13 cigs in my packet. We had been bombed and strafed by the Luftwaffe, now we were about to get a taste of what it is like being on the receiving end of their nine mile snipers. Less than half a mile away there was a battery of 25 bounders, probably Canadian. As we looked on, we could see the ground begin to erupt around them. "Those poor buggers are copping it" someone commented. Suddenly it was our turn; we had fired plenty of shells but had never been on the receiving end. It took us about two seconds to recognise the whooooosh! of a shell coming over, even a German shell. We had not dug any of our own trenches, as there seemed to be enough to take a whole army. When the first shells came over we all dived for the nearest trench, but unfortunately someone had fouled the nest as it were. As we piled in on top of the poor lad to be first in, he cried out let me up! it's full of shit. Keep your bloody head down or it will be full of blood, came an unsympathetic retort. When the shelling stopped, the artificer who had heard us discussing the number 13, came over and handed one of the lads a piece of shrapnel about two inches long. He said it was still quite hot when he picked it up. As he passed it round for all to see, would you believe it, it had the number 13 stencilled on it. I tried to keep it for my two boys, but the finder would not part with it. The nearby hangers were like a colander but still standing when we first arrived, now they were on the brink of collapse. Some of us thought we could spend the night in one, but not now. The Germans used many thousands of horses to carry their equipment, but alas, those poor beasts of burden did not volunteer any more than we did, and were just as much a part of the casualties as the men. Now and again, we would come across a partly dug pit ready to burn or

bury the dead horses along with sheep and cattle. However, as the Germans left in such a hurry, our own Royal Engineers had the lousy job of clearing up the mess to keep down the risk of infection and the stench that we could smell for miles. We all hoped we would not be positioned downwind of such a stink. We were always looking for new ways of feeding our faces, one cook tried to heat some large tins of pork and veg' by the side of his stove, but forgot to pierce the tins, as expected they burst, scattering pork and veg' all over the place. Killed by flying pork and veg' well, not exactly a glorious exit. While all this was taking place, the final phase of the Normandy landings was getting underway with the battle of Falaise a few miles south of Caen. In mid-August, we were part of a bombardment like that of Caen. I cannot be sure, but I think we were a part of the battle where thousands of German troops were being squeezed into the Falaise pocket in what was known as operation Goodwood."

"Falaise, a town a few miles south of Caen was in the firing line and suffered the same devastating fate as Caen. As we moved through village and town, all the people were waving and cheering, throwing flowers and greeting us as liberators. They had little food to offer, but some did hand us nice fresh fruit, however the wine was most definitely an acquired taste. We would stop for a few days, usually in a wooded area, and then we were on the move again experiencing an entirely new dimension of warfare as the Germans were in full retreat, hotly pursued by the Allied forces with more tanks and guns than we could shake a stick at. As some infantry units had 25 pounder Howitzers at that time, we were often deployed with our much heavier guns, with four times the firepower to break down any strong pockets of resistance. As the chase slowed down, we only moved a few miles at a time; we could increase our range until it got to almost the maximum of 15.000 yards, then move again. We were all very heartened by the reception from the local people and felt great. One of our officers told us, just how important we were during the battle for the Falaise pocket. Well it was damn obvious we had done a lot of damage to the enemy. We dared to think that the war could be over by Christmas; the sights we saw further strengthened our hopes as we passed through mile after mile of burnt out tanks, guns, lorries, but most upsetting in a sense, as we saw people's houses and farmsteads smashed, most of them, just for the sake of it. There is something not of this world about a bombed out village, to describe it as eerie would be an understatement. Anyone who has passed through these wrecked and charred towns and villages will remember how they felt, and how strangely they were affected. The only living things

left in the villages were cats. Frightened, furtive creatures would suddenly steak across the street from one ruin to another. Even the birds were quiet. You cannot help noticing the absolute shamelessness of war in such places. Charred wooden walls, plaster figures of Jesus and the Virgin Mary smashed to pieces in the front garden of what was a cherished homely cottage. Bedding sodden with urine and feces, a piano up-ended and riddled with bullet holes. We somehow found it easier to look at, if we blamed the Germans not ourselves," Looting was not allowed but we all did a bit just for the sake of it. One or two lads could not resist looting a few treats such as toilet paper, razor blades, and even a few toffees. Sad to say their success rate was often zero."

"Gun pits and slit trenches were a thing of the past now that we were moving every two or three days. Wearing our steel helmets, or tin Bowlers as we called them, was a thing of the past as they were a nuisance most of the time. Unless strapped on tightly they would fall down over one's eyes, and in any case, we lost a certain amount of confidence in them as soon as we landed when we saw those three make-shift graves by the beach, one helmet had a three inch gash through the front. By now the Germans were being pushed back right across Europe. When we heard that Paris had been liberated, we felt that we were on a roll. It now became a case of into action for a few hours, fire a few rounds, and then move out. It seems we were doing a kind of leapfrog with our sister battery. We rarely saw them even though we passed each other repeatedly. Sometimes we were in such a hurry that one brawny Liverpool lad dispensed with the lifting gear. He would carry a 100lb shell in the crook of his arm, ram it into the breach, and shout, "send the f..ker on it way lads".

Life goes on at home.

School log.

(August 28th 1944)

Reopened school. 69 children admitted. Of these 69 children, 27 were evacuees from the London area. There are now 36 evacuees from London.

THE SOMME

"As we moved across the Somme river valley, my thoughts went back to the years of the first World War. Mary's farther was stuck there in the trenches of the Somme valley for two years. His salvation came near the end of the War as he was badly wounded by shrapnel and gas. He was shipped back home only months before the Armistice. We passed through the same area of the valley and over the river Somme in only a few weeks. As we got nearer the coast, we passed a number of wooded areas, and were intrigued by the pathways cut neatly into the depths of the forest, with huge camouflage nets suspended from the trees. We could see long ramps almost hidden in the undergrowth. As we drove through this area, we saw more and more ramps in equally wooded areas. They too were covered over by camouflage nets. We learnt that they were runways or ramps from which the V1 flying bombs that Hitler wanted to launch against London. Fortunately, they were never used."

"We all felt relieved that they were put out of action before Hitler could launch them over the channel to bomb our homes and families. The destruction of those ramps made us feel that we really were fighting not just for King and country, but our own doorsteps, wives, and kids. One night I had the most frightening vision of German soldiers marching up Alldis street, bashing our front door in with the butt of their rifles and throwing Mary and the kids into the street. I woke up in a cold sweat and just wanted to get this bloody awful war done with. Thankfully, it was only a dream. I told one or two of the lads and strangely enough, some had had a similar dream over the past few weeks but did not like to say anything. We passed through dozens of small villages and hamlets over the next few weeks, the villagers chalked the name of their respective village on the canvass sides of our truck. We were stopped by people asking how things were, and when had this or that place been liberated, sighting the villages we had obviously passed through. We felt like conquering heroes, until an officer had to spoil our moment of glory. He came straight to or truck to see what all the fuss was. When he saw all the village names on the trucks, he blew his top, get this lot scrubbed off now! Do you want me to send a bloody telegram to Hitler telling him how we are doing? He saw my stipe and bawled at me at the top of his voice, "AND YOU SHOULD KNOW BETTER" In fear of losing my stipe I, in turn bawled at the lads to clean it off now! We did as we were told, muttering that Jerry would know by now he is losing so much ground. In fact, if we had had any idea of the overall situation we might have understood a little better. With the Germans losing communications with some of their units, it may well have been a help to know which places had been liberated, but why waste breath explaining to the lower ranks. Soon, we were to eat our words as shells started falling from the sky. Within seconds, everyone had run for cover, and we were on the move in double quick time. The villages were a lot safer if we were not there. That was indeed a timely reminder that we still had to finish this bloody war. I was swanking about the food our cooks managed to scrounge, but we were met by a real heart-breaking site of dozens of dead chickens, ducks, and geese, smashed eggs, and machine-gunned pigs, sheep, even cows and horses".

We were in a place recently that was a German H.Q. and before they left they killed all the cows and poultry ~~but~~ but we surrounded a couple of very young turkeys and a rabbit and they soon ~~soon~~ surrended so we had a good ~~supper~~ for once with a few spuds

P. T.O *Darling*

"After we were ready to take post, I went and had a closer look, and could see they were not fit to eat. Fortunately, the lads took my word for it and did not bother to look for themselves. We were cautioned that some of the houses and out buildings could be booby-trapped. Something as simple as a length of string tied to a hand grenade across a doorway could blow a leg off! Thinking it is not worth it we kept well away. I felt o.k. that evening when I managed to get my head down for a few hours, but during the night, I had to make a number of emergency landings, if you know what I mean. It seems I had a touch of dysentery, and did not always make it in time. I had some spare gym shorts that I could use until I could get myself cleaned up properly. My horse blanket be it only slightly soiled I very nearly threw away, but decided that as it had served me well so far I would hang on to it for a bit longer. After a quick rinse, it soon dried out on the bonnet of the truck. I went to the M.O. after breakfast, though I could not face anything more than a drop of tea. I told him about the dead sheep and pigs, and that I had the runs. All he could say was that the usual treatment of M and D meaning, medicine and duties was of no use to me. An aspirin and rest will not help your dysentery either. Here, try this; and gave me a tin of evaporated milk and told me to keep away from the cookhouse. I felt sorry for him; all he wanted to do was his best for our welfare but was frustrated by the lack of the right medicines. Nevertheless, I could not keep it all to myself, I told one of the lads to wash the tin after I had handled it then he made a good brew up of Kamp coffee with the condensed milk. The dysentery left me feeling very feeble and washed out. That afternoon, the sergeant sent me back to our waggon lines for a couple of days rest and soon I felt a lot better. Letters from home were few and far between, as we were all over the place. I was waiting for news of our baby that was due the second week in October. I knew Mary would be alright with my mam and my sister Lena close at hand, but it is still a bit worrying being so far from home with such a feeling of helplessness. All I could do was hope and pray that everything was fine. We were soon on the move again and crossed into Belgium early in September. As we approached the outskirts of Brussels we received a tremendous reception as we passed ruin after ruin, but to our disappointment we went through the city nonstop. We took up new positions in a school about four miles *outside the city; I was glad really, as we felt more comfortable in our more accustomed environment. We were lucky enough to stay in one place for a few days and managed to get some washing done. Some of the lads managed to get a 48-hour pass to go into Brussels for a break. However, we were soon on the move again and crossed into Holland. We hadn't been there very long when we were on the move again and finished up back in Belgium not very far from Antwerp. We never knew exactly what was going on, but heard that the port at Antwerp and the Scheldt Estuary was a massive port and needed to be captured by the allies before Jerry could do too much damage. Thanks to the Canadians the Scheldt Estuary and the port of Antwerp were captured reasonably intact. Our time near Antwerp was only a few days but for the first time I managed to get one over on the sensor. I was able to tell Mary where I was. At the close of my letters, I used to end with your loving husband Bill and named the children in turn. Terry xxx Ken xxx Ann xxx. But this time I wrote love from me of course, then' Mam twerp, Terry twerp' 'Ken twerp' and 'Ann twerp'. I was glad that the sergeant had not spotted what I had done, (or did he?) and amazed that Mary twigged my subterfuge. I was in 'Antwerp' of course."*

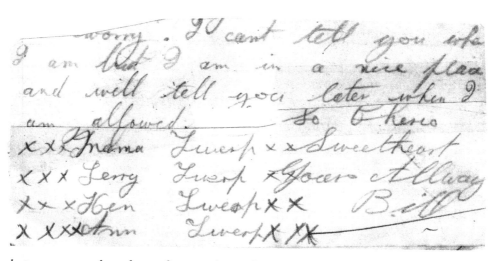

"We changed sites every other day, often without firing so much as a fart in a bottle. We were just beginning to think we had been forgotten, when we were on the move, and move we did. Right back into Holland. Even though it was the middle of September, sat in the back of a canvas-covered truck that was never built for comfort, hanging on with one hand and trying to smoke a fag with the other was not my idea of a day out. We travelled all day along roads that were the victims of so much heavy traffic and as you would expect were full of shell and bomb craters. As soon as they were filled in, they were just as bad after we had been through. All we managed was a one-hour break for a pee and a brew. In that order. We learnt afterwards that the stop was not just for our benefit, a gun had run into a crater and bounced off the road damaging one of the wheels and had to be winched back out of the way to get a new wheel fitted. The fire in a hole in the ground was a very handy trick to know at times like these. We didn't know at the time, but we were about to be part of the battle code named "Market Garden". A hectic and exhausting time lay ahead as the allies were determined to capture the bridges at Arnhem, Eindhoven, and Nijmegen before the Germans could evacuate their troops to the Reich and had time to blow the bridges to halt the allied advance. We eventually got to our gun *positions, and by the time we had set everything up and ready to 'take post' we were lucky if we got more than a couple of hours sleep".*

"On a dark, bitter cold mid-September morning 1944 all hell was let loose, our firing rate was 3 rounds a minute in the half-light of dawn, and even more as the sun came over the trees, and we could see better what we were doing. Though it was hard work, we preferred this type of deployment instead of waiting for orders all the time. As usual, we had no idea where or what our target was. At first, we thought there must be some big town ahead that was going to get the same treatment as Caen and Falaise. The order was given to cease-fire as hundreds of Halifax bombers came into sight. We expected a massive raid on wherever we had been shelling. We could see hundreds of planes as they passed overhead a few miles in the distance. Then we could see some of the planes falling from the skies, and thought, poor buggers. Not until they had nearly dropped out of site did we realise that they were gliders, hundreds of them. We learnt afterwards that there were something like 30,000 paratroopers dropped over two or three days. What happened that day was a terrible chapter of the war, told in many books and films since. We didn't know it, but we were about five miles from Nijmegen being the only bridge caught intact during the first offensive. Being nine-mile snipers, we were never told what was going on. It seems the attempt to capture the Arnhem and Eindhoven bridges some days ago failed and now tremendous efforts to repulse the German counter attacks to hold what we had gained was a nightmare. We were pulled back a few miles, about half way between Arnhem and Nijmegen but were unable to use the roads during daylight because they were needed for supplies. We had a hell of a time for nearly two weeks, we were shelling, God knows where from a farmyard or village square, as tank followed truck after tank after truck along the narrow roads in the Dutch countryside. When the traffic stopped, we were on the move as soon as we were ready to roll. We would travel for an hour or so, and then stop to make sure we were clear to carry on a few more miles. It felt like all the Germans, and all the Allies were fighting over the same bit of Holland and Belgium. One lad put it into context very well. He said it is like your next-door neighbours on each side of you fighting in your back garden, churning up the plants, wrecking your greenhouse and shed. The experience we gained when supporting the chase from the Falaise gap across France, stood us in good stead. Getting rapidly in and out of action presented no problems. Well, there was just one problem; we could not get any proper sleep. We were firing, or at least in a permanent state of readiness day and night. It took time to get ready to move at night on roads that were pitch black unless we had a moonlit night. Our trucks were under orders to keep their lights covered unless it was absolutely necessary. During the day, when we were in action, the only one to get a half-decent sleep was the driver. He took his ground sheet as far away from the gun as possible to escape the din. Some of us tried to get our heads down in the back of the truck for a few minutes, but it was hopeless. We seemed to be going forward, then doubling back to take up a position just as advanced as the one we left, but a mile or so to the left or right. We were so dizzy we hadn't a clue where we were half the time. During one of our breaks, we saw where some of the gliders had overshot their landing grounds. There were about eight in a very muddy field, but only two had landed safely; the rest were in varying states of disintegration. Some had caught fire, leaving the charred remains of the equipment still inside, then we realised that the gliders were carrying men as well as equipment. We could see that some of the gliders had made a perfect

landing, only to be crashed into by a following glider with devastating consequences to both men and machines. Later that day, some of the lads made a closer inspection, and saw that they were made of nothing more than a wooden frame with a plywood floor; the wings were covered with a canvas like material. It was a sobering thought that so many men had to risk their lives in such contraptions. The battle of "Market Garden" was a disaster, with thousands of casualties on both sides. We wondered if it really was worth all the death and destruction. Only one bridge was captured intact, the one at Nijmegen, notwithstanding all the recent chaos, several incidents stand out in my mind, like the time we encountered rifle fire. We had just pulled into position one afternoon and were getting ourselves organised when we heard a sound like very angry and very large bees. We had experienced bombs, shells, and being machine-gunned from fighter aircraft, but this was something new and took a few minutes to realise what was happening as we all dived for cover. The sergeant attempted to reassure us in an Irish sort of way. He said, "It's alright lads, they're only stray bullets, they're not firing at us". Another time we came to a halt on a road behind dozens of trucks. The cause of the holdup was because the Germans were bombing a bridge a mile or so ahead of us. We found ourselves behind three tanks and dozens trucks. There did not seem to be any anti-aircraft guns defending the bridge; one or two Bren guns opened up, but could not reach the elevation required to get a proper shot at them. The planes appeared to have a virtually free run. The tank crews jumped out of their tanks and dropped into a ditch, others jumped out of a truck and ran under the tank. We jumped out of our truck and sheltered behind a stone wall. It was a relief that Jerry was not interested in us, they were after the bridge. About six planes came in one after another and dropped their bombs, but not one fell near enough to the bridge to cause any damage, the whole operation lasted little more than twenty minutes and we were on our way. I could not help thinking that the pilots were deliberately missing the bridge just to get this damn war over. The infantry used to call us 'the nine mile snipers' but we got a bit of our own back one day. As I said, we were doubling backwards and forwards. We passed about a 100 infantry men dug in along the side of the road thinking the enemy must be ahead. They just stared at us in disbelief, until one said, "where the bloody hell have you come from". Knowing that they dubbed us the nine mile snipers, we couldn't resist retorting; "What are you hiding for; why don't you get up where the action is" It was all in fun, and knowing this, they gave us an ironic cheer. At some future date, they may have defended us against the "nine mile" jibe. Once on our travels we saw the biggest vehicle ever. Was it a secret weapon? No! It turned out to be an American mobile laundry and bathhouse. We thought we were doing well to get a bath or a dip in a river once a month and clean under clothes whenever we stopped for more than a day or two....About this time the letters from home ceased and, as I found out later, our letters were not reaching home. I just had to hope that Mary was not worrying too much, not knowing where I am or how I am. In fact, the enemy had cut the supply lines in their efforts to prevent the final push toward the Reich. We found evidence of this later when the roads were littered not only with German, but allied trucks too".

A HIGH PRICE TO PAY

"By now, October, I was still waiting for news of the birth of our baby even though it was unplanned, 'I blamed those Camellias, and the early nights last time I was on leave.' Nevertheless, we were both as pleased as punch, and looking forward to the happy event. It was getting a bit cool by about four o'clock as the days got shorter and was I was glad I kept my horse blanket. We saw many things we would rather not see. It was about two o'clock in the afternoon on a dull, overcast day. There was a strange quiet about the village as our convoy slowed to a halt in the cobbled square. Three men came walking down the street towards us, two of them, frogmarching a third between them. A little girl about ten or twelve years old was following a few yards behind them, weeping bitterly. One of the lads could just about make sense of their conversation as they neared the truck. After a lot of shrugging of shoulders the two men were determined to carry out a summary execution then and there, and wanted us to form a firing squad, saying he was a collaborator. We all said that we couldn't shoot anyone just on their say so, nor would we want to. A few minutes later in a wooded area at the end of the village, we heard a single shot; we can only assume he met his maker on that dull day somewhere in Holland. The fourteen man ration packs slowed to a few packs a week, but we still had plenty of biscuits. The food we managed to scrounge from the villagers and abandoned gardens was fresher and better than our rations. One of our cooks was a proper time served butcher and thought nothing of slaughtering a pig. Fresh pork and garden peas made a welcome change. The peas had been frozen in packs wrapped in a kind of greaseproof paper; it was our first experience of frozen food. While not looking a gift horse in the mouth, we wondered why we were getting special treatment, but it transpired that they were provisions taken off the Dutch. Who had in turn pinched it back."

An English language newspaper article of the time read.

FOOD THE GERMANS CANNOT TAKE.

From Our Special Correspondent.

STOCKHOLM Sunday.

Large stocks of Danish dairy products are lying in Denmark's refrigerating plants; I am informed by free Danish circles here. It is earmarked for Germany. Germany's war-strained transport cannot handle it, so that much needed food must stay in Denmark.

"When things calmed down a bit and the situation had stabilised, we bivouacked on the outskirts of Nijmegen with our towing vehicles well away from the battle lines. All the vehicles and guns of A and B troop were parked on a side road in a quiet part of town with houses down one side of the road and a large grass square on the other. We had some great games of football with an old rag filed shopping

bag. We had some temporary billets down the road about half a mile away. One day, one of our drivers was doing a bit of maintenance on his vehicle. He decided to move it backwards a few feet to check the tyres. Unknown to him, a toddler had left the safety of his front garden, and was playing underneath the truck. The driver only let it roll a few feet, but the child died instantly. Despite all the deaths and carnage we had witnessed, we were all devastated. No blame could be attached to the driver, but that did not make him feel any better; the child's parents must have realised what a tragic experience it was for him and likewise attached no blame to him. Shortly after that episode, we moved to another position in the town not wanting to be a constant reminder to the locals of that terrible tragedy. Then we moved to a new position some miles away and had our first post for nearly a month. I received the long awaited news from Mary telling me I am a dad for the fourth time. A girl, born on the 14th of October weighing in at 10 lbs. fit and healthy. Then she went on to tell me that she felt fine. In our letters during our time apart, we thought of names for a girl and a boy. We seemed to agree on Carol Mary, or George Anthony. Even though I was not there, I could feel the happiness in the letter and the sense that she was doing well. Grandmas and granddads were thrilled to bits. Terry, Ann, and Ken, were as pleased as could be with their new sister and have been as good as gold. I was more than happy to call her Carol Mary but felt sad that I could not be there for the Christening".

Oct 22
L/Bdr Gibbons W 1109419
89/13 Med Rgt
A Troop
B.L.A.

Dear Sweetheart

I got the letter last night that I had been waiting for, at first I thought you had not had the baby when I saw the dates 14 Oct and 17 Oct then when I went to open the first one I see where ma had just put on "baby girl born 14 oct" I could not get the second letter opened quick enough. There were tears in my eyes while I was reading because I was so glad that you had got just what you wanted you said it was everything you wanted it too be, I wish I could have just one little peep at my new daughter
P.T.O Sweet

"I was very disappointed that there was not a photograph with the letter, but as you can imagine, film was hard to come by. I expect I will get a photo as soon as Mary can arrange it. I would love to write a really soppy letter telling her just how much I love her and how I am looking forward to a new life after the war, but all our mail is censored by our officers. It did not feel right somehow to write such a letter even though they never betrayed any confidences. However, not all was lost. About a week later, we were issued with one green envelope each; these could be sealed and posted without being censored.

By a stroke of luck, we were able to wet the baby's head with real Champagne. (I kept the cork for years) We were offered the opportunity to buy a bottle of champagne each. Some of us did although most of the lads felt we were being taken for a ride. Perhaps a local wine merchant and the Major had done a deal to make a few bob for their retirement fund, but who cares."

things are going on very well out here as you will read in the papers. You say the baby is everything you wanted it to be and the nicest we have had. I can only say it must be nice for you to say that. I notice you always go in for Saturday babies. I am eagerly waiting for a photo of her. Well I wet the babies head with Champagne, we got hold of three bottles between four of us and we drank the babies health in good style

"A few days later after our evening meal, the post arrived. As I waited impatiently for my mail I felt sure I was going to see a little angel, and I did. I was ecstatic as I saw my little girl looking out at me from the photograph and Mary looking as pleased as could be. It was the best early Christmas gift ever. The lads drank a toast to Mary and me, wishing us all the best and hoped we would all be home soon. I had to pretend I was going to the lavatory; I didn't want my mates to see me on the verge of tears. Here I was, in the middle of nowhere, far from home, and no means of doing anything about it."

"Jerry started to shell us at mid-day and early evening. The shelling, though fairly intense only lasted about ten to fifteen minutes, so we knew when to take cover and just wait for it to stop. Anyway, it ceased all together after a few days. One day, a couple of lads came from the bakery about a mile away. They told us they were in the Arnhem push as we were. It may seem odd, but that was the first time we knew for sure we were part of that particular battle. As I said, we did not see our Colonel very often, so had little notion of how we were doing. He enquired about our ration of tea soon after we landed in Normandy. Nearly six months later he paid us a second visit while we were having something to eat round the gun. We all stood to attention and one chap put his mug on the spade of the gun, for which he received a right bollocking. He spotted my stripe and was not best pleased with me either. The gun is not for putting mugs of *tea on he shouted, take it off now. He would have had a fit if he knew what we carried on it when we were on the move. As the winter set in and the weather deteriorated suddenly. November was one of the most miserable periods of the war so far. We did hardly any moving or firing, everywhere was wet through and sodden as rain followed rain followed rain day in day out. We had no idea if we were winning or losing the war. One morning we had our third visit from a brass hat. He came to see for himself what our conditions were like, and found them appalling. He told us he would get us our forth blanket right away and some straw for under the ground sheets of the tents; the fourth blanket was part of our winter issue anyway. We all had our great coats but we were still bloody cold unless we could find a place to stay for any length of time and get a fire going. He was true to his word as we got our blankets and straw that same evening. The blankets were a Godsend. In addition, miracle of miracles he brought an issue of woollen gloves. I had my trusty horse blanket, my ground sheet, four blankets on top of me, my woolly gloves, and cap comforter. However, the straw was much less of a success as it soon disintegrated into bits resembling pine needles, but at least we were a lot warmer. That was the only time anyone of high rank had shown the slightest interest in our personal welfare. Some of us managed to keep warm in a sort of scout hut and kept a fire going in the little pop-bellied stove all the time we were there. We managed to 'borrow' some coal, it was smashing. No one bothered us at all, maybe the 'brass hat' who paid us a visit, had a word in the right quarter to leave us to our own devices so long as there was no trouble. Remember the 'mug of tea on the gun, well, as I said the colonel in Normandy would have a fit. The spades of the gun were loaded with logs, a bag of coal, and some dry twigs and anything else that would come in useful, all stored in an empty ammo' box strapped to the spades of the gun. Of course we had lots of bits and pieces in the truck. A few weeks before Christmas, we had a bloody awful time. Our site was in the grounds of what had been a large market garden just on the edge of a small village."*

> I saw in the papers that
> there was a shortage of
> potatoes at home, all what
> we are having are full
> of frost they are almost
> uneatable still we just
> cruise along and take no

"By now, the gardens were full of dead flowers and rotting water-logged spuds. The only veg' to survive were the sprouts. We tried some, but they were bloody awful too. After a couple of days of inactivity, some of us had a stroll across the village, we came across two football pitches, where the ground was slightly higher than the surrounding area, and appeared well drained. When we saw them, there was a lot of grumbling that we would have been a lot better off there than where we were. I do not know if it was by accident or design that we had not used this as our gun position, but the fact that we did not, probably saved many lives or at least many casualties. The next day we came under fire from a

German 88, it was just one isolated gun, but they certainly made our lives a misery for a while. They kept up the firing for days, with no particular sequence. Four or five shells would whistle over for ten minutes, and then it might be two hours before we got any more. We were all on edge the whole time. If they were only doing it as a nerve-wracking exercise, they were making a damn good job of it. About two o'clock in the morning we were ordered to 'take post' but were baffled by the orders. Our tormentors were on our right, but we were given co-ordinates to our left. Evidently, the 88 was not our target, and it made us feel very vulnerable to be firing in one direction while someone was firing at us from another. In fact the German 88 was responsible for our fourth casualty. A lad had been with us since the first days of training at Marske. His gun was about 150 yards behind ours to the right. He was hit in the back by a piece of shrapnel. We did not know about it until next morning; his mates told us he walked to the ambulance that took him away, he was laughing and saying, "with a bit of luck I'll be home by Christmas". As usual, we received no information through official channels, and all hoped he would make it home in time for Christmas. When our tormentors were finally silenced, we had a couple of days of relative peace. Strolling across the other side of the village, we happened upon the football pitch again. To our horror, they were full of shell craters. It seems that the Germans had occupied the village, and knew precisely where we could be, this time I took my hat off to the 'brass', they probably saved many lives. We heard some days later that that young lad died on his way home just in sight of the white cliffs of Dover".

"We received orders to be ready to move the following day, and damn quick it was too. Why, we had no idea, the one long journey we took some time ago was the dash towards Arnhem. Now we were wondering what to expect, would it be the usual five or ten mile dash? Our presumptions were sadly misguided. Rather unusually, the drivers were briefed longer than usual as we loaded up and prepared everything for the off. We received the order to move out at 6:am. It was bitter cold, and pitch dark; we had no idea where we were going. Are we going into action? Definitely we thought! As we were belting along at well over 30mph, it may not seem very fast, but in the dark, on potentially bomb cratered roads towing a heavy gun, it was fast. We went nonstop for hours, then suddenly we realised as the day dawned that we were back in Belgium as we could see all the villagers waving little Belgian flags. The roads were so icy they were throwing ashes and straw on the roads so we could get a grip. We heard that the Americans were having quite a scrap to hold on to Bastogne. Where ever that is! We heard nothing official, nor did we expect anything official. We learnt from the Belgium's themselves why they were so relieved to see us."

"They were afraid of being over-run by the German offensive through the Ardennes forest. We thought they were worrying over nothing. Moreover, we did not know exactly where the Ardennes forests were or if we really would see any action. The following days and nights confirmed that we certainly would. It was bitter cold, everything we got hold of was

frozen, yes even 'it' if we went for a pee. We spent weeks moving all over the place firing hundreds of rounds, fed up, bitter cold, and pissed off and just wanting this bloody war to end. The real picture did not emerge until a few weeks later. It transpired that we had been engaged in a strategic position in what was to become known as ' The battle of the bulge' We learnt that even though we were quite a few miles from Bastogne, we helped to prevent the break-through by the Germans, north of the American positions and to push them back once they had been stopped. We were proud to have been part of that phase and make a real difference. Occasionally we would see a newspaper from home, albeit a week or two out of date but we did get an idea of how things were. Our unexpected break came when we were pulled well back to a village called Wespelaar about twenty miles from Brussels".

"Life goes at home"

School log.

(December 20th. 1944)

Children assembled in the hall for the Christmas concert this afternoon.

(December' 21st)

Christmas parties in the classrooms this afternoon.

"We hoped we would be stopping here in Wespelaar for a while, as Christmas was only a couple of days away. We all made a special effort to put our tents up nice and tight and keep everything ship shape and Bristol fashion in a sheltered corner of the village. The people made every effort to make us very welcome. They asked if they could take over from our own cooks and make us a Christmas dinner as a special thank you. Our basic rations were fourteen man packs. Now and then we had what was termed a fresh ration day. With some good husbanding of flour, fat, and potatoes, we were expecting our lads to come up with something a little more fitting for Christmas dinner. However, the ladies of the village came up with a surprising amount of 'extras' by dipping into their own little bits and pieces. It was the best Christmas dinner we could have hoped for and more than we expected. Because of the numbers involved, we could not all dine together, nor eat exactly the same menu, but the ladies of the village did us proud. In the evening, some of the lads went to church with the villagers. Even as a Catholic at the time, I felt that I could not go and give praise to God after seeing so much death and destruction. One or two of us thought how could we pray for victory and deliverance, at the same time as the Germans were praying to the same God for their victory and deliverance. Nevertheless, I must admit, my thoughts and prayers were with Mary and the children back in England".

When I awoke this morning about 7 o'clock I lay thinking of what the children were doing and whether they would be up, I guess they would as they get up early on Xmas morning. I was imagining them all excited and flying about showing you what father Christmas had brought them and I was thinking to myself how I would have have loved to be him this year, do you remember when we was trying to fill their stockings and they kept on rousing as though they was going to wake up it seems such a long while ago, but never mind I will be doing it next year. It

"The next day, Boxing day a grand dance had been organised for everyone. They told us the band knew some English dance music, good we thought and looked forward to a pleasant evening. After a few umpah's and local folk tunes we thought we were in for a real treat as the bands leader said they were going to play some English dance music for their honoured guests. Well, it was true; they did know some English tunes. 'Roll out the barrel' 'Run rabbit run', and the piece-de-resistance, 'Hang out your washing on the Siegfried line. We used to say, there is nothing like English ballroom dancing, and that was nothing like English ballroom dancing, but we all had a great time and forgot for a few hours that there was a war on. We all felt as if we had deserted our American allies, but there was nothing we could do about it, just hope for the best."

"As we got to know some of the villagers, we began to see how their lives had been turned upside down, and inside out. Although the Germans did not occupy the village all through their occupation of Belgium it was nevertheless very frightening, particularly for the children. The Gestapo used to drive round the village from time to time in a big black limousine. One Sunday morning a young girl on her way to church, realised she had forgotten her prayer book and ran back to her house to get it just as the car came round the corner. They followed her and accused her of running back to warn someone of their approach. The girl was taken away without explanation never to be seen again. Alas, we had to move on and leave our newfound friends who did wonders for our morale as our spirits had been at rock bottom, we never knew where we were, and quite often what day it was".

HAPPY NEW YEAR

"We moved out of our little village about a week after Christmas, and had the most uncomfortable journey we had ever experienced. The roads were icy, the snow was falling, the wind was bitter cold, our feet and fingers were freezing, and we were here to fight a bloody war. Happy New Year! We seemed to be getting on at a steady pace until we came to a hill, well, more like a long slope. Even with 4xwheel drive, we could not get the lorries up such an icy slope. The site of waggons being winched up one at a time made my heart sink. We were there for hours, and getting even colder. Of course, when we realised that we would be stuck for quite a while we got a brew going and just sat it out until it did eventually become our turn, another two hours we were all up and on our way and looking forward to getting warm with another brew up and some grub inside us. We arrived at our position in the early hours and towed our gun into a field. It was a pretty field, with nicely trimmed hedges on three sides, a few trees, and covered with two feet of very cold snow and blowing a blizzard. As I said we were here to fight a war. There was no let-up in our routine, we had to be ready to take post as soon as possible after getting to our positions. We were issued with woollen gloves some four years ago, and our unexpected second pair just a couple of months ago, nevertheless we all needed to beg borrow or steal some kind of gloves or mittens, even a piece of blanket rather than use our precious warm woollen gloves in the wet slushy snow. The shells were so cold we dared not handle them without some kind of cover. One lad found some oven gloves and tied them round his neck on a piece of string. Anything was better than our wet hands freezing to the metal casing of the shells. Our feet were getting colder by the hour even though we were moving about a lot. An advance party is often sent on in daylight to find us a half-decent cover if we were expected to arrive after dark. We usually found our own billets when we arrived in daylight. However, on this occasion, after we had prepared the gun for action, I was one of the off duty squad looking for the officer from the advance party to see if he had any information about a billet for the night. If nothing was found to be suitable, so be it. We could either sleep in the truck, or pitch our tents. He was not supposed to leave until he was sure we were all ready for action. After looking around in the dark, a corporal informed me that he had gone back to the lines and was most likely asleep somewhere. I protested that he had no right to do so! "Oh well, he's had a hard day you know". Hard day my arse I said. It looked as though we were in for a cold night, what's left of it. The next day we found a deserted school, I am ashamed to say I thought nothing of smashing a window and climbing through it. Some of us tried to sleep on two desks put together thinking it would be a bit warmer off the floor, but it was hopeless, as we turned over, we would start to slide off. After a few attempts, we gave it up as a bad job and got down on the floor. Some of the other crews had put their tents up and laid a tarpaulin on the soft snow thinking it would be a bit more comfortable, this may have been a good idea initially, but the heat of their bodies soon melted the snow. When they woke up they found themselves quite dry, but in pools of very cold water sloshing around under their ground sheets. To illustrate just how cold it was, one crew experienced an incident that happened at dawn. They received the order to take post, reported ready, then set a number of shells on the ground. The

shells have a copper band round them about four inches up from the base, if it became frozen into the slush, the soft copper band could be damaged. The copper band was made to engage with the riffling of the gun barrel to spin the shell so it was more accurate when fired. This was the one and only time the copper band came detached in firing the shell. It left the barrel and went out of control traveling base over apex, or arse over tit, as we would say, making a swishing noise. We felt very uneasy when we heard one of those shells nearby as it could land anywhere. Our snowy torment continued for several more weeks somewhere in snowy Belgium as we moved from one position to another. We pretended to be delighted to learn that we were to get an issue of firewood, but why? We were surrounded by bombed out houses and wooden structures of all kinds by the thousand. We had our own supply of clean dry firewood squirreled away on the back of the gun carriage. When the issue of wood arrived, it was very green and too damp to burn, even with a splash of petrol. It was a shame to throw away several large sacks of firewood we could not use, so we gave it to some villagers to dry out indoors in exchange for enough ersatz coffee to make a few brews. I remember watching a tank weighing something like thirty to forty tons unable to get a grip trying to negotiate round a corner on an icy road and watching the crew pushing the rear end round by hand on the glass like surface. Eventually it got a grip and ploughed across the gardens to where the road was a bit clearer. Another gun position provided some of us with alarm; we arrived in the middle of the night, our gun position being on a low field behind a frozen ridge. The first round we fired sent the gun skidding back, and several of us narrowly missed having our legs broken. Before we could fire any more, we had to use picks and shovels to get through the frozen soil and thick ice to dig a proper gun pit so the gun spades could get a bite in the ground. We had another surprise a little while later when we saw what we thought were some donkeys being led towards our position. However, they turned out to part of a mountain artillery unit. Of course, there is always a smart arse to put us right. He said the poor buggers are a sterile hybrid of a mail donkey, and a female horse. That's exactly how I feel one lad said amid cries of so do I. One lad swore our maps were wrong, and we were in Switzerland. For all we knew we could have been. Someone shouted you would do better with bloody polar bears it was so bitterly cold."

"What prompted our colonel to pay us an early morning visit, we can only guess. This was only the third or fourth time we had seen him. Being in no mood to jump up and stand to attention, we carried on doing bits of jobs. Those who had no jobs allotted, soon found something to do. Maybe that upset him, as he demanded to know why we were still unshaven at nine o'clock in the morning. Someone said we have no clean water sir, but this he rejected as an excuse, saying there was plenty of snow we could melt. He was so far removed from the conditions we were fighting under, we had not undressed for weeks, and when we did get some half-decent cover, it was far too cold to do so. We managed to keep ourselves clean despite having no regular change of underclothes or socks, and no bathing facilities whatsoever. There were, of course many houses with baths of one kind or another but they were either smashed or full of debris and no one wanted to bathe in cold water. It really annoyed us when the top brass adopted that sort of attitude, but made no attempt to improve our conditions"

School log.

January 17 th 1945.

Nurse Smith called in school today to see three children about spectacles.

January 22 rd

Dental inspection by Miss Sellers all day.

23rd January.

Dental inspection continued all day. Weather very cold and snowy 112 children absent. Dental inspection finished.

School log

January 29th 1945.

School dinners did not arrive until 1-5 pm. School afternoon session began at 1-50 pm.

February 2nd

The attendance for the week was only 63-9% due to the snow and cold and cases of measles and mumps.

"Despite our physical discomfort, we still had our moments of fun, or so we thought. Looking round a wrecked and deserted village street one day, we saw pictures of Hitler posing with the German infantry and realised that we were actually on German soil. We took great delight in throwing snowballs and stones at the pictures until we were warned not throw things at the pictures as the Germans anticipated what we would do, and as any retreating army would do, they booby-trapped some of them. There were tales of British troops doing a bit looting for souvenirs, but we were rarely in a position to look for anything. As we were still in quite deep snow, we used some perfectly good bed sheets to camouflage our gun. Mary wrote to me one time, saying that the little extra money I sent home was a Godsend as she was able to buy some sheets from Sam's stall in the market for the children's beds. I could have wept to think of the waste of war. I promised myself I would take some home when I get my leave, or should I say 'if' I get my leave. After a few weeks at this site, the snow started to disappear but the ground was still frozen solid. Rooting around for something to burn, one of our lads found some papers hidden a barn, he said they're written in German, what do you expect you silly bugger we all said, and little more was thought about them. It is a good job we didn't burn them, but passed them to an officer, who in turn passed them up the line to B.H.Q. A few hours later, it was panic stations. The papers were plans of a minefield, and we were right in the middle of it. To add another dimension to our plight, the spade of a gun had dug into the side of one".

"Not knowing what it was, one lad used it to chop wood on thinking it was a rock. As the ground was still very frozen, we were assured that they were not anti-personnel mines and were safe to stand

on. You can imagine the four-letter word preceding 'off'. We were to pull out at first light and not wait for the engineers to make the mines safe. As our towing trucks kept on the road, they gingerly winched out the guns as we kept a very safe distance. A Sergeant from the Royal Engineers told us that they were perfectly safe to stand on, as he demonstrated to us we all said sod that for a game of f..kin' soldiers, as we all crept away on tiptoe, and onto the road with just the kit we needed to carry. The rest of our stuff we slung in the back of our trucks. As the dawn turned to daylight, the sun blazed down on that little patch of icy field somewhere in Germany we were mightily relieved to get on our way. We travelled all day with only a couple of stops of about an hour. Eventually we were billeted in a deserted monastery; it was almost dark and getting colder by the minute. We slept on the stone floor of this cold abandoned place of worship in the middle of nowhere; Some of the lads' grabbed the few remaining cushions to place on the stone floor, the rest of us rolled up in our great coats, gas capes, and anything else we could find. My horse blanket was a Godsend. Well we were in a monastery. No pun intended. I wondered what Him up there thought. Walking up and down the well-worn stone steps to the big oak doors caused quite a problem. Our legs would go like jelly after about half a dozen steps to the massive oak doors, carrying all our kit, including our rifles, bedding, even a little stove we managed to 'borrow' complete with some paraffin. It seems we had forgotten how to walk up steps or stairs after being on the level for so long, but after a day or two, we got used to them. Rumours had been going round that a leave rota was being arranged. That evening the Major and a couple of officers came down and announced that leave was indeed starting, and explained how the system was going to work. Senior N.C.O.s were drawn separately from the lower ranks, so a balance was kept. The lucky ones would be going in about two weeks' time. We all waited eagerly for our names to be called out, everyone hoping he would be one of the first. In fact, it was to take many weeks before anyone got any leave. I was disappointed at having a late number, but as it happened it was for the best, even though I did not think so at the time."

MONTY'S MOONLIGHT

"The improvement in the weather meant we were soon on the move again. We took part in some of the mopping up operations in Holland, and while not knowing much about individual deployments. I do remember that we felt that we might grow webbed feet. Many of the lads were moaning that the Royal Engineers were nowhere to be seen. Nevertheless, we just had to get on with it. Mopping up was a very apt description, as the Germans and the Allies had breached many dykes and dams to flood massive areas of farmland".

"Montgomery had instigated the use of searchlights on some of his operations, and this became known as Monty's moonlight. It allowed us to cross a flooded area in the early hours of the morning under the searchlights, we were fascinated by the system employed to overcome this flooding. We had seen the

advantages of the Bailey Bridges before, but these were like a railway lines. As we drove along the flooded roads, we crossed over many a 'Bailey Bridge' that had been put in place across a river or canal just in time before the water rose to high. It truly had been a colossal undertaking. Once we crossed the flooded area, we took part in many minor offences in order to get over the myriad of canals and rivers with the use of even more Bailey Bridges. Sometimes we would get a couple of days breather if there were a build-up to cross a river or canal. We never knew where we were half the time, but we were past caring. We were wet through, fed up, and still with no leave in sight. We pulled into a village under cover of darkness, the Sergeant said our guns were o.k. until dawn, then we had to camouflage them until the opening barrage; we discovered later that there were many more artillery units doing the same thing but we did not see any of them. I suppose that that was the general idea. As the sun popped over the horizon, we had to camouflage our guns and trucks. There were so many of us we ran out of camouflage nets that were not in shreds and had to make our own from what we could find. Any surplus vehicles were hidden under the trees and covered as best we could. As you would expect, it became a bit of a competition to try to spot each other in the distance. Our position was in the large garden of a house on the edge of the village, our guns and trucks were nicely hidden under some trees. There were a few scrawny trees and bushes we could use, so we threw our camouflage netting over the gun, threaded some tree branches, and other bits, and pieces through the netting, and felt very proud of our achievement. As we stood across the road and looked back, it was almost invisible to the casual observer, especially a spotter aircraft. The family occupying the house did what they could for us, but as soon as we got the order to take post, the few people still in the village were sent to our lines a couple of miles back, where they would be a lot safer. Their resources were very limited, but they did offer what turned out to be the best offer we had had for a very long time, clean clothes, great! We had to find some soap for them but as we had not been doing much washing for ourselves, we were pretty well stocked up with the stuff. There is always someone to spoil a good thing and take advantage of people. One officer demanded they wash his greatcoat, and we all hoped it would shrink or take days to dry out. The British Tommy was always popular, one day; the lady of the house explained to us the reason why they were so willing to help us. She said "British Tommy, immer locking" 'always laughing' the French were miserable all the time, and the German soldiers were gruff and always seemed to be bad tempered. One lad acquired an imaginary dog, and at times, he would try to teach it to beg. Later, he added a few imaginary chickens, which the dog was always chasing, we played up to him, saying the dog was chasing the chickens again and stopping them from laying. A couple of lads from another battery came by, and as we stood chatting; our mate went into his dog chasing routine. Our visitors looked at him pityingly and tapped their temples enquiring if he was suffering from shell shock. When we said no, that dogs a bloody nuisance, as it stops the hens laying. They wondered off thinking we were all crackers. Just before we were to start our barrage, we had a visit from a film unit wanting to get some newsreel footage of us in action. I know many reporters risked life and limb to report the news to the people back home but this was a bit of a comic disaster. Rather stupidly, they asked us if we would fire our guns for them. Of course, this was out of the question after all the work trying to keep our position quiet. We told them to bugger off and sent them to battalion headquarters. How did we know if they were genuine reporters? A couple of hours later they came back with a chitty giving them permission to film, and another one if they got hurt, or worse. They had to report to the casualty clearing unit. The only thing worse than being hurt, was to be killed, but they still had to report to the casualty clearing unit. How they could report to the medics if they were dead is anyone's guess, but orders is orders. That's the army for you. They set their cameras up just as we got the order to 'take post'. We all thought we could be on Pathe news in a few days, and were quite excited about it. For the next couple of hours we were far too busy caught in the heat of battle to pay any attention to our visitors. When we did get a few minutes breather we looked around for them but they were nowhere to be seen. It transpired that as the first shell was fired, their camera, tripod, all their equipment disappeared in a cloud of flying sods and detritus of all kinds, including the news team, we never saw them or any others for quite some time. We thought our camouflage was good until a haystack opened fire. That stack had been there in the next field ever since we arrived on the site about a week ago, but had no idea that it was concealing a gun. We were sorry to leave this gun position as we got to know one or two villagers when they came back to see if their houses were still intact. Our next gun position was just inside the German border but we did not know it at the time. We found a position on the corner of a short lane at the edge of a seemingly deserted village. While we were hanging about, one or two of us had a wander round. At the end of the lane, I saw an isolated bungalow. As I crept round the back, I tried the door, to my relief it was unlocked, so I crept in and wandered around to find myself in the main bedroom. With the aid of a very dim lamp, I could see on the dresser a gold watch and a ruby pendent. Not being able to resist such an opportunity, I put them in my pocket."

"As my eyes became accustomed to the gloom, I could see a man and presumably his wife staring at me with a look of terror. Not being sure which country we were in, or if the people spoke German, Flemish, Dutch, or even double Dutch made introductions something of a hit and miss affair. All I could think of to say was "guten morgan" in my best German. This seemed to reassure them that I meant no harm. After a few minutes, we were sitting around the kitchen table drinking a substitute coffee made from acorns, and very good it was too. I discovered we were just inside the German border. A revelation that frightened me at first, but I was soon reassured with their broken English that they were not Nazis or anything like, they were simple folk caught up in this bloody awful war. Even though they did not give any kind of hint that they saw me take the watch and pendant, I did feel the pangs of conscience getting to me, but thought they could have suffered a worse fate by a greedier soldier. When I did eventually give them to Mary, and told her how I got them, she said "you cheeky devil. I don't know how you dared." Many things went on during my time abroad that she would not have understood or approved of. After the war, I learned that they were of no intrinsic value. I felt really bad about taking them as they would have more value to that frightened couple."

48 HOURS IN BRUSSLES

"As well as the home leave rota, another scheme started to allow some troops a 48 hour pass to go into Brussles. Mine came due during the preparations for the assault across the river Rhine. It was obvious to us that a big build up was taking place with smoke screens day after day. We were in the garden of a big detached house facing in the direction of the river Rhine, albeit a few miles away. I thought to myself, in better circumstances this would be a beautiful place to live. It was the best gun position we had had for ages even though half the roof was missing with shell holes in what bit of that beautiful house was left. There were no civilians in the vicinity, they had either fled or been evacuated by our forces to avoid any leakage of information. We could not help thinking that Jerry must have known we were getting ready for an offensive with all the smoke day after day. Of course, the old saying that idle hands do the devil's work we couldn't help but have a nosey round the houses, and hope we could organize a decent nights kip in a real bed for one or two of the off duty lads. Once inside what was a beautiful five bedroomed detached house I could have wept. We looked up at the sky, through the hole in the roof and thought better of it as it was far too dangerous. The beds were wet through and looked ready to fall through to the floor below. In the part of the cellar that was not full of bricks and rubble, we found some sausages and pork dripping, wrapped in waxed paper stored in a bucket of dust-covered cold water. Not to look a gift horse in the mouth we all had a good sniff, and the consensus was that they were typical German sausages with lots of spices and were probably fit to eat. At the far end of the garden, we found a chicken coup with a few chickens scratching about; they very kindly provided us with a nice clutch of eggs, but two of them were cracked so we though best not to eat them. One lad wanted to kill a couple of the chickens for dinner. However, when we asked him where will he get any more eggs for tomorrow's breakfast he shut up. In the larder, we found a few spuds and an abundance of cooking utensils in the kitchen draws and decided to make some chips. While the chips were cooking, someone chucked a sausage in the pan. After a few minutes, some of the braver ones had a taste and were unanimous in thinking that they were o.k. and chucked the rest in a separate frying pan with some pork dripping. We all sat round the kitchen table with our sausages and chips as if we were at a banquet. Not all of us had sausages, the sergeant asked volunteers to forego their sausages in exchange for a couple of eggs each. The thinking behind this seemingly odd request was that if the sausages were a bit suspect at least some of us would be fit enough to tackle Jerry"

"Although the enemy knew that a big build up was taking place we were told not to walk about too much, you never know who is watching us. This suited us fine, we were so pleased with our billet we were content to stay put for a while. As the days passed, we were aware of a good deal of activity in the village behind us, and were a bit worried when we saw a field hospital as well as the usual casualty-clearing units being organised. To add to our apprehensions we heard talk of German 'dummy' paratroopers being dropped to cause confusion behind our lines. Of course, the wise crack came back that we were already confused and did not need Jerry to help us. We were told we would be opening *the barrage that night so get some grub inside you and prepare for a busy few days. We heard later that 1,000 guns of the British 2ⁿᵈ and the U S 1ˢᵗ and 9ᵗʰ Armies battered the crap out of Jerry in that particular offensive. Just as it was going dark, one of the lads said he thought he heard someone crawling about at the top end of the garden, I hope no one is after our bloody eggs he said. A couple of us grabbed our rifles and went to investigate. We found a figure hiding in the long grass; we shouted, "halt! who goes there"? The last time I shouted that was at the gas works back in Portwood all those years ago, I never thought I would ever shout it in earnest. Whoever it was, hearing our English voices stood up with a plaintive call of "where am I". The silly sod had somehow got separated from his unit that were on their way to mark out with white posts, the route the Buffalo's (amphibious tanks) had to take to the river. He said when the truck stopped for a few minutes; he dived behind some bushes for crap, no sooner had I settled down, I heard the waggons leaving. Running down the lane with my trousers neither up nor down I was left behind. I had no idea where I was, and thought you were Germans at first site, and was crapping myself a second time. We soon assured him we were friendly and sent him back for our H Q to deal with."*

I NEARLY MISSED THE RHINE CROSSING

"We started our bombardment, having been told that the objective was to knock out previously identified enemy positions to make the crossing less hazardous. This was to be the only time we got a clear picture of the part we were to play. We even knew the name of the town where the assault was to be, a town called 'Wesel' on the far side of the Rhine about four or five miles from our position. We had no idea that we were so close to the enemy. The realisation that the German positions were within our range, made us realize that they had their own "nine mile snipers". That made us feel uneasy when we heard the sounds of gunfire in the distance. I knew my leave to Brussels was due any time soon, and had been looking forward to the break as we all did. If anyone suggested that I would experience a lack of enthusiasm to go when the time came, they would have thought I was crackers. Whether it was because we knew what part we were playing, or because we realised that this could be the final assault into Germany proper, and bring an end the war. I, like many of us thought that the Rhine was the border between Germany northern Europe. However, that was not the case. The Rhine forms only part of the border, we were already in Germany. Nevertheless, we felt that crossing the Rhine was like crossing over the last real obstacle to the Third Reich and victory. I wanted to cross the Rhine with the Regiment. Many of us had been together since Marske. I felt as though I might miss out after waiting so long to be able to make a real bid to help to get this damn war over and see Mary and the kids just that little bit sooner. However, I said nothing as that could make things difficult for the lads sometime in the future. We were in the middle of our barrage when I got the call to go. As I was getting my things ready I looked across to witness the town of Wesel being battered to bits as our shells exploded. Although I could not see the town in any detail, I could see the burning buildings as the red glow of the flames reflected in the water along what must have been a two mile stretch of shoreline visible across the flat pastures leading down to the mighty river Rhine. Even the off duty crews came to have a look. Then we heard the most frightening noise ever. A rocket firing battery called a Z battery, started up. It went on none stop for about an hour. What an unholy racket they made even though they were about a mile behind to the left and right. The noise was deafening as cluster after cluster flew over every few seconds. I am sure some of us felt sorry for those on the receiving end, though no one actually said so. With the bombardment in full swing I thought that our 48 hrs.pass would be postponed for a few days, but I got the call at 2: am and off we went. There were just two from each battery aloud to go at any one time. We picked up about ten more lads from other batteries along the way. As we left the battlefront, the noise of our guns became quieter and quieter until we could not hear them any more as we trundled along the deserted Dutch and Belgium roads in the dead of night. We arrived on the outskirts of Brussels at about eight o'clock in the morning. The driver said we were not allowed to go into Brussels until nine o'clock. No explanation of course, but we thought it was to give time for the previous lot to vacate the billets and get some breakfast. We asked the driver where we were. He pointed to a village about half a mile across the fields. To our amazement, it was Wespelaar, the very village where we stayed at Christmas three months ago. I had with me a couple of pairs of girls' shoes and a

pair of women's boots to augment my spending money. I decided that the shoes would be very much more appreciated by the family that made us most welcome over Christmas rather than the bars in town. I had a word with the driver, he said you randy bugger, be back in about an hour. I could not be bothered trying to explain, so I just set off running down a lane towards the village. Luck was on my side as I recognized the houses where we were made most welcome. They were so surprised to see their "uncle Billie". The little girl's faces lit up when they saw the shoes; by pure luck, they all fitted perfectly as did mama's boots. Alas, I did not have any for papa but he was pleased for his wife and children as they admired their new shoes. I could only stay for about half an hour, but it was the most gratifying half an hour I had throughout the whole War. To bring so much joy with a simple act of kindness was better than any leave. As I said, only a limited number of men were allowed away at any one time, my companion, Bob, was a chap from another troop, not my first choice for a weekend companion, but he was decent enough. We were billeted a couple miles from the lively part of Brussels, the same place we stopped at just before we were to engage in the battle of Arnhem thou' we did not know it at the time. After we made claim to a bed and our blankets, it was nearly dinnertime. Bob could not wait to get into town, but I was happy to get some dinner then to sit on my bed and write a nice long letter to Mary and the kids. I was surprised to see Bob, quite sober, back in time for the evening meal. As we sat in the NAFFI, he said he had trawled round a few bars, but did not enjoy it on his own. He came back for some grub as the things on offer were more than just food, and very expensive. He wanted me to go into town with him later. I said o k if you want someone to hold your hand. About seven o'clock a few of us set off to catch a tram at the end of the road. My mate's miming gestures, worthy of Shakespearean actor, landed us smack bang in the middle of the red light district. Most of the lads wandered off to have a look round. Bob could not wait to sample the delights. As we got closer to the town centre, we could see that the place was very busy and crawling with Military Police. They told us to behave ourselves in terms that were easy to understand. We noticed that some of the women were wearing very smart coats made from best woollen army issue blankets for officers of course. We heard that the M.P.s would stop the offender, take the coat, cut the buttons off, hand them back, but keeping the coat. The army in its infinite wisdom did not want to be seen stealing anything from the civilians. After a few drinks of watery larger, we were getting a bit fed up and felt that our high expectations were sadly misguided. Then our luck changed as we found a bar full of other forty-eight hour pass lads. As the night got going my mate disappeared. He was gone for over an hour. I knew what he was up to so I didn't bother, he was a big lad now and could look after himself. We both said we must not miss the last tram back to our billet, but of course, we did. We cadged a lift part of the way, and then had to walk the last mile or so. The walk back took us the best part of an hour and a half, and wondered if it was worth it. Bob said he had the best shag in his entire life, and worth every penny. Probably the first! we all shouted, much to his embarrassment though he had no idea how much it cost him. The next morning Bob found out the true cost of his dalliance, a banging headache, empty pockets, and a worrying thought that he might have caught a dose of clap. We spent the rest of the morning in our billet until dinner, and then we had a walk round a nearby park in the sunshine. In the evening, we called in a local bar for a few drinks, and were made very welcome. The following morning, our driver came earlier than we expected. We had hoped for the best part of another days leave, but by 10 o'clock, we were on our way back to our lines. Upon returning to our battery in the afternoon, I was surprised and oddly pleased to see that they had not begun the crossing without me. I only just made it as they were all packing their kit in readiness for the crossing at dawn in a few hours' time. As I said, I was keen to be making the crossing, and making my own little bit of history. Others were, to say the least miffed at not getting their 48 hours in Brussels. Four o'clock, it was just coming light. Trucks loaded, guns hitched up and we were ready. We were told that the river was about twenty feet deep in most parts, so if we were hit or capsized for any reason try not to panic and shed as much weight as you can. One lad said if I shit myself that will shed a few pounds. Driving across those pontoon bridges we marvelled at the engineering skill of the Royal Engineers, and the speed required getting them in place. It seems that they were assembled upstream, and then floated down to be anchored in place the secured at each end into the bank. I could not help but think they must have been in some bloody awful schemes back in England in order to perfect these skills. After an uneventful but nerve- wracking ride down to the riverbank followed by a short drive across the river that felt as thou' it was about ten miles wide, we came off the pontoons and all lined up ready to move out. We knew that the Germans have been pushed back rapidly, but looking at the devastation we had inflicted on the town of Wesel and surrounding countryside as a whole, we were not surprised. Events started to happen thick and fast, so numerous that it is hard to realise that so much happened in so few weeks. We would stop in a farmyard, fire off a few shells, then move out to yet another village, and then we seemed to be forgotten for a few days".

"During one of our brakes, we heard of a warehouse full of shoes, so we drew lots to determine who would go first as we could not all leave the gun at the same time. I was one of the lucky ones to go first. There were no civilians about so I started to look for some shoes for Mary and the kids. All the shoes were boxed in sets of two left shoes, or two right shoes in an effort to stop pilfering by whoever was transporting them. In normal circumstances, say, in a shop, it would not be a problem, but those that had beaten us to it had emptied shoes all over the floor to try to speed up their searches. After about half an hour, I managed to find three pairs of black lace-ups for the kids and two pairs real leather court shoes for Mary and felt pleased with myself. In any bunch of men there's always one that is a bit slow and often relies on his mates to help out, but no one could have foreseen what happened to our very own silly bugger in that warehouse. He took his own boots off to try on some civvy shoes for himself. When the time came for us to get back to our positions, he was panicking because he could not find his own army issue boots. We all scrambled around and found them and off we went just in time to let the next lot go. A few days later, we went into action on the outskirts of a town that had been subject to a massive air strike. There were German bodies everywhere, so we had no desire to go exploring around that particular place. A German soldier's leg lay only a short distance from our gun position, one lad said jokingly; I wonder if it has a good sock on it. I had to find a piece of carpet to cover it up. We saw many German corpses, a lot of them still in their trucks and some hanging out of tank turrets, none of them had what one might call a clean death. A group of four, or was it five bodies blown to bits, scattering limbs and belongings all over the place, blood spattered letters and photos' of their loved ones, I thought, that could just as easily have been us. We had to try to look upon them as inanimate objects and get on with the task in hand. We passed by a farm that had been the

site of much fighting and found the stables still smouldering. Not only could we smell the burning straw but also burning flesh, we could see where one of the horses had tried to jump over the half door of its stable but couldn't break free of its tether. As a result, the poor animal was burnt to death just a few feet from safety. Nearby, a dead German soldier lay by a wall with a long handled grenade in his hand. We saw another dead British soldier being taken away to add to our tally of the three on the beach at Normandy, the half dozen or so in the Jeep and the officer who went to help his comrade after the shelling in the woods. We heard that a number of paratroopers had had their throats cut as they landed in Holland during the "Market Garden" assault. We came across a British soldier with a very firm grip on a boy in a German uniform who looked little more than fourteen years old. The boy was crying and calling "Mutter! Mutter!" Looking out of our truck, we said "let the little bugger go" the British officer holding him said he's just killed my f..kin' mate! How does a man react when a boy of fourteen or fifteen, who had just killed his comrade, so near to the end of the war cries out for his mother?"

"Some of the lad's went on little forays when they had the chance. One lad came back wearing a yellow silk scarf he found in a warehouse just up the road, so a few of us that were not on duty went to have a quick look to see what we could find. As we approached, we could see dozens of civilians milling about as well as officers mingling with the lower ranks. As we approached the only available entrance, we saw a young lad standing by a box the size of a tea chest handing out axes. Not wanting to be missing out we just took one each. We found the place was full of wooden crates and boxes of heaven knows what, but we were quite content to look at the ones that had been opened already. We had just started to have a good rummage, when a Sergeant Major stood at the door and called out for everyone to be quiet. We could see ourselves on a charge and me losing my stripe and my 9ᵈ a day. However, to our relief, the Major barked out an order, telling all the civilians to leave the warehouse. As the last one left, he said right, carry on lads, we don't want bloody 'Johnny foreigner' getting in the way. My haul was not fantastic; I could only find a few bits of cutlery, and a few pairs of thick woollen socks, but best of all, a load of hair clips for Mary."

"She said in many a letter that they were unobtainable at home. I filled a canvas bag with about a dozen cards of all kinds of plain and decorated hair clips, there must have been hundreds of them,

Mother's Medal

enough for the entire street. In one box, I found a medal; on it was inscribed (DER DEUTSCHEN MUTTER.) meaning mother's medal. After asking around some of the German woman they told me it was a (bronze 3rd class) for producing four children for the fatherland."

"I also found a deaths head ring. This was the emblem of the dreaded S.S. To the best of my knowledge, no one in our unit, or for that matter, anyone in the army stole from any of their comrades. However, no one liked the deaths head ring and told me to get rid of it. I was looking to the future thinking it might be worth a few bob after the war, but it disappeared shortly afterwards."

SOMEONE UP THERE LIKES ME.

"We knew the war was coming to an end, but there was still a sting in the tail. It meant saying goodbye to all my mates, particularly Curly. I did not know it at the time, but that was the last time I saw him for the best part of twenty years. All thoughts of promotion had long been abandoned by me so I was surprised when, out of the blue, I was promoted to full bombardier. I had the task of taking charge of a gun with another troop, moreover my promotion was backdated three weeks so I became 'War substantive' immediately. Usually, all promotions have a three-week probationary period to enable personnel to be demoted if they do not measure up to the job. I was quite happy as I got three weeks back pay. If I made a serious mistake, as full Bombardier, I would have to take the blame. My new crew were beginning to get a bit rusty not having been in much action lately, they were getting slow laying the gun, but there was not a lot anyone could do, we couldn't go on a scheme as if we were back in England. A couple of days after tacking charge the crew were once again slow acting on firing orders. I said the only thing I could think of, and it seemed to do the trick. I told them all, in no uncertain terms, that we were not firing at the German army for the fun of it; we were here to help and protect our own infantry units, you know, the lads at the thick end of the fighting, not cushy nine mile snipers like we are. We are trying to protect them from being shot at by the German artillery; do you want the Germans to win? From then on, we were the fasted gun in the east. We went into action on a very wet and soggy afternoon and had a great deal of difficulty getting our gun into position in a very wet field. We had to chain the truck to a tree to drag itself up the field; the truck in turn was used to drag the gun off the road and into the field. Once we were far enough into the field we un-chained the gun without too much bother but still had to man-handle it round to face something like the right direction. (Remember Brecon) After we had fired about ten rounds, the gun was unstable, as the spades could not get a firm hold in the wet soil. Because of all the bouncing about the gun developed an oil leak in the recoil system. Our gun artificer had to get it under cover, so we had to tow it to a nearby barn for them to work on it. What a ball-ache. We heard, through the grape vine that we were to take part in a big night barrage to dislodge one of the last German defences. The word 'last' seemed to breathe new life into the men. We all got stuck in and built a raft of heavy planks from a nearby timber yard, then filled some empty ammunition boxes with soil to make a sort of breast work to stack round our gun when we got it back in position. The gun was taken in the afternoon so I went a couple of times to see how things were getting on. Eventually we went to collect our gun and got back just before midnight to groans of couldn't you have left it until morning. I said it was only a few hours ago you wanted to get stuck in. Now's your chance! It was hard work winching it into position, we dragged our boxes of soil and built some more rudimentary barriers round the side and front of the gun hoping it might just help to hold it in position. Leading up to the start of the bombardment, we were running around like blue arse flies getting ready to 'take post' and reporting ready to receiving orders to fire. After following the correct procedure the order came through, I remember repeating it, and the number one pulling the lanyard, and then... nothing. When I came to my senses I found myself on the ground with an

121

excruciating pain in my hip, I could feel what I thought was blood running down my right leg, as I felt down the side of my leg, I was relieved to feel it was cold gritty water, not warm sticky blood. For a moment I did not know what had happened, I thought we had been on the receiving end of a German shell. As I looked in the general direction of our gun, I could see that we had had a 'premature'. In other words, the bloody gun had blown up. I could not bring myself to go and take a closer look, I half expected all my mates to be blown to bits. As we were near the command post, I ran for assistance. Perhaps if had not been so close I would have had to steel myself, and go and see if I could do anything. I burst into the command post shouting, "we have had a premature"! For god's sake, get someone out there I think some of my mates have been killed. Prematures were very rare and while some could be devastating, others were relatively harmless, depending on where in the gun the explosion occurred. The Command Post Officer, having heard the explosion knew it was a premature from his own experience as he too was once on the receiving end of one. He realised by my agitation that the situation was serious. He notified battalion headquarters for the medics to report right away. Then, gathering some assistance, he was on his way to the gun leaving me sitting there in the command post with my nerves in pieces, and trembling like a jelly. About ten minutes later, he came back, and to my relief, he said it's all right Bill no one is seriously hurt. As I was the only one in the command post, I was not sure if he was just saying that so as not to make me feel even worse. However, after a few minutes some of the lads came in and were surprised to see me, they thought I was dead as I could not be found anywhere near the gun. One or two of the others were being sick outside. I was only about ten feet away from the gun, but I was just in the right spot to avoid serious injury. The number two was closest as he was the one to pull the firing lanyard. He was hit in the eye by a tiny piece of shrapnel, and subsequently lost his eye and was sent home. None of us envied him going home so soon, even though the war was not yet won. We thought the loss of an eye was too high a price to pay for early demob. The Liverpool lad was some distance away as he had gone for a pee, he sustained some shrapnel wounds in his arse as he was thrown to the ground, the M.O. removed the bits there and then in the command post, and he did not even report sick afterwards. Another lad was near the charge pit well away from the gun so he was o.k. whereas another lad was knocked into a trench and broke his ankle. While we were all trying to come to terms with what had happened, and how bad it could have been, the cook was summoned from his bed, along with a couple of orderlies. They soon made a bucket of tea and found enough mugs and extra sugar to go round. It was a very welcome distraction amid all the mayhem. By now, it was nearing five o'clock. After checking us all, the M.O. gave us all a couple of aspirins each then suggested we all went to get some sleep if we could. The command post officer told us report in at noon. After a late breakfast, a few of us had a wander down to the gun position. As we looked at it, we were amazed that we all survived. As we stared in disbelief, we could see that the shell had exploded in the chamber and blown the barrel off; it was resting on what was left of the gun, but pointing in the opposite direction. As this was the strongest part of the barrel, made of 4" hardened steel, it gives you some idea of the force of the explosion. The horns that hold the massive springs were blown to pieces, the wheels were unrecognisable, and the tyres were in shreds. We were all amazed that no one was seriously hurt. As I thought about what happened, I felt a shudder down my spine. However, Jerry was not to know what happened and was in no mood for any let up. Our sister batteries carried on just the same. The artificer had been collecting various parts to help with the enquiry into the mishap. He found the arse end of the gun buried about three feet deep. Finding the block, called for even more digging, it was eventually located about three feet down in the soft soil. It was a very graphic indicator of the power of these guns. As we looked around in disbelief, as a number of curious on-lookers joined us. A couple of lads from our sister battery asked us "how many of 'em bought it?" When we told them what happened, they were, to say the least 'gobsmacked'. Some other lads told us of the exact same premature some time ago killing all the crew of ten. A premature explosion is exactly that. There is no doubt in my mind that it was a faulty fuse. Some weeks earlier, we had orders to double check the numbers on all the fuses, and report to B.H.Q. if we found any matching those on a list we had. However, on this occasion the fault was missed. The top brass thought these were responsible for other 'Prematures'. We learnt that the faulty fuses were not only traced to the arms factory, but the operative assembling the components. It was a woman who had been drafted into war work against her will. Strongly resenting this, she had been deliberately passing faulty fuses, either through resentment, or in the hope that she would be sacked. Whatever happened to her we never found out, but we all hoped that she would feel guilty for the rest of her life. I did not tell Mary about the gun blowing up, until long after the war was over."

A NEW GUN

"The next day, I was detailed to collect a replacement gun. When I heard we were going to a town, just over the border in Holland and as it was to be an overnight stop I asked if I could take some of my crew with me. My request was turned down until I pointed out that, as we did not have a gun there was not much they could do and it would help them to get over the trauma of this bad experience. I thought, what would you want them to do! Throw sticks and stones a Jerry? It was a good job I kept my mouth shut. About an hour later, I was told that I could take three men with me as well as the driver, and to be ready to roll in an hour. I chose three names out of a hat, being the fairest method I could come up with. Arriving at the depot in the early evening, and looking forward to a night in town, as we did not have to collect the gun until the following day. The truck had to stay at the depot under guard along with all our other equipment. We never thought to ask the lads at the depot, if the nightlife was any good. It was a pity; we could have saved ourselves a lot of bother. We were quite happy with our bivouac in the church hall as the weather was quite pleasant. We hoped things would be a bit livelier in the town centre, and it was, but not as we had hoped for. Evidently, we were still in range of some German artillery and soon heard the unmistakable sound of German shells falling only a mile away. This made us think hard about going out even if the shelling stopped. We decided to stay put and enjoy our surprisingly generous rations given to us in case we were too late to get some grub. (We were) Along with a few beers that we managed to scrounge from the N A F F I, we were all happy bunnies. After our fill, two of the lads went to see what was going on in town, but were back in half an hour, they said everywhere was boarded up, no trams, and the streets were deserted, so we settled down and had a few games of cards. As we sat there chatting and reminiscing about the premature and what might have been, one or two of the lads wondered if we could crack on to be more traumatised than we actually were and get our ticket home. It was a big temptation to get away from it all, to get undressed properly and sleep uninterrupted for a change. I felt sure I could have got away with it, but I could not lie to myself. Whatever the outcome, I would always know the truth, and despise myself because of it. I soon quashed that idea and told the lads never to mention it because it could scupper someone who is genuinely traumatised. We took our replacement gun back to our lines the following day, but could not use it, as there was no dial sight available. We thought we would have an easy day or two but we were sadly mistaken. You would have thought we were back in England. Clean the gun, clean your kit, clean this, clean that; the dial sight arrived two days later, just as we were preparing to move. Things were becoming chaotic among the German forces. We heard of hundreds surrendering, and of others throwing away their weapons and uniforms, and then taking to the woods. One mild night when most of the lads were asleep, I sat outside our tent on an ammunition box. It was so quiet; the war seemed a thousand miles away. Looking down, I could see pinpoints of fluorescent light around my feet. Little that I knew about nature I felt sure that 'glow-worms' didn't crawl about on the ground. I rubbed my boot in the soil, only to see it light up, as if kicking the embers of a fire. I found a stick and wrote my initials in it, hoping they would remain visible for just a few seconds so I could see my name *in lights for probably the one and only time in my life. Sitting there alone, it suddenly occurred to me that the enemy could be hiding in the woods behind our position, even though the infantry had cleared them out a few days ago. Still, we were now at the stage of worrying only when there was something to worry about. I learnt the next day after telling one of the more leaned lads about the glow-worms, they were female wingless glow-worms, cleaver sod, I thought."*

School log

April 13th 1945.

President Roosevelt died last night at 10-30pm. The flag was flown at half-mast all day and a talk was given to the children after the morning service on President Roosevelt and his great friendship to this country.

"At noon the following day, hundreds of German soldiers walked out of the woods a mile or so up the road, with arms aloft carrying white rags as they surrendered to the allies. Another time we passed a column of about a hundred German prisoners walking, not marching, guarded by one diminutive corporal. As we passed each other, he shouted what do you think of this lot then, as if to claim them all as his very own bounty of prisoners. As we moved clear of the woods, we had a nasty reminder that the war was far from over. A German plane suddenly appeared. Flying low over our column with such a deafening roar, we didn't have time to panic until it had passed over. The Major shouted, "Get the hell out of here". We didn't need telling twice. Later he said there is no point getting killed with the bloody war so very nearly won". The bombardment ceased almost as suddenly as it begun. When we had a look at the damage, we were all relieved that we were away from our guns. A truck not much more than fifty yards away was on the end of a German shell, and was little more than a twisted wreck and burning out of control. Then we realised that it was full of shells, within seconds, we were back behind a heavy stone wall forming the front of a house. As the truck was hit, it blew shells all over the place, we estimated that the truck would have at least twenty still on board. The rest of the battery joined us, as this was the safest place to be as the shells began to get hotter and ready to explode. From the safety of the building, we watched as our driver was trying to go and collect his loot, but the Major told him he would put him on a charge if he stepped outside. As we crouched down watching the truck burn and waiting for the tyres and petrol tank to explode. Only one of the shells actually exploded whilst we were there. We knew that the driver had a fetish for ladies fancy underwear, we could see silk knickers, bras, and underskirts flying up into the air, some landing in the branches of nearby trees, covering the area of a football pitch. It looked as if the devil and his disciples had had an orgy. However, that was the funny side of things. We were to learn that a lad from another battery half a mile down the road had been killed and another had a piece of shrapnel lodged in his jaw. We moved from there without firing a shot. It was so bloody frustrating at times, knowing that the enemy was only a few miles away, but not receiving orders to shoot back at them." As we pulled away from the devastation, the Royal Engineers were preparing to shunt the burnt-out and damaged trucks off the road so we could get through."

BELSEN

"Rumours began to circulate that a prisoner of war camp had been discovered a few miles away near a small town called Bergen This had no significance to us at the time. However, as the rumours began to take hold, and become more fantastic, people began to believe that something terrible had happened. I could not believe it when we were told that thousands of dead and dying bodies were strewn about that prison camp. The camp was "Bergen Belsen" concentration camp. The first such camp to be liberated by the allies. Some of us thought we might go and have a look, just to satisfy our curiosity. We asked a senior officer if we could go and have a look at what we had been fighting against. We were ordered not to go under any circumstances. Later we learnt that as the allies were getting closer to the camp, the Commandant, under a white flag meeting with Allied senior officers, called for a quarantine boundary be drawn round the camp as there were thousands of dead and dying prisoners as a result of Typhus. In fact, the whole camp was infected with Typhus. We protested that we had had our Typhus jabs last year but the order was rigorously drummed into us, anyone caught even thinking about going there, would be on a charge with no excuses. We had no way of knowing just how terrible a place it was at that time. Some top brass were there, with reporters, medics, doctors, film crews. It seems that all human dignity had been abandoned, and cruelty and starvation was part of Hitler's new order. A new order that the people of this little town called Bergen could not, and would not believe. It was so far removed from the stereo-type prison camp one would expect to find. It was a concentration camp, a name we had only recently heard. A number of local dignitaries, along with trade's people who had supplied the camp with food for the guards, were treated to a trip round the camp. To say that they were appalled would be an understatement, but the 'top brass' were not entirely convinced that they were unaware of the suffering, even if they didn't know the full extent of what went on in that camp. They were forced, along with hundreds of ordinary townsfolk, to stay there for days on end to help to bury the thousands of corpses by way of a punishment to make them realise just what their so-called masters of the Third Reich thought of human life that did not conform to their ideals of 'Racial Purity'. As the first such camp to be liberated by the Western Allies, it received instant notoriety. One lad, sent back to our lines was so badly traumatised by what he saw he could hardly describe it. He went as a medical orderly when Typhus had been identified in the camp. He told us... strewn over an area about the size of ten football pitches, lay thousands of dead and dying people. Huts were full of men women and children all suffering from Typhus, dehydration, dysentery and an appalling lack of human dignity. Outside, pits were full of corpses not yet covered over. I could hardly tell the difference between the living and the dead. Those not in the pits or in one of the dozens of stinking huts were lying all over the place with corpses around them, an awful ghostly procession of emaciated aimless skeletal people with no hope of life, unable to see the terrible sights around them ... Babies had been born there, a mother, driven mad with hunger, screamed at me to give her 'milch für meine kinder', and thrust the tiny mite into my arms, then wandered off unable to shed just one tear as she was so dehydrated. He said, *as I opened the bundle, I found that the baby had been dead for days and stunk to high heaven. As he told us what he had seen, he really was in a bad way, with tears in his eyes, his whole being was trembling uncontrollably. As he wandered off he said, "That day was the worst day of my life". Rumour has it that he was repatriated soon after. Poor kid"*

NATURAL JUSTICE

"Let me tell you something official about that first camp to be liberated by the British 11th Armoured Division. They were first on the scene on April 15 1945. The commandant of the camp contacted the British to tell them of the Typhus. A cordon was put around the camp with strict orders regarding exit and entry. It was designed for 10,000 prisoners but eventually held about 60,000. Most of whom lacked any food, water, or shelter. Even though there were no gas chambers at this camp, some 28,000 prisoners died of disease and starvation. Many more died in the weeks after their liberation by the British Second Army. After reading more about that camp, and dozens more like it, I am glad I did not go. Anna Frank died there just weeks before the liberation. After the camp was photographed, documented and cleared, it was burnt to the ground with flame throwers mounted on Bren carriers. On a note of natural justice, nearly all the camp guards made to clear up their atrocities, died of Typhus, and we believe many German civilians along with them".

School log

April 20 th 1945

School dinners taken out doors to day. Dinners were delivered half an hour late.

April 23rd

Dinners were not delivered until 1.25 p m. Began school at 2 pm

"What was to be our last position in action was one we occupied shortly before my leave was due. Once again, we had no real idea where we were. We got fire orders and co-ordinates for one gun, our gun, to fire five rounds, when we received the order to cease-fire, to our amazement; we heard a voice over the Tannoy: "congratulations gentlemen, you have just hit a ship". We were dumbfounded, we were unaware that we were anywhere near the sea. Actually, we had been firing at a ship sailing up the river Elbe to Hamburg. The observation officer must have been so pleased to hit such a rare target, hence his congratulations. I just wish I had known at the time, that those five shells we fired were our last. Maybe I would have said a prayer and given thanks for my deliverance. We had another piece of great news. Quite simply, the voice from the Tannoy said "Hitler is dead" The death of such a tyrant was the best news ever as we all cheered and shook hands with as many blokes as we could and kissed as many girls as we dared. The eagerly awaited day arrived when I was to go on home leave. Not knowing if I should leave any of my kit with my unit, I asked a chap in the quartermasters stores what was the best thing to do. He told me if I lost any of my kit, I would have to replace it on a payment slip. If I lost my rifle, I would be on a charge or even a Court Marshall. Not wanting to lose out, I packed everything in my kit bag and took it all home including my rifle and tin 'at. I scrounged a

French kit bag for the shoes, tin 'at and a few bits and pieces. The journey home was uneventful, and very very very slow, or so it seemed. The weather was lovely and warm. As the white cliffs of Dover came into view the cheering on deck was as loud as any football match when England score a goal at Wembley. I defy anyone not to feel utterly moved by such a sight and the feeling of going home at long last. The customs officers were all blind as bats as we all, to a man, went through with kit bags full of bounty. One senior officer was seen pushing a pram full of pots, pans, and bedding, topped off with an army blanket to hold them in place. Was the pram part of his booty, or just the contents, or both. Well, I thought the best of luck to him. When I saw the army blanket I could have kicked myself, I had forgotten my horse blanket, well, I thought it could still be there when I get back but I had more important things to think of first."

MY LITTLE ANGEL

"Words cannot describe the feeling that was welling up inside me as the train pulled into Edgeley station. As I walked, well, almost ran down the station approach, my mind went back to that dark, wet, morning half a lifetime ago. I caught the tram from Mersey square, and felt like getting out and pushing the damn thing up Wellington road to the top of the hill. Mary was expecting me about teatime. The moment she saw me with my kit bags she thought I was home for good, but I had to explain that I could not just leave because Hitler is dead. The kids were so excited to see their dad for the first time in nearly a year. The joy of my homecoming, and the delight of holding our little baby girl for the first time was priceless. The black and white photo' Mary sent me just a few weeks after Carol was born certainly did not do her justice one little bit; she was a little angel with bright blue eyes and blonde hair. Mary felt a bit uneasy with the shoes I brought home, but I managed to convince her that they were from Belgium. The children were happy with any kind of new shoes.

REAL STEAK

The butcher had given Mary an extra meat ration for me as a thank you. He managed to get a piece of frying steak, about 8ozs. I could not persuade Mary to have some; she said it was my treat from the butcher. Army personnel were not issued with ration books during the war. When a serviceman went on leave, he was issued with a ration book to cover his needs for the duration of his leave. A ten-day leave a ten-day ration book. It was a matter of course to let your butcher and ration book shops know when a family member was due home on leave. I savoured the moment as we all sat round that little scrubbed pine table with a freshly washed and ironed tablecloth for the occasion. The only thing to spoil the occasion was the fact that we did not have enough chairs to go round. The twins had to stand up between the table and the wall, a practise that lasted for quite some time after the war. After tea, we all sat in the front room on the three-piece suite and felt a bit posh for a while. The simple things in life became more apparent as it was good to hear the news regularly, as well as familiar music on the wireless, like proper dance music by Victor Sylvester, and Jack Payne, and the sense of stability after all the chaos of war. We planned to take the children on a trip round Bell Vue zoo. When, to tremendous relief we heard on the wireless that the Germans had signed an unconditional surrender. We felt that a trip to Bell Vue was just our kind of celebration with our new family. The BBC announced that the next day May 8th would be Victory in Europe day. (V E-Day,) a day for national celebrations. We listened to Alvar Lidell as he announced that Winston Churchill is going to speak on the wireless at 3pm the following day the 8th of May. I will bet you could hear a pin drop over the whole country as we listened to the voice of Winston Churchill."

"Hostilities", *boomed the familiar voice* "will end at midnight. The evildoers now lie prostrate before us. Britain had stood mighty against the most tremendous military power the world had ever seen. And she had fought back from the jaws of death, out of the mouth of hell while all the world wondered"

That speech by Mr Churchill was the best news ever; it was a tremendous relief to us all as he said that all hostilities would end at one minute past midnight. My Ma' and dad made a little tea party for the twins and Terry round at mill cottages. They wanted to make the day feel like a special day for all of us in the summer sunshine amongst the Rhododendrons and Lupins in the garden of Mill cottages in the summer of 1945.

Me >

Once again, I have to disappoint you, we had some photographs of our little tea party, but like many things, they were lost in the midst of house moves. Nevertheless, as you can imagine grandma found a few red white and blue pennants to drape across the trees. We can just about remember tiny snippets of that little party we had in the garden of Mill cottage.

School log

8th May 1945.

Victory in Europe day. The Germans surrendered unconditionally. Thanksgiving service held in school at 9. am this morning and then school was dismissed for two days national holiday.

June 1st 1945

Keith swindles, a boy in class 2 aged 10 years was killed whilst boarding a tramcar. He ran back to the pavement and was caught by a motor lorry.

"We tried to explain to the children that the war was over, and hope that daddy will soon be home for good. We did not expect them to understand, but we were so happy and just wanted them to share our joy. I was due back the next day, but was delighted to here on the wireless that all servicemen on leave were to get an extra two days leave by way of celebration. I thought a couple of pints in the Dog and Partridge tonight will do me very nicely thanks, only to have my delight snatched away as quickly as it was given. I was in the back yard thinking how soon I could rip down the Anderson shelter and start some sort of garden for the kiddies. Mary came out to me with a mug of tea and, with just the beginnings of a tear in her eyes; she said the man on the wireless said the two days extra leave was not for those on leave from overseas. This was indeed a bitter blow. It seems that it would be unfair to make those waiting to come home from abroad to be made to wait another two days. This only demonstrates the woolly thinking of the army at times, as if a serviceman would not be willing to wait, so he could have two extra days at home. Anyway, I was going to have my two extra days come what may. After a glorious ten days, plus two, seeing friends and family I was all too soon on my way back to my unit. I had a rail warrant to get me from Stockport to Dover by whatever trains were available and off I went."

THE WAR WAS OVER, BUT ONLY FOR SOME.

"After what we hoped would be our last goodbye, I boarded the train with far more reluctance than ever during all the time I was in the army. However, this time, I boarded that train in the knowledge that I would soon be home for keeps, little knowing it would be about eight months before my demob'. At Dover, with some of the lads from our last deployment I boarded a troop ship bound for Calais. As I watched the white cliffs of Dover disappearing in the distance, my feelings were the exact opposite as they were two weeks ago. When I re-joined my mates in Calais, I was surprised how many there were as I only saw one or two on the way to Dover. There were about two hundred of us; we thought the war was starting all over again. Officers were calling for rank name and number to check us all in. Eventually we were sorted with a brew and fry-up in the N A F F I, and very welcome it was. We had instructions to board the train on platform 7 by two o'clock. We had no idea where we were going or what was to become of us. We trundled along all afternoon, and then stopped about six o'clock for an hour so we could get some grub and a toilet break. Then off once more for about another hour. When we stopped, it was almost dark. Nevertheless, off we went again in our more familiar army trucks with our kit thrown unceremoniously on top of us. After about an hour, we pulled into what we later learned to be a displaced persons camp at Aachen just over the German border. After yet another roll call, we were shown to our billets just outside the perimeter fence and left to our own devices. We had no idea of the scale of the problem caused by these poor unfortunates."

"There were millions of 'displaced persons' all over Europe after the end of hostilities. This camp, though under the jurisdiction of the British army was like the League of Nations. There were Poles, Latvians, Lithuanians, Yugoslavs, even some from Nazi concentration camps, and God knows where else. It was our job, the British Second Army to keep order until they were repatriated to their country of origin as soon as possible. As for us on the ground, our job was to keep the piece. Our immediate priority was to provide shelter, nutrition, and basic health care. Most of them suffered from malnutrition and the results of cruelty and were just as much victims with the terrible loss of life, property, and dignity as anyone unlucky enough to be caught up in this bloody awful war. However, the human spirit is much tougher than you might think. The majority of camps soon set up churches, synagogues, newspapers, sports events and entertainments, even maternity units. As the scale of the problem began to manifest itself long before the end of the war, the 'International Tracing Service' was set up to administer the repatriation of millions of displaced persons spread all over Europe. One day in late June, we were soon brought back to the reason we have been fighting this war for the past six years, Democracy! The Major asked if anyone was interested in the forthcoming general election back home. This came as a bit of a surprise to us, as politics was the last thing on our minds. We were given a chance to hear someone speak on behalf of each of the main parties. Sad to think now, but we were somewhat baffled by all this politicking. Most of us felt that Churchill was the saviour of Britain and her allies, but thought that Attlee might be better in peacetime having been in the coalition during the war. Having said *that, I did not send in a vote, nor do I recall anyone else doing so, but I felt that finally things were getting back to normal."*

Life goes on at home.

School log.

"July 5th 1945

School closed all day it being used as a polling station for the general election."

"*The camp was practically deserted during the day except for a few walking wounded, but about five o'clock in the evening about four hundred foreign workers drifted in, all were in make-do and mend clothing, and looked a sorry sight indeed. There were quite a lot of woman, most of them no more than thirty years old and all in need of a good bath. This was our first of many encounters with what one could only call the pitiful fallout of war. We did our best to feed and clothe them whilst we were there, but it was a mammoth task. After a week or two, some of us were glad to be moved to a camp a few miles west of Hamburg, being the only part that escaped the bombing of last December. The locals told us of trees beginning to blossom in January because of all the heat from the incendiary bombs dropped by the allies. Even mother nature did not know what was going on. Many Germans in the towns and villages we occupied declared that they were not Nazis; we heard that Hamburg was the only place where Hitler was booed during one of his famous beer hall rants before the war. We heard the news that the American air force have dropped a massive bomb on Hiroshima in Japan killing thousands of people in one hit. A few days later, we heard that another bomb had been dropped on Nagasaki. Then we heard that Russia had invaded Japan at about the same time. We were all convinced that the war will be all over in a matter a weeks if not days and we would be going home a lot sooner than we dared hope*".

DANCING GIRLS

"A trip was organised for us to see a show to keep us out of mischief, and to stop us moaning all the time. Looking out of the back of the truck as we dodged and swerved round the badly repaired shell and bomb craters, we could see mile after mile of destruction. In some places bulldozers had to be brought in to clear the streets of debris, not just debris, but some poor bugger's house or shop? Along street after street scarcely a wall was standing. Looking back, maybe we were being cruel thinking it serves them bloody well right, but we did not start the war. The show took place in a large theatre that had somehow survived all the bombing. The variety show was first class, even though we did not understand most of it, but we enjoyed the dancing girls. After a few days, we were found a duty that was amusing, interesting, and very educational. We were to cross back over the river Elbe to join some other lads from what used to be our sister battery making our numbers up to about 40. We were going to another 'displaced persons' camp, mainly to show the British presence. Not knowing what was in store for us, we all hoped it would be better than the last place. Some German civilians in three large rowing boats rowed us across the river. Being very wide at this point, it took over half an hour to reach the other side. When we were all accounted for, we were herded onto some German trucks driven by German drivers. We all felt that we were going to be taken prisoners ourselves for a minute. When we had settled in our new camp, an officer came and outlined our duties. These consisted of the mind numbing duty of walking round and round the camp just to be seen. There were Russians, Yugoslavs, Poles, Latvians, and God knows how many more assorted nationalities with the females outnumbering the males by two to one. As you would expect in a British camp, the sexes were segregated well away from each other, particularly at night time, but the ingenuity and sex drive overcame the most rigorous of curfews. Truth be known it did no harm to help to foster international relations and keep the peace. If they broke the curfew, no one bothered. We had a talk given to us by someone from a kind of displaced persons welfare group. He went over the same ground as the chap at the first camp. He said that just because the allies won the war we were not to treat them as if we were conquering ogres. All the inmates, (not prisoners) are to be treated with respect and humanity. Most of them have suffered more than any of us during the past five years. Our orders are to see to their medical needs, food and general welfare. Anyone found to be mistreating any inmates will be on a charge and dealt with most severely".

FLIT DOWN THEIR KNICKERS

"One day a new batch of D P s came in and we had the unenviable job of delousing them. This was done with a kind of Flit gun filled with DDT powder. There were no female army personnel at the camp, and the brass did not ask for any help from the woman in the camp. It was up to us to do the job. Some lads were embarrassed at first when told to spray up the women's skirts, front and back, and down their knickers. While most of the newcomers were in good shape, there were quite a number still dressed in concentration camp striped pyjama like pants and coats; they were so thin they could hardly walk. There was a sick bay in the camp, but few would admit to being sick, it seems that the big buxom German nurse was keeping a few patients sleeping in the sick bay to justify her presence and her insatiable sexual appetite. The self-confessed camp stallions would call in for an 'Asprin' nearly every day, but got more than an Asprin. A collection of clothing was gathered from the German civilians living nearby whether they liked it or not. It was meant to be in some small way, reparation to those in the D P camps. We made sure that the first inmates to benefit were the ones still in the concentration camp pyjamas. The rest had to queue up outside one of the huts made ready for the purpose. As one would expect, there was a mad scramble for the best coats, trousers, and sweaters, the resulting chaos soon got out of hand with the ever-present threat of a third world war breaking out. The only way to stop this free for all was to close the 'shop' and tell them, through a number of translators, that if they could not wait in an orderly line, I would close the shop for a week with an armed guard on duty day and night. Nevertheless, I could not deprive them of a half-decent coat for too long. There was real chill in the air felt by inmates through their flimsy clothes. I had to come up with a strategy to suit everyone. Late in the afternoon I put the word out that, the 'shop' will open from 10 am until 12 noon for women and 1pm until 3pm for men. If there is any repeat of yesterday's behaviour, I will close the 'shop' until we have some kind of order. Fortunately, now that I am a full bombardier I can enjoy a nice cup of tea and write a letter to Mary. The next day, orderly queues were formed and everyone was happy with their lot. Some girls would lift their skirts to show they had no knickers on, so they could get another pair, we knew they deliberately took their own off and put them in their bra' or bag if they had one, but we just let it go. There were many offers of sexual favours for a better frock or bra' and not surprisingly some of the lads were entering into the spirit of the free enterprise culture. I did not blame them one little bit, and I was sorely tempted once or twice. As the camp was taking fewer inmates we moved to yet another one in the middle of nowhere. This time we were there to protect our late enemies. The surrounding area was dotted with smallholdings and slightly larger farmsteads. It seems that gangs of marauding ex-prisoners not wanting to be repatriated were living rough and terrorising the area, raiding farms, raping and pillaging, even committing a murder. We were told by our commanding officers not to take any unnecessary risks, as we will all be going home soon. One night we were on duty along with about a hundred and fifty troops on a massive operation to surround a large area containing several small farms, the idea being that if any of the farms were attacked we would move in and arrest the culprits. Baring in mind what our C.O. had said, most of us were ready to shoot first and ask question later. We stood about all night shivering our balls off, but not so much as a rabbit was about on that bitterly cold night, so we were sent back to camp and heard nothing more about it. All went quiet from then on".

A SORRY STATE

"There were lots of occasions when we would see dozens of former German troops trudging past us when we were out and about. Most of them looked as if they had walked all the way from Normandy as they were in such a sorry state. They passed us in single file without a word. When we did manage to speak to some of them one of the questions we were frequently asked was of concern me: "When are the British joining us Germans to fight the Russians?" This sounded ridiculous to us, we had been told to respect our gallant Russian allies. We really were ill informed about how things were on the diplomatic front. We noticed the willing acceptance of authority where local German labour was used by the army. In every case where one German was in charge of half a dozen men, he would bully them all day long, and thought it to be quite normal. On the few occasions when I was in charge of German workers, I found I could be tolerant as long as I showed my authority at the first sign of decent. As usual in times of shortages, the black market was thriving, cigarettes, food, and sex being the standard currency. We were in a privileged position, as we could buy plenty of cigs' from the N.A.F.F.I. making life a bit easier in a society where the barter system was the norm'. It was a pity we could not sell sex in a bottle, we could have made a fortune"

"Our next move was rather sudden. To boost the army's numbers, about twenty of us were taken to a large displaced persons' camp containing about two thousand D Ps, most of them Russian. Apart from our own officers, the Russians had their own army officers to keep order. Stalin treated all prisoners captured by the Germans as traitors and deserters. The fact was that after the war was over, they were free to go back to their units for demob'. Little did we know they were quite happy to stay put for a year or two in the safety of the camps. Squabbles broke out from time to time; often it was about two things, food, and fags with sex a close run third. Nevertheless, the Russian officers soon put it down. Except the one time a naive young Scots lad, who had formed an association with a Russian girl went to meet her one day only to see her being held down on a box outside her hut while a man was cutting off all her hair. This was the punishment meted out by the French, Belgian, and Dutch people to some girls who had collaborated with the Germans. The fact that this punishment was being administered to a girl for being friendly with a member of the Allied forces showed just how much the Russian officers had been brainwashed then, in turn passed the message on to their charges. The young soldier was so incensed by what was happening he set about those holding the girl down and managed to free her. She ran to her hut, the lad ran to his billet near the camp gates. After a few minutes of calm, we could hear the shuffling of hundreds of Russian boots as they came across the square towards us; and it was not to ask us for a dance. There was a large tarmacadam square between our billets on the outside, and the D.P.s' huts across the square. The British officer in charge turned out the men, about 40, with loaded rifles, and a Bren gun carrier, the sight of which temporarily halted the mob, but after more shouting they started advancing again. A senior officer ordered the men to fire one round over their heads, if they didn't stop, fire directly at them. Fortunately, our interpreter made it very clear that we meant what *we said. After the first shot, the hostile D.P.s beat a grudging retreat thus avoiding an international incident. Local vehicles brought in their rations by arrangement with the Army Control Commission. It was stew served out using a ladle with a one size fits all system. A big man got the same as a slip of a girl. The ladle also doubled up as a weapon to keep thieving hands off the bread, as once again one piece of bread each, be you 15 stones, or 6 stones. Pathetic, was the only word to describe the utensils and receptacles nursed by each inmate being, along with their spoon or fork, their most treasured possessions. Some had biscuit tins; some had pans, bowls, even a chamber pot. One sight that had us all doubled up laughing was an inmate with a sausage in his chamber pot. Most had lost or bartered their dish and spoon as issued to each inmate, in exchange for a few fags. They really were fed like pigs, with their individual trough. Some D.P.s ventured out of the camp. As they were not prisoners we just let then go, and some did not bother to return, just what happened we did not know or really care that much. Things seem to settle down for a few weeks, but the temperature dropped like stone as soon as the sun went down. We were all in the same miserable mood. Nowhere to go, not much to do, we were all really pissed off. I should be at home by now, working, bringing home a bit more money, playing with the kids and enjoying a pint of Robbies in the Dog and Partridge or The Crown beer garden on a nice summer evening."*

GOOD OLD FOOTBALL.

"A little salvation in our humdrum lives came from the Russians; they challenged us to a game of football. There were only three of us from our glory days back in Hailsham; it seems like last century since we were there. The game was to take place under some sort of loose F.A. rules, but once we kicked off, they soon went by the wayside. Strolling down to the football ground, we were surprised to see such a good setup. It was something like our non-league club grounds, with a stand down one side. The game was to be thirty-five minutes each way as most of our opponents would not be very fit. At half time, we were all knackered, including the Russians, the usual half an orange would have been very welcome but there was little fruit of any kind. We had to be happy with mug of sweet tea. How wrong could we be, thinking or opponents may not be fit, maybe they were not very fit but they were determined to give it their all. With the score standing at 3-2 in our favour, we called for the ref ' to blow the bloody whistle, but he said he was playing injury time. Then unexpectedly they scored an equaliser, the ref ' blew his whistle and ran like hell to a waiting staff car and off he went. When we got back to our billets we had a word with the referee, he said there was no way he was going to let us beat the Russians and cause a riot. He said the whole world needs referees now. I suppose he was as much of a diplomat as a referee, and a good job too."

"A week after that interlude, dozens of British army troop transport trucks began to ferry the Russian inmates out of the camp, presumably back to their own units, or was it prison. Our lads were told to stay well away. Stalin labelled all Russian prisoners as traitors to their country and the communist cause, and would be punished as such. A few seemed to escape the round up, maybe their turn would come soon enough. Restrictions being relaxed, we started forming the odd friendship. I had previously spoken a few times to a lad about twenty-five years old, using German as a common language. He looked a bit of a wide boy, and seemed more intelligent than most and had a thirst for knowledge. I called him Roscon, being the nearest I could get to pronouncing his name. Eggs were known to be fairly plentiful in the rural areas, but for some reason we were still on powdered egg in our rations. One day Roscon suggested going on an egg safari. I spoke to the sergeant about trying to cadge some fresh eggs to supplement our rations and managed to borrow a 15 cwt. truck. We still carried our rifles whenever we were away from the camp, but Roscon wanted to take a Sten-gun, saying the Germans were more afraid of a Sten than a rifle. I said we were buying, not stealing. Two or three American cigarette could buy half a dozen eggs, so why steal. Off we went, me and two of my lads with Roscon. At our first stop, as we made to get out of the truck Roscon took hold of my rifle, we had to be very firm with him before he would hand it back, phew!. A lot of the farmers were not too sure about Roscon as he was still wearing his Russian tunic, but we did all right with our egg safari. I gave him ten eggs to foster good will between us, the rest, about thirty, were soon wolfed down as fried egg butties with a nice mug of tea. He wanted to go again but we were told not to go around scrounging like beggars. It was an object lesson in being polite and actually asking for things instead of thinking brute force was the preferred option. Roscon could not understand *why we were always moaning about being in Germany for so long and saying sod Churchill, and sod Montgomery; we would be shot if we said the same things about Stalin."*

"As before, I was tempted by the goods on offer from some of the women, but thinking back, I am glad I didn't. Most of them were pleasant enough, but with distinctly Mongolian features. A couple of days later, I saw a group of about a dozen girls getting on a British Army truck. I asked the driver where he was taking them, he said to the clap clinic. Say no more! Time passed and we were on the move again. There was never any reason given as to why we were moving, where to, and for what purpose. I lost count of how many moves we made".

STRENTH THROUGH JOY.

"What was to be my last tour of duty, though I didn't know it, was the most idyllic of the whole war. Eleven of us were posted to a village to enforce the prevailing curfew. A Sergeant, 5 gunners, 2 drivers, (with trucks) a wireless operator and a cook and me, making a total of eleven. We were billeted in the village hall in an isolated spot down a quiet lane. The lads had the biggest room, the sergeant and me had the office, (with heater) luxury indeed. In the spotless kitchen there were two German women busying themselves with even more cleaning. They offered to stay on as our cooks, however, we were not allowed civilian cooks, so one of them was made the cooks orderly and the other cook became a cleaner. wink! wink! We formed ourselves into two sections, after the necessary duties were done; the lads passed the time in any way they wished, so long as they kept out of mischief. The area we patrolled was mainly countryside with the odd farm, or tiny hamlet. On our first patrol, we came across an elderly couple guiding a cow slowly down the lane close to curfew time. We had orders to arrest anyone breaking the curfew and lodge them in the local police station about two miles down the road for attention the next day, but here was a problem, what to do with the cow. After a few English/German words and gestures, we ascertained that the cow was sick and they were doing their best to get back to their farm as soon as they could. Not one to be hard on people just for the sake of it, I asked them to get home as quickly as they, and the cow could go. We got to know some of the villagers as they began to accept us as friends, not conquering ogres, as they had been lead to believe. For some odd reason a poster was still stuck on the wall in a little back room. "Strength through Joy" being the slogan of the" Hitler Youth". We asked the 'cleaners' why he was so popular with the young. They told us that during their early teens throughout the 1930s they were totally transfixed by Hitler. After the school leaving examination, they joined the HJ (Hitler-jugend) Hitler Youth. We felt that we were sharing in the responsibility for National Socialist Germany. Shortly after we joined, we were sent to an H.J. camp for six months. Those six months at the camp were the happiest days of our lives. We were working in the fresh air with lots of other youngsters and making friends with peasant girls, students, working girls, hairdressers and many more from so many backgrounds. There were over 6,000,000 unemployed when Hitler became chancellor of Germany, and he seemed to be our saviour at the time, can you blame us for wanting a better future".

"As we began to settle into a routine, all kinds of odd things happened, like the time we found a small suitcase in the road one evening. We all dared each other to pick it up, but after being told about booby traps albeit some time ago, and the Major telling us not to take any risks we left it for someone else to find. My leave was due in about seven days' time, but would I be able to go. My face began to itch like mad. Having suffered the extreme discomfort of Impetigo (skin disease) in the early days of my Army career, I feared the worst, the postponement of my leave. I knew what it was, and was loath to see the M.O. However, knowing how quickly it could spread, I had little choice. As luck would have it, the medics were only a few miles down the road. After just one look at me, M.O. said I was

in luck saying they have just received their first supply of a new wonder drug called penicillin. He gave me some tablets, explaining how costly they were, and how I was lucky to be his first patient to get this treatment. With a feeling that they could not be that good, I returned to my billet with very strict orders to stay clear of any contact with other men, the kitchen, and use a dedicated toilet and pin an order of explanation on the door. The Army was very worried about contagious diseases, any man with the slightest signs of skin blemishes was immediately isolated from his unit. But as it was not so bad I was allowed to return from whence I came so long as I kept stickily to what I have been told and keep my towel and shaving things well away from anyone else's. To my relief, the penicillin worked wonders, not just on my skin, but my morale too. It meant that I would be able to give Carol a big hug on her first birthday".

Southwood road school still helping others.

"October 15th 1945)

Collection of oranges for a girl of Greek St High School who is ill in Stepping Hill Hospital and needs oranges for her illness."

"During my journey home, my face began to itch again, but as I looked in the mirror in the toilets there were no visible signs of skin blemishes, and put it down to my imagination. After three days at home, and trying not to be too close to the children I just had to go to the Doctor. He was somewhat sceptical, thinking I just wanted a sick note for a few more days leave, he said I should go back to the army medics' and let them give you some more of that new wonder drug. Alas the next day I felt very unwell. Not wanting to give my infection to the children, and knowing I would not be able to get to my unit in Germany looking like a spotty kid, I went to the only place I knew, Great Ducie street in Manchester, the place where I had my medical some five years ago. I arrived at nine o'clock hoping for a quick turn around and be home again by dinnertime. After a cursory glance, the doctor arranged for me to be taken to an Army skin hospital about forty miles north. I asked if someone could let my wife know how and where I was going".

BLOODY HELL!

"On my arrival at the skin hospital in the afternoon, a specialist dermatology doctor examined me. He said I have a recurrence of my Impetigo. Bloody hell I thought, I hope they have some Penicillin. I joined four other lads in a little ward and told to make myself comfortable. After a few minutes, an orderly brought me a very welcome mug of tea. Feeling rough I got undressed and got into bed only to be told by a nurse that no one was to get in bed 'till nine o'clock. Feeling bloody awful I declined to get out of bed. Shortly afterwards, another nurse came in to see me, it seems someone had informed on my reluctance to stay out of bed. He took my temperature, and promptly transferred me to a confined to bed ward with two other lads. The following morning the orderlies were doing their best to keep the beds nice and straight for the doctor's ward round. To my amazement, we were told to lie to attention when the doctor came to look at us. It did not matter if you were dying, so long as you did it in an orderly manner. When I moved my position in bed, an orderly would rush to straighten the covers. You can guess by now, that's right, I would move even more just to watch him run around like a scalded cock. The doctor, on seeing just how awful my skin was, told me about the new drug called Penicillin. He was somewhat surprised to learn that I knew about it, and that I had already had some treatment when I was in Germany a few weeks ago. Nevertheless, he went on to tell me all about it. I think he was showing off with his knowledge. I was somewhat surprised to have a visit by Mary and my mother, the orderlies could not have been more friendly, and even brought us afternoon tea and a sandwich on a tray so we could all eat together but not too close of course. When the orderlies left to give us a bit of privacy Mary said a policeman came to tell me where you were, I was frightened to death when I saw him, I thought you had had an accident or something. I asked Mary if any of the children had any signs of a rash or spots. I was relieved to hear that no blemishers were visible particularly on Carol and reassured me that she would keep a very close eye on them all for the next week or two. I told her if there are any signs of spots, she must take whoever was showing signs to the Infirmary right away and ask them about Penicillin and never mind the doctor. I was discharged after ten days and dismayed that I had been 'Y' listed. Normally a man absent from his unit for three weeks was struck off the strength and sent to a holding unit. If he were lucky, he might find his way back to his own unit but could easily finish somewhere else. When I protested, I was told that the 'Y list' period has been reduced from three weeks to one week, and I was to report to the Royal Artillery barracks at Woolwich. I felt so let down having to go to Woolwich, I decided, by way of compensation to spend the night at home. Mary was surprised and delighted to see me as I walked up the path at about seven o'clock and suspected I had jumped ship as it were. The next day I was on my way to Woolwich, the home of the Royal Artillery. I had heard how very strict the discipline is there, so I reported in with a smart salute; I was surprised when the officer did not return my salute. He looked at my discharge papers from the hospital then said if I didn't live far away I could go home for the night, I said I lived in Stockport south Manchester, he said have you any friends or relations nearby, no sir. To think, I could have had a couple of extra days at home. After a bloody awful night's sleep *in a crowded billet, I went on parade in civvy shoes, collar and tie, but I still had my battle blouse and fatigues with me. Having left all my Army kit back in Germany, including my horse blanket, I was expecting to be put on a charge for being improperly dressed but as there were no N.C.O s' in evidence, the parade was being taken by a lance bombardier. I was o k. as I out-ranked him so he was not likely to challenge my improper dress. Various work parties fell out for transport to pick them up, leaving the rest of us to our own devices. The N A F F I was at the far end of the barrack square, so after breakfast I decided to take a stroll to find a cup of tea and something to read for an hour or two. After dinner, I thought I could go for a look round the town. My second stroll was not such a success, as I went to pass through the gates; the sentries stopped me, saying that only work fatigue parties or special passes were allowed out before 18.00 hours. I was so bloody annoyed I could not help myself but to bawl at them saying the f...ing war has been over for months! All they could say was that they have their orders so you will just have to accept it. This was indeed a blow, so I put my thinking cap on and managed to get out of the camp the next morning by pretending to be with a working party. However, I was as bad burned as scalded. Once I got out, I realised that the weather was cold; I had little money and nothing to do. I went to the pictures a couple of times, but I was fed-up to the back teeth. One day I saw an officer from our sister battery and told him about my frustration at not being able to join my unit in Germany. Even though he did not know me too well, said he would try to help with my request to get back to Germany. Shortly afterwards I heard that because of the overcrowding. I had a choice to make; a week's leave, or back to my unit in Germany. Mary could not believe it when I walked in the back door just as it was getting dark. As usual, the clocks seem to go extra quick when I am on leave. After only four days, a police officer came to tell me to report to Woolwich the following day. On arriving, I found myself on orders for posting to a holding unit. When I went to draw my kit for posting, the quartermaster said that new rules had just been issued, meaning I would have to sign a pay form, thus creating a debit. As I had spent the previous few weeks either on leave at home, or in hospital, most of my clothing was civilian. Being away so long my mates would quite naturally assume that I would not be back, therefore sharing out what bits and pieces that were of any use. I needed several items of uniform such as boots battle dress and shirts; and sign a pay form. In other words owing the Army about a £100 when I am demobbed. I fought a battle for the replacement of a five-penny field dressing and there was no way I would sign a pay form and put myself in debt. As it turned out, I only got £90 war gratuity. To spend over five years in the Army and finish up with a 'minus' £10, gratuity, not bloody likely! On parade the next day the officer in charge asked me why I had not drawn my kit. I explained the situation to him, so took me to the stores where the Quarter Master said rules is rules and could not do nothin 'about it. After tea, I went the N A F F I .to write to Mary to console myself. I did not tell her about the uniform fiasco it would only upset her. About ten o'clock the next day the officer said go and collect whatever you need on a 'no pay' form as soon as you can, we are leaving at about four o'clock. How or why, he persuaded the Q M stores I have no idea. I had a field day at the stores. I got more or less a full kit of boots, battle dress, and a brand new great coat as winter would soon be upon us".*

I MIGHT AS WELL STOCK UP.

"Knowing I would soon be demobbed I managed to stock up with extra underwear, shirts and socks, even some field dressings, this time for nowt! The Quartermaster on duty that day said he was due to be demobbed in a few weeks, so help yourself. The next day we arrived at a camp near Dover to be told we were in a holding unit for a few days then on to service abroad. This, as the name implies, was a unit where troops were stationed in England awaiting posting to various units still needed to keep the piece. All the staff were busy sending people overseas, while they sat tight. All ranks were entitled to at least two medals, three if they had been out of Britain. However, by a process of elimination, two ribbons only served to declare that the recipient had never been abroad and consequently had not seen any action. A number of schemes were organised to keep us occupied, as our Artillery group had no big gun to play with, we were issued with little guns for rifle practise and the good old standby, lectures on personal hygiene. The only fighting we saw in Germany at this time was between the sexes, the only issues with personal hygiene, was the danger of catching a dose of clap."

"As you know by now the army have a system for everything not least demobilisation. Most of us still to be demobbed, felt very hard done by but we had to be patient. If millions were demobbed at about the same time, it would be chaos. It would mean finding millions of jobs, food, and welfare, an impossible task at the time. We were placed in numbered groups ready for demob, mine was group 38. I thought as I am married with four young children and worked in the building trade, that maybe I would soon move along the queue. Nevertheless, I just had to be patient for a bit longer. I am glad I didn't know just how much longer. Whilst at this camp I was offered 'B' release, but after speaking to a senior officer, I refused, as I thought I was nearing my demob date anyway and didn't want to miss any of my army gratuity. Shortly after my refusal of 'B' grade status, I was asked if I would consider signing on for another year with the rank of sergeant with married quarters for Mary and the children. At first, I thought it would be like a long holiday for Mary and the kids, and then I realized that I could be sent anywhere north south east or west. I realised that not only God but the Army work in mysterious ways. Mary and the wider family just wanted me home for good. Besides, the council might want our house if we were away too long. We were under the command of a senior officer and a sergeant, and were both very keen to make a good impression in front of the lower ranks. When the courses finished and we were back in our routine, the news came through that the entire unit were next for posting back overseas. It may seem odd, but if I am going abroad, let us get it over with. I was in a state of limbo just hanging about for weeks on end".

"The two Sergeants I mentioned, had only four and ten days respectively to wait for their demobilisation. We were surprised when they both asked permission to accompany the unit overseas; it seems they wanted to show off their three ribbons at their local cenotaph service as having done service overseas. I suppose it was not their fault they were not sent abroad. Permission granted they could hardly wait *for their time to leave. About six o'clock in the evening we boarded a liberty ship similar to the one we used in June 1944, and crossed the channel, this time to Ostend. Having been fed and watered on the way over, and managed a bit of kip the usual fiasco ensued at the dockside until we eventually boarded a train as dawn came over the horizon. We finished up in a Belgian regular army barracks in Mechelen used by the Germans during the war. Even though the town was deserted at that time of night, the two officers were as happy as a dog with two dicks. One could be forgiven for thinking they were opening the second front as we all marched through the deserted streets with them as pleased as punch with chests out and arms swinging remarking loudly, let us show these foreigners what the British army can do. A retort from the darkness; most of us have been doing it for ages sir. Two or three days later one sergeant returned to England for his demob' his mate remaining another week. No one dared tell them that the qualification period for the medals was six months. Our deployment here was a complete waste of time. There were very few D Ps in during the day as they were out mending roads and clearing tons of bricks and all manner of debris. They were so well behaved we felt like a spare prick at a wedding. I soon managed to wangle a pass to go into town with a few of the lads, using the excuse that I would keep an eye on them. Arriving in the town about eleven o'clock in the morning. I took them for a look round without getting too carried away. We eventually ended up in a bar, and soon the lads began to sense what kind of place it was and some of the younger ones were a bit embarrassed when a girl began to run her hands up and down a lad's inner thigh. The Madam was doing a bit of wheeling and dealing, and suggested the young lad bought the prettiest girl a drink. I knew that drinks were about two or three francs, but the poor lad got stung for ten francs. About an hour later, he emerged with a beaming smile and a look of "bloody hell" on his face. Of course, we were merciless in our piss taking and telling him to see the M.O. in case he caught a dose of clap, but he was o k. Thinking of Mary, I told them I was not in the mood and didn't want to spend my money too soon. Madam said "you no like my girl", I said I thought she was lovely. Madam was a little annoyed and said, "don't you have a cock". I said " I've got two" when the laughter had subsided one girl said "you got two, I lay you" The girl I said was lovely approached me and said, I finish at eleven o'clock tonight, so come back here and we can go to my flat, have a little supper and wine. She paused, then said do not worry about any money, but do not tell madam or any of the girls or I will be in big trouble. I was ready to go back to camp, but three of the lads said they had not had anything yet, meaning sex. So we all trundled from one bar to the next until we found a likely looking place, some of the lads disappeared for a while, whilst me and the rest had a few classes of beer that was like gnat's pee. Then we went for a kip on the sunny side of the park. We found the rest of our troop wandering around the town centre wondering what to do next. After a couple more beers we were on our way back to barracks. I told them about the blonde-haired woman in the bar down the road. They could not understand why I had not taken up her offer. I told them if there were any trouble I, being an N.C.O. would get a bollocking for leading you lot astray. A situation that could see my demob' date put back. We arrived at the barracks at a quarter to twelve. The guard commander ticked off our names in the pass out book, when he came to my name he said; The Sergeant has been asking if you are in yet, does he want to see you? I explained that he was only snooping, as we were not exactly bosom friends. The next day I heard that he checked in again at twelve thirty just to try to catch me out. It is a good job I didn't take advantage of what was on offer last night. On the move again, we were shunted from pillar to post, as nobody wanted us. There were no duties no roll calls for anyone; no one seemed to know what to do with us. We were beginning to feel like displaced persons ourselves. Eventually we did settle down for a few weeks somewhere in Germany and oddly felt more at home. I grew to like the German people and the country as a whole. As we got to know the people, we all said that it was incredible that we could have been at war against each other for these past six years as we were so much alike in our culture and customs. The only thing that was missing was a sense of humour like ours. Not only did they lack our humour, but could not understand why we were so obsessed about it. Some lads were posted to various D. P. camps. I and a few others that were due for demob' were left alone. A dance hall in town begun to hold dances once more. With no real mates at this new camp, I decided to go out on my own just for the sake of it. I managed to cadge a lift into town and was surprised to see so many German civilian men and woman, and only a few servicemen. I stood there for a few minutes wondering what to do, when a Sergeant called me over to his table, he introduced himself and his two lady friends. I can only remember one girls name; it was Maria the German equivalent of Mary. I offered to buy them a drink, but to my relief, they declined my offer, I was glad because I was a bit low on funds. After a couple drinks and a chat, the Sergeant said it was time for bed, and he did not mean his own. He said it was too late for me to walk the two miles back to camp; you might as well make the most of it. He said if you get a bollocking for being out late just tell them that you were with me last night. I agreed, as I did not feel like a two-mile trek in the bitter cold. Maria showed me to her bedroom and left me for a moment, I took my boots and battle blouse off and lay back on the pillow just as she returned a few minutes later wearing a nightdress and little else; she would have found me fast asleep in another couple of minutes. She was not sex mad; some company and a bit of affection, was all she really wanted. She had lost her husband during the first part of the war in 1941. Her only child died at birth and, like most Germans at the time she had no idea what the future held. I visited her several times while stationed there and enjoyed her company for what it was, two people thrown together with a mutual need. We moved on three days before Christmas and settled in a small town somewhere in Germany. Both the town and the barracks had seen better days, but nonetheless we were happy to learn that quite an array of entertainment was laid on for us over Christmas and New Year, with dances, variety shows and carol concerts. However, owing to the distinct lack of suitable venues they were all ticket affairs, most of which had been allocated long before we arrived. But in any case, a carol concert sung entirely in German was not something I was looking for. There were quite a few A.T.S. girls and members of other women's services, but apparently, they were a bit haughty and would not look at anyone below the rank of General. The Polish DPs celebrated Christmas with the traditional coffee, cake, schnapps, and lots of singing, both solemn and uplifting. Others celebrated Christmas in their own way. I was friendly enough with the lads in our billet, but they were youngsters out for a bit of fun. Going alone into a large hotel bar one night, there was a mix of German civilians, British soldiers, and many other nationalities. I was chatting to some lads stationed in the village, when a couple of German lads about eighteen or nineteen came in. They looked cold an exhausted, but before they had time to sit down a waiter ordered them out, thinking they just came in to get warm. I was surprised as they turned to go without so much as word, one of them collapsed in a heap on the floor. Despite this, the waiter insisted that his companion should drag him outside. I could not sit there and let this heartlessness go on. As no one else intervened, I got up and told the waiter to leave them alone; he looked surprised but did as I asked. By this time the lad had lost consciousness so I said, call a doctor for the poor lad. The bartender said there is a police station across the road. This infuriated me; the lad's companion said not a word. Shortly afterwards a female doctor came through the door with an irritated demeanour, she had a quick look at his papers and called for an ambulance saying he carried a card stating that he suffered from a heart condition and needed certain drugs. I was not so sure if I should believe her or not but had let her take charge of things. While we were waiting for the ambulance I got into conversation with the doctor as she spoke good English. I said I could not understand the apparent callousness of the bar tender and others as they stood by and did nothing. She tried to explain, saying that all the hospitals were still full to bursting all over Germany, so people just put up with the situation. She then began to open up a bit more, telling me that in one large hospital nearly every German patient was missing at least one arm or one leg. She went on to tell me that any German male between eighteen and forty who needed treatment in a Russian administered hospital had at least one limb amputated even if they had nothing wrong with them to make sure that they could never take up arms again in any future wars. My next stop was to be my last before my demob'. We were billeted in a huge rambling mansion with overgrown gardens, just waiting to be cared for. I came upon some stables housing half a dozen beautiful horses. At first, I thought they were Army horses so I went over to the lads who were detailed to look after them. One of them used to work as a stable lad at Newmarket, the other one was hoping to be a vet after his demob'. Until now, I never came into direct contact with the colonel, but heard plenty of tails about him. Once, for some unknown reason he decided to inspect his men on horseback, he overheard a soldier call him a silly old bastard as he passed. He turned back and said, "I don't mind being called silly, or even a bastard, but don't call me old." This may have given the impression that he had a sense of humour. Nevertheless, there was a less pleasant side to his character. One late afternoon, approaching two young lads on guard duty, he asked them if they were cold, when they said yes sir, he said; "I'll hold your rifles while you go inside and have a quick brew and a warm". Even though they knew it was wrong to hand over their rifles, they could hardly refuse a Colonel, but when they returned they were both put on a charge for leaving their post and surrendering their weapons. He was a bastard after all."*

MY LAST CHRISTMAS AWAY FROM HOME.

"Christmas eve 1945 and nowhere to go. There were a few barrels of free beer in the NAAFI but after spending an hour there, I was more than ready to snuggle up in bed and think of what Mary and the children will be doing in the morning and trying to console myself that this was definitely my last Christmas away from home. New year's day I received the best news ever. After hanging about for weeks on end, one of my mates came dashing into our billet shouting that my name was on orders for demobilization on the 28th of January. I was ecstatic! I would actually be on my way home in just a few weeks' time. I wrote to Mary right away but did not give her the date just in case it was changed. One line from the letter she sent in return was priceless. She said tears were welling up in Ken's eyes as she told him that daddy was coming home for good."

"I just wrote that I could be home by the end of January. Having no idea how long the demobilisation process would take, I tried to keep Mary informed of my progress and to expect me home very soon. Those four weeks passed much quicker than I could have wished for in my wildest dreams. One evening meal was some kind of meat pie, as took a bite; I felt a piece of my tooth brake off my top dentures. Knowing the army had a dental unit nearby I went to see if they could repair it in time for my demob'. Fortunately, most of their work was on the civilian population; so I was lucky to jump the queue and get my dentures fixed the next day thus saving me some money when I get back home. Still in a state of limbo, all I could do was to keep all my bits and pieces ready to go as soon as I got the day of my departure. I had no interest in finding any souvenirs, but felt I had to try to find something for the kids. I found a German signal lamp for Ken and a brand new tank Aerial for Terry, and some lovely new white socks for Ann. I was just glad to be on my way home to that cosy little terrace at 55 Alldis Street".

"Finally, the day dawned. The 28th of January 1946, another day to remember. As I said farewell to my mates, some of us had been together since Normandy. The only sad note for me was that Curly was long since demobbed and wondered if we would ever meet up again. I shared out a few unwanted bits and pieces amongst the lads, and off I went with about twenty others. The train was filling with army personnel from several other camps; they too had been on D.P.camp duty since the end of the war. By the time we got to Ostend at ten o'clock, what seemed like thousands of men and women of all *ranks from all over Germany were boarding ships. As we trundled up the gangplanks onto yet another Liberty ship, and another scramble for a little corner to call your own with the usual bully beef wad and mug of tea, we were all eager to get moving rather than moan about things. Just as the dawn broke we could just make out the white cliffs of Dover as they loomed out of the cold January fog, I did not cheer this time I felt far too elated to even speak let alone shout or cheer as most of my companions were doing. I am sure I could actually see the ship's Plimsoll line rising above the level of water as we all scrambled off the ship to get on British soil. One lad reminded me all too vividly about the time we landed in Normandy as he kissed the ground. Even after we landed, we spent ages trying to make sure we got on the right train. After about six hours travelling north, stopping every few miles to let people off. Wondering where we were going to next, and when will we get to Stockport. If I asked the guard all I got was a grunt, a cheese wad and some bloody awful tea. Finally, at about six o'clock in the evening, I found myself with half a dozen others hearing a corporal shouting out where we are. We were at Ashton-Under-Lyne. I shouted out is this the nearest to Stockport we will get. He said you had better get demobbed first a get yer money. I was off that train like a greyhound out of a trap. We were shouted at for the last time to get on the truck parked just round the corner as he looked for stragglers, believe me there were no stragglers that day. Next stop was Ladysmith Barracks a couple of miles up the road. I will always remember No 7 Military Dispersal Unit. As I waited to collect my demob suit, shoes, and whatever I could scrounge. I decided to be hard faced and stuffed my underwear, socks, and pullovers to the bottom of my kit bag as well as half a dozen field dressing's hoping that the sergeant would not want to know what I had. As it was getting late in the evening the Sergeant in charge just wanted to get rid of us all as soon as possible. I received a full kit of civilian clothes without question. All they wanted in turn was all my discharge papers, sign here and here and here. Collect your money at the end table. With my very last salute, I said thank you sir as he shook my hand and wished me good luck. Once we had been officially discharged from the army we were on our own. How am I going to get home? I will bloody walk if I have to I thought? Then someone shouted if anyone wants a lift to Stockport, jump in the grey truck round the corner. Some lads wanted the other side of Ashton, two others were dropped off in Staley Bridge and one in Hyde. As luck had it, the truck was going was back to his depot at the Armoury on Greek Street. Half an hour later I jumped from the truck, shouted good luck to the lads still to get home, ran all the way down Greek street, across Wellington road just in time to jump on a tram elated at the prospect of a new beginning as husband and father. Just as before, the tram driver seemed to have the brakes on all the way up to Great Moor. I got off the tram by the Congregational church at the bottom of Lake street. The same church where the members were always there for Mary, and the children. They wrote to me from time to time with messages of hope and a prayer, and a very welcome postal order for a shillin' or two. I ran up Lake street to the passage on the right leading the back of our little house. I turned the corner and even in the dark, I could see the roof of our terrace, I sank down on my knees, and said, thank you God, thank you thank you thank you. After a few minutes, I composed myself and carried on to our back gate, it was so dark I went over on my ankle on the uneven cobbles and very nearly fell to the ground. I thought how ironic it would be to sustain an injury only a few steps from home. What an anti-climax it was; the house was in darkness! Still, at least the door was on the latch so I could console myself with the best brew in six years. After my second cup, I heard the excited chatter of Mary and the kids as they ran up the path. They pushed their way past her, and jumped all over me, those excited treble voices calling joyfully "Daddies home! Daddies home", will live with me forever. Mary said the waiting was unbearable and just had to take the kids to the pictures. I could not wait to go round to mill cottage to see my precious little bundle of joy 'Carol' and of course mam, dad, and Lena and Gordon who were waiting for me. With hugs all round, and a promise to call round in the morning we walked on air back round to Alldis street. Mary said she had promised the Harrop's we would let them know as soon as you get home no matter what time it was. As you can imagine after welcome handshakes and hugs all round, accompanied by the usual cup of tea we said good night to them and put the kids to bed. After some supper we lay in bed, talking half the night away and looking forward to making plans for the future, we kissed goodnight and the great adventure was over".*

So concludes Dad's memoirs,

"I Had An Ordinary War."

I think this is how dad would have continued his story.

NEW HOPE

I arrived home to a warm welcome and a freezing winter. It was in fact the snowiest spell for many a year. The whole country was almost at a standstill. With millions of sheep frozen to death, and cattle suffering it was awful. My gratuity for a total of 1,857 days of army life, was the grand sum of £90… about a shillin' a day. Adjusting to civilian life once more was far easier than I could have hoped for. I think having the children to think about and how I was going to provide for their future was the best incentive I could have had. I remember they kept calling me granddad for the first few weeks but kids are so resilient, they soon got used to calling me dad and seeing me off to work, if I had any, and then coming home for teatime is the stability and the bedrock of family life. I brought a German signal lamp back for the boys, and was lucky enough to scrounge a doll for Ann from a lad on the train home. After a week or two at home mending things, getting my bike fixed up. I used some of the panels off the air raid shelter leaned against the wall behind the coal shed to put my bike in. It had been round at mill cottages during the war so it had not suffered any damage; even the tyres were still slightly inflated. I had a few tools in the bottom draw by the range in the back room. Mary said every time she opened the draw she would look at them and wonder just how long would they languish there. Doing a bit of painting and playing snowballs with the kids, was all very nice but I had to think about finding some gainful employment. However, some things are never fair. I sat on the doorstep with a mug of tea, felt for the one, and only time how much I have missed over these past five years. I was heading for what could have been a bout of deep melancholy. Then one of the children brought me back life with those words that only a father can hear "can I help you daddy" The war ended in May 1945. I was demobbed quite some time afterwards as you know it was January 1946. The weather was about as bad as it could be making things even more frustrating. The jobs market was dire to say the least. It was a case of first demobbed first to find work. Any indoor jobs were like gold. Even as a skilled plasterer, I found it difficult to find any indoor work at all. The war had been over for nearly a year and the promise of vast numbers of new housing to be built was still to get started. Practically no new house building was getting started simply because of the worst winter on record, coupled with a shortage of timber, cement, copper and lead. Building repairs were not affected quite so much, as they were more labour intensive needing fewer raw materials as most repairs were done with recycled timber and lead pipe. As I said, the winter of 1946 went on record as the worst for many years. Before I got married, I tried to make my own way in business as a plasterer but found that the lack of a motor vehicle, having to manage with a second hand handcart and the threat of war turned out to be a bad time to start my own business. Now the war is over, I feel sadly let down, as things are equally frustrating as they were back then. My younger brother Charlie by seven years was still in the army in Italy. Tommy Carroll, my life-long friend went down to London with his wife Annie at the end of the war to find work on the thousands of bomb-damaged houses. After several weeks of fruitless searching for a decent job, my six months dole money awarded to me through the army, would soon be coming to an end. I was getting more and more frustrated at not being able to find my way in the world. I began to feel very bitter about the past six wasted years and wish I had taken up the Army's offer of a stint as a Sergeant. Unless I could come up with something fairly soon my gratuity would be spent with nothing to show for it. We still had some money in the post office savings bank but that was sacrosanct. I began to think that maybe Tommy had the right idea after all. I felt a bit ashamed of myself thinking that he had had an easy time during the war, being home, earning a wage, sleeping in his own bed. Then I told myself it was not his fault that he was not fit enough to join the forces. He did his best to help the war effort as part of the home guard and fire-watch throughout the war. He was lucky enough to find a room for himself and Annie his wife, and start a new life in war-torn London. After a long talk with Mary and the family, I thought I would give it a try".

NO ROOM AT THE INN

"With my bag of tools, we said our goodbyes as I boarded the train for London. As you can imagine all the feelings of that fateful day in 1940 came flooding back, with interest. In London, I joined Tommy and Annie but with a strange feeling that I had deserted Mary and the children. After a few weeks, I had to come back home. Not only was my heart not in it, sleeping on Tommy's settee was little better than many of my army bivouacs. The chances of finding a house to rent for me, Mary, and three children with the right schools nearby was impossible, and the fact that we were paying rent for Alldis street too. I would love to have stayed at my gramas' in Sidcup Kent, remember, the one that sent me a postal order on my birthdays. But it was too far away from the work that Tommy managed to secure. I had been away for over five years, and Mary wanted me home in Alldis Street for good. I must say I was glad she wanted me back as I felt that I would be letting Tommy down. With what was left of my army gratuity and reluctantly, the few pounds from our Post office savings I tried to pick up where I left off before Mr Hitler so rudely interrupted me. I went to see Mr West. Remember, the builder that built our house in Brinnington. He was not in a position to start any building as raw materials were difficult to secure for new houses. I said I was willing to take on any kind of plastering work or labouring work of any kind. He remembered me and was sorry that he did not have any work for me. Nor could he promise anything in the near future. I had the distinct feeling that he was sorry for me after fighting for King and country only to be out of a proper job. I managed to find bits and pieces of general building jobs to pay the rent and keep us fed. However, not all was lost, towards the end of summer Charlie, my younger brother was demobbed. He too was a plasterer, so we pooled what money we could spare and spent £25 on a 1935 Austin 7 Ruby Saloon car. However, the one important document that was missing was a driving licence. With a bit of fancy footwork, I wangled a licence by writing in pencil in my Service pay book, 'driver' past 1942. I then rubbed a grubby finger over it to give it an aged look and took it to the general post office on St Peter's square. Thinking that I could play on their sympathy, I explained that in the heat of battle I lost the actual license and never had the time to get a replacement. After about a week had passed without a letter, I thought I might have to take a driving test. However I was in luck as a new driving licence dropped on the mat shortly afterwards. Charlie did the same trick with equal success. With some new tools, petrol coupons, headed paper, and business cards we created "Gibbons Brothers" plastering contractors. That little car made all the difference; we could get around and look for work. If anyone offered us some plastering work to do, or indeed anything to make a few bob, we could get stuck in immediately. That poor little car really earned it's keep as we carried bags of cement on the back seat with tools and heavy wooden hod thrown on top and we were on our way in every sense of the word. When we found enough work, we employed Lena's brother-in-law Norman. Born in 1928 he was too young to serve in the forces during the war, but did national service later."

On the photograph you can just make out the small 's' at the end of "Gibbons Bros" In the photo' on the right the three men leaning against the tiny Austin seven saloon are uncle Gordon in the pullover, and dad holding what looks like a newspaper. The one in the middle could be Uncle Charlie, but I am not sure. It appears in the photograph on the left that things are looking up as they now have a little van. The three little kids are unknown to me.

Dad's memoirs are entitled 'I had An Ordinary War.' Well maybe he did. Nevertheless, we must all be proud and thankful that so many men and woman at home and abroad fought not only for King and country, but as my dad said, he was fighting for something far more precious, Mary and the kids.

PART THREE

I would like to dedicate the final part of this trilogy to my brother Terry who passed away in October 2003 and my sister Ann who passed away in February 2013.

CONCRETE AND CUSTARD

(School dinners)

I remember in no particular order, a number of bits and pieces of our lives during the latter stages of the war. Things that may seem unimaginable in Britain today. However, at the time these difficulties were not just a part of our lives, they *were* our lives. Things like second hand clothes, odd wellies, Marmite butties, sugar butties, bread and scrape, mam out cleaning, dad in the Army, dolly mixtures dolly tubs dolly blue cast iron wringer and donkey stones and, believe it or not, quite often no underpants. One of my earliest memories is just a flash in my head and lasts for only a few seconds. It would be about 1941 when Ann and I were barely three years old. (Terry must have been at school.)We were in our twin trolley as mam pushed us through the front door at Alldis street. I can remember holding the door back so we could get through. (that's it! 30 seconds from 73 years ago.) I am not sure if we, as little kids, actually heard any German bombers flying over, but I do remember that cold dark shelter as we got a little older.

The air raids were always during the early hours, around 5: am. Mercifully, the worst of the air raids were over by the time Ann and I were old enough to remember very much about them. I just remember the tail end of those very frightening air raids. One night, well, early morning, the air raid siren wailed up and down with its usual eerie pitch. We were literally dragged from our beds, hurried down the stairs to the back door, mam grabbing coats and blankets; I distinctly remember crying because I could not find my shoes and would not move without them. I was whisked, bare foot down to the shelter in double quick time hanging on to mam's coat for dear life. We would be encouraged to sleep as we listened to mam's reassurances that we were safe because daddy was soldier. I do not recall hearing any bombs booming in the distance, but suspect that mam could, and it must have been very worrying as she sat there in near pitch darkness, huddled round a paraffin stove trying to keep warm. The drone of the bombers in the distance, trying to keep her little brood safe hoping and praying for the all clear to sound. There was no such thing as a portable wireless; and it was often too dark to read anything. An hour or so later, the all clear sounded to signal the end of the raid. Quite often, me Ann and Terry had dropped off to sleep for a while, only to be woken up and back to bed to try to sleep once more.

Often, after an air raid I can remember lying on my pillow and hearing the Tramp! Tramp! Tramp! of German jackboots. A noise caused by the pulse rush of the blood in my head, a sound I would compare to today's Doppler ultrasound. It felt as though the Germans were marching up the cobbled passage to our back gate. I would pull my knees up to my chin, thinking they were going to grab our feet and cut our toes off. I would close my eyes and huddle up tight with my twin. As little kids, we slept in the same cot until we were too big for it, then to a single bed at Alldis street. Round at mill cottages, Grandma, Lena and the couple from next door at number 3 with their little boy would be in the mill's own air raid shelter built for the workers. Granddad, being on fire watch round the mill would call on us to see if we were all right. There were times when we had air raids for several nights in succession. That was bad enough, but nowhere near as bad as London and Manchester. It's a wonder we were not traumatised for life. I can remember, albeit hazily, times in the shelter when we would huddle round the paraffin stove and look up at the sky through the gap at the top of the door, more often than not we could see the stars by the million as there was no light pollution due to the blackout. Even to this day, as I look through my back bedroom window at home in Bredbury, and look in just the right direction so I cannot see any street or house lights anywhere, it really reminds me of the blackout all those years ago.

WE THOUGHT SCHOOL DINNERS WOULD BE POSH

Being brought up to eat what was placed in front of us, we were quite excited to be having school dinners for the first time thinking we might get some posh food, and thought it was going to be great and something new. Most schools did not have any kind of kitchens, just somewhere for the teachers to make a cup of tea. Southwood road was no different. The week before the school dinners were to start, the council delivered some folding tables and extra chairs to form a dining area in the assembly hall. All went well as the food was delivered at about half past eleven in what looked like milk churns, (they probably were) with mashed potato in one, some kind of meat stew in another, and vegetables namely carrots peas or cabbage in a smaller one. Quite often the food would only just be warm enough to enjoy but that was our hard luck. Treacle tart was usually in a tray and custard in a big enamel jug (the aluminium jugs would be part of a Spitfire by now) a thick skin forming over the 'cuzzy' helped to keep the heat in. However, the treacle tart did cool down all too quickly; as it cooled, it would set like concrete. Hence concrete and custard. Another time we would have a salad with mashed potato but I cannot recall if we had any meat with it. We had Tatterash at least once a week with meat of unknown origin. As you may remember in the school log entries, the dinners were sometimes late, making for rumbling bellies. I remember on one occasion when the tatterash was off, by that I mean that the meat was sour and smelt awful and was quite inedible. I cannot recall any recriminations, apologies, or money back, but it was a long time ago. All kids make up names for things to make them seem more interesting or funny. Treacle tart and custard, was concrete and custard. Tapioca was frogspawn, salad was rabbit food. Liver was yuk! I cannot recall ever having chips; it must have been because of the shortage of fat or drippin' plus the fact it would not be practical to transport chips in a milk churn or on a tray. Sometimes we went home for our dinner. However, if mam were out cleaning, me Ann and Terry would let ourselves in the back door, sit round the table and share a pile of Marmite and drippin' butties. We didn't realise that mam probably did not have enough money for our dinners. It would have been about 4ᵈ each per day totalling 5/- for the week for the three of us. I don't know why mam didn't did not apply for free dinners as some mothers did as mentioned in the school log.

The air raids on and around Stockport began long before I can remember. With raids on the gas works, Woodford aerodrome where heavy bombers were built. Fairy Aviation in Levenshulme and the railway viaduct being the main artery north to south. One bomb fell just a few doors away from grandmas' on Marsland Street Portwood on a cold snowy dawn raid in December 1940 killing two people. It was a combined 'high explosive', and 'oil bomb'. (See picture on back pages.) Because the picture is of poor quality I need to point out that the snowy effect really is snow. I think the same aircraft dropped a "stick" of bombs as it flew over Stockport hitting Portwood, Cale Green, Garners lane and Cheadle heath. Heavy down pours of rain often flooded our shelter to a depth of two or three inches. Mam had to throw some bricks down on occasion for us to stand on until we could get in, and then lift our feet up onto the makeshift wooden benches. We could not store anything in the shelter such as blankets because it was too damp even in the summer. When it rained during the day, Cherrytree granddad managed to pump out most of the water with the stirrup pump he had as part of the fire watching kit he kept at mill cottages. He tried to divert the rain by digging a gutter round the front of the shelter to take away the rainwater, but it seeped in again below ground level soon afterwards. There was never time to make a hot drink to take into the shelter and presumably, we did not possess a flask in any case, but we did have our little blue paraffin stove to keep us warm, little knowing that the paraffin created more condensation and actually made things worse. Candles and matches were a very precious commodity, being the only source of light or heat that most people could afford. Mrs Rogerson always kept a few candles and matches under the counter for regular customers. I suppose that's why we always used a 'spill' of paper to save our precious matches when we lit the stove from the fire. I remember Terry saving the bits of used candle wax or tallow and warming it on a tin lid by the range then rolling it out flat with a milk bottle then pressing a length of string down the middle and then folding it over and rolling it repeatedly under his hands to form a candle. They did work after a fashion but were never as good as Mrs Rogerson's candles. The air raids during the summer months were still during the night time of course and obviously just as dark and traumatic even thou' the weather was a bit warmer. As we got a little older, we could retain a little more in our memories of the air raids, having to get out of a nice warm bed to the sound of a dawn chorus we did *not* want to hear, the sirens. Sitting in a dimly lit damp air raid shelter just waiting for the all clear, then go back to bed for an hour or two. No sooner did we get to sleep in spite of the trauma just suffered, we were up and off to school within hours. The kids and teachers were often very tired; if a child fell asleep during lessons following a longer than usual air raid the teachers were very understanding as they carried on as best they could. As a result, the academic levels were not as good as they would have been in peacetime. The curriculum was quite rudimentary as there were very limited resources.

About mid-1944, although we did not know it at the time we were entering the last year of the war. We were growing up and remembering things such as R.A.D.A.R. Although radar had been used in various forms since the battle of Britain, it was kept top secret, and was all very new to us. All the kids in the street thought it was something like Flash Gordon's ray gun. We made up our own reasons for the name. The "ray" from Flash Gordon's gun and "dar" from the shooting sounds we made in our mock fights. We thought it could shoot a beam of light at the German planes and blast them out of the sky. We ran around the streets with a rolled up length of burning newspaper or cardboard shouting, Radar! Radar! Radar! Until we ran out of paper. A plane without propeller? That's impossible. We soon found out it was called a jet. Radar and Jets, wow, it felt great. After the war, it was revealed that the war office, together with the ministry of food came up with a brilliant piece of subterfuge. A Pilot named John Cunningham nicknamed, "Cat's Eyes Cunningham" had become the most famous night fighter pilot in the R.A. F. During May 1941, successfully claiming 14 night raiders using A.I. (Airborne Interception) the aircraft version of what later became known to all as Radar. In order to cover up the use of this new form of radar. The R.A.F. claimed a select group of British pilots ate carrots for up to two years to develop superior night vision. Cunningham, a modest individual, detested this nickname. This ruse, though not known to the general public as a ruse, was equally successful in getting people, especially children to eat more carrots believing they would be able to see in the dark. (Carrots contain vitamin 'A' thought to be good for our eyesight). Another ruse was the one saying that newsprint was good for the treatment of piles. However, seriously, Children's welfare was always a priority during the years of shortages. As well as a diet of Ostermilk and National dried milk, every child in the country had an allowance of a regular supply of supplements and vitamins. We had concentrated orange juice, the best I have ever tasted. 'Scots Emulsion' was a sort of milky white substance and tasted of nothing in particular. A thin watery medicine called 'Fenning's Fevercure' tasted awful to Terry and me, but Ann loved it. The nicest one of all was a thick caramel like malty substance, 'Cod-liver oil and malt' we all loved it and couldn't get enough. I am not sure if Rosehip Syrup was government issue or not, but I do remember it. I think Carroll would qualify for the infant allowance, but by the time Tony was born, the welfare state had kicked in and such schemes were probably being phased out.

HOW DO WE MAKE JET NOISES?

We used to run around with arms outstretched, making Spitfire and dive-bomber noises. neeooooowww kik kik kik brreerrrrmm. Now we had a new noise to make. As we had no idea what a jet sounded like we would run around arms outstretched making swishing and whining noises like Flash Gordon's space ship. We even tried to make our very own 'doodlebug' noise made from a flat piece of wood by cutting it three or four inches long by one and a half inches wide. When mam was not looking, we made a hole about half an inch from one end with a red-hot poker, then thread a piece of thin string through it about three feet long knotted at one end. As we swung it round and round as fast as we could it made a sort of whooshing noise just like a doodlebug. However that was one experiment that was soon forgotten as it was hard work for little reward. In warm weather, we would dig out the 'gas tar' from between the cobbles with a stick then pat our hands in the dust of the dry gutter; rub some of the dust on our hands so we could roll the tar into acorn-sized bombs. Then we would find a nice piece of privet hedge stem about 16 inches long, strip off all but the last four or five leaves at the top then push the end of the stem into our 'gas tar' bomb then squeeze it tight, we had to dip it in cold water to make it harder and we were ready to go. We would hold the top of the stem and wing it round and round and round, then let it go soaring in the air. It was great fun until it landed on someone's washing leaving a tar stain. Mam would be very angry with us when we got tar on our cloths and hands. We had to run round to granddads to get him to clean it off with some Paraffin and Lanolin soaked wool scraps. As well as the local authority taking railings at the beginning of the war, we were called upon to give as many aluminium pots and pans as we could. There were constant calls to save paper, tins, and rags; even bottle tops and wooden bobbins, in fact anything and everything. Ann and I would call each other Squander-bugs, thinking it was a very funny name. However, it was all deadly serious. The message the government was constantly drumming into people, was not to 'squander' resources.

To illustrate this, we would unwrap the margarine and put some of the contents in the dish, when we had finished the packet of margarine we would scrape every last morsel from the paper then fold the paper to use for covering a storage pot, or wrapping foodstuffs. It was the same thing with sugar, undo the blue paper bag very carefully, and pour out some sugar as required. When all the sugar was used up we would undo the corners of the bottom of the bag to tease out the last grains of sugar. Quite often, there would be as much as a quarter of a teaspoon to be had from the  folds. If we were lucky enough to get some brown sauce or camp coffee, the last dregs would be shook up with a little drop of water then poured into the next bottle or used in tatterash.

Following it to its logical conclusion, we would finish up with a bottle of water so we only used this method of scrimping three or four times with each bottle then used the fourth lot of dregs in 'taterash. Another clever trick if you did not have any Oxo or gravy browning, was to hold a half a teaspoon of sugar on a large spoon over the gas ring, after a few seconds it would caramelise and ha Presto! Gravy browning. And so it went on and on. Anything that could be saved was saved. Some of the shortages would seem ridiculous today. Simple things that were taken for granted before the war such as hair clips, matches, scented soap, candles, clothes pegs, camera film, paper bags, (it was illegal to use wrapping paper) writing paper, pencils, ink, polish, buttons, sewing cotton, string, cutlery, pots and pans, make-up and shoe leather, the list goes on. These little inconsequential things all added up to make life one long struggle.

SOD BLOODY HITLER

By now, people were fed up sleeping in those awful air raid shelters. As the raids subsided, most people were beginning to get blasé and stay in the warmth and comfort of their beds and sod bloody Hitler. School air raid drill was still practiced on a regular basis, but many felt that they were unnecessary now that the allies were pushing through France. The school curriculum was very limited because of shortages of almost everything especially text books, and writing paper in general, coupled with the regular air raid practice, and the *real* air raids, we had an education of a different kind. I cannot recall any kind of detention during our time at Southwood road school. The usual punishment would be 100 lines relating to our misdemeanour. I think it must have been because of the possibility of an air raid just at the wrong time. If we were sent home at the right time, the school could not be held responsible for our welfare during an air raid. We were taught to make the most of things and waste nothing. To that end, all the schools did a great job of collecting waste materials of all kinds. Greatmoor Council School won the salvage cup thirty odd times during the collection campaign. Waste paper was the most easily collected by the kids. Tin cans jam jars, books, and even wooden cotton bobbins, as you will have read in the school log entries. Our school won many prizes for collecting waste. However, apart from collecting waste, the teachers did an amazing job with the children in their care in such difficult times. Raising funds and putting on shows to help keep the children and parents involved in the war effort. We had visits by a number of Lord Mayors as each in turn served their term of office they supported a number of initiatives and help for the many charities connected with their office.

A TRAM TICKET FOR A SPITFIRE.

One such initiative was for tram passengers to purchase a penny ticket. Mam told us that penny tickets were on sale on the trams and busses to help to contribute to the lord Mayer's fund to buy a spitfire from the people of Stockport. Mam said if the air raid sirens sounded during the journey, the conductor would call out to the passenger to, "come on, our lads up there are fighting for us, so come on, buy some Spitfire tickets to help them to defeat bloody Hitler." The tram kept moving as a kind of defiant gesture.

The ticket F 4097 was The Mayor of Stockport's Spitfire fund. (See back pages.) Other charities during the war gave help to refugees from the Channel Islands, help for Russia, a clog fund and many more. During the late summer of '44, things were a lot quieter once the bombs and doodlebugs were much less frequent. Mam being a keen rambler with her friend Margaret before the war, loved to take us on outings when the weather was nice and warm. I remember paddling in the Ladybrook stream that ran through Bramall Park. It was, and still is about eight inches deep along by the gatehouse. We loved to stand in the cool water and lift any big stones very gently to see if there were any bully heads (*fish*) basking under the edges, and then try to catch them before they wriggled from our grip and put them in a jam jar to show mam. They were about three to four inches long with big, or bull heads, hence the name. Other more elusive ones to catch were Catfish and Stickle backs. The former having whiskers and the latter having spikes down its back. We spent so long in the cold water, that when we got out, our legs were bright pink. In some streams, we would search for "Indian chalk". It was quite simply red sand stone, but our name was better. There was an abundance of this red sandstone as Stockport is built on the stuff. We would rub the wet stone on our arms, and then with our hands, we could rub some on our faces and play cowboys and Indians as well as fighting the Germans. I remember a time as mam sat under the trees writing letters to dad as we played about and ate our jam or Marmite butties. Though she was not the type to keep a diary, I do recall seeing a diary after the war with references of the 1,000 bomber raids over Germany around late 1944. I wonder what she was thinking as she wrote of those events in her diary on those sunny afternoons as we played in the stream. It is a pity the diaries are long gone. As well as our outings with mam, we had our own outings and got into all kinds of mischief. We would sneak round the back of the Dog and Partridge and throw sticks or stones up at the pear tree for a few very disappointing rock-hard pears. However, somewhere along Moorland road, there was a corner house with no wall round the front garden and a very tempting apple tree just a few feet away from the footpath. We used to wait for the blossom to appear then wait for ages until the apples were ripe. As soon as the apples 'fell', we had to test them to make sure they were ok. Next, conkers. I am not sure, but I think the trees on the very wide grass verge opposite the Davenport cinema were horse chestnut trees. They had very sturdy wooden benches cut into six or eight segments to fit all the way round them, but alas, the trees and benches are no more. In the never-ending quest all around Great Moor to find the biggest and best conker, watched by all the little kids, Terry and Freddy Pennell being the biggest would throw sticks for hours just to knock a few cockers down then make a mad scramble for the biggest. When we were satisfied that we thought we had a winner we dashed home to place them near the warm oven to help them to dry out and make them very hard so we could swank about having a 2er or a 3er even a 6er some would exaggerate beyond silly, and no one believed them anyway. If we had the patience to wait, eventually, all the conkers would simply fall by the hundreds. Another exiting trick of the time was to place a farthing on the tramlines and wait for the tram to squash it flat enough to bring them up to the size of a ha'penny and wafer thin. I do not think we ever tried to pass them off as a ha'penny; we probably would not get away with it anyway. Sometimes we put a ha'penny on the lines as many as four or five times just to see how many times a tram needed to run over it to double it in size. It would be rolled out like a piece of pastry, not something we did too often, as it was expensive; we could by two pieces of hard liquorice stick for a ha'penny and loved to see each other's black tongues and lips.

A NEW DOLL FOR ANN

October 14 th 1944. Ann and I were playing out one afternoon when Mrs Harrop called out to us to run home quick, your mam has a new baby sister for you. Cherrytree grandma and aunty Lena were sitting in the back room. Lena had a tiny little baby in her arms. We had no idea where it came from, and no idea why the nurse was there. Ann, Terry and I were thrilled to bits. Ann wanted to know what kind it was and what it was called. She wanted to nurse it there and then, and asked if daddy knew about it. A couple of weeks later in accordance with the Catholic faith, not to mention the fact that our Cherrytree grandma made all the arrangements weeks earlier, she was Christened Carol Mary. In one of dad's letters, there is a reference to one or two boy's names. Dad seemed to favour Anthony or his brother Bert's middle name George if it was a boy. However, he was quite happy with Carol Mary. They must have talked about it before dad was posted abroad. We played out less as the nights drew in, and spent some of our evenings helping mam as she unravelled a woollen jumper that was beyond its best. She would either use some of our old jumpers, or buy one or two off Mrs Miller for sixpence each. A shillin' would always buy a nice frock to cut down to make a miniature version for Ann. Sometimes Mrs Miller would come across a frock or coat that she knew would fit a particular child and save it for them. She lived at 27 Alldis street and was the saviour for lots families in the Greatmoor area. She was a one-woman recycling company; All through the war and the very difficult times that followed, she trudged with her pram round Davenport park road, Bramhall lane Mile end lane, filling her pram with all manner of surplus shoes and clothing of all shapes and sizes. Without her, many a family would have been hard pressed to find warm clothing in those difficult times. However, as the war dragged on year after year even the people of those more affluent areas were feeling the pinch. Mrs Miller had to travel further afield to find what we needed. I remember going down the street with mam to her 'shop' with Ann and Terry many a time. The front room was packed high with all manner of clothing. Warm jumpers on one table, shoes in the cupboards on each side of the fireplace now with the doors removed, wellingtons under the table, and coats hung everywhere. I remember having a pair of odd wellingtons, they were the same size but with different patterns round the front. I cannot recall if I was ridiculed at school but I suspect not, as the difference was not so noticeable and most of us were in the same boat anyway. Frocks hear, trousers there, clothes every flippin' where. Whilst none of the clothing was actually dirty, mam would always wash and iron them to make them good as new.

To make up a ball of wool mam would find the end thread of a knitted jumper to start unravelling it. The next step would be to wrap the thread round the back of a chair to form a skein of wool, and then she would 'ponch' it up and down in some warm soapy water and leave to dry on the end of the wrack in order to remove the kinks from the wool. After a few days when the kinks seem to straighten out, Terry, being the biggest would be called upon to hold the skein of wool over his outstretched hands using his thumbs to keep if from falling to the floor. As mam wound the wool, Terry would dip each thumb in turn to allow a strand of wool to peel off as it was wound into a ball. After a minute or two came the cry, maaaaam! my arms are aching, mam would say don't be a big baby and carried on winding the wool into several balls. Sometimes, mam would unravel a jumper and roll it directly into a ball if it was the right kind of wool. When she had enough ready to knit a jumper, it was set aside. Our next door neighbour at number 53, Mr Harrop, who, apart from being a very good neighbour was a good joiner and would make a frame from bits of wood gleaned from granddads mill. The usual size was 4 feet x 2 feet with borrowed hessian tightly fastened over the frame to make it easier to make the rug. During the cold winter evenings mam would cut up an old coat or two into strips about an inch wide and 4 inches long to make a 'peg rug'. We would help mam by arranging the different colours of materials into piles ready for use. Of course, the colours were quite often black or dark grey, we were in our element if mam managed to find a red or green coat at Mrs Millers for a few pennies. We would watch mam make a hole through the hessian with a length of wood shaped like half of a long clothes peg. Hence (peg rug) she pushed a strip of the coat through the hessian and back again in a way to form an equal length of 'pile' on the upper side of the hessian. As mam got nearer to finishing the rug, we were all very excited as we waited for Mr Harrop to undo the frame so mam could finish off round the edges. Being quite small for a hearthrug, we would wrestle each other to lie on it, as they were always so soft when they were nice and new. One time when dad was home on leave, he managed to draw a good likeness of his Royal Artillery cap badge using some bits of crayon, and a bit of black lead on his finger as a marker. I can remember the finished rug looked very good. Mam would say the new rug was a present for all of us from daddy. More often than not, we all had a 'new' jumper for Christmas, but decorations were something mam could not afford, even if there were any in the shops. At school, the pupils of each class made their own decorations. We cut up strips one inch wide and six or seven inches long out of newspaper, coloured magazines were best if we could find any. The teacher would mix a bit of very precious flour with water to make a paste so we could make loops into streamers to decorate our classroom. I cannot remember if we had a Christmas tree, but I think that maybe we did have something in the assembly hall. Christmas at home too, was equally austere and make do and mend. Christmas 1944, leaves me with little in my memory to describe how it really was. Like any little kids at that time, we just accepted what we were given without any thought that we were badly done by. I have only a disjointed recollection of my time at Southwood road school at that time; I do not remember the air raid drills or gas mask drills. But I do remember we had a little bottle of milk during our morning break, the teacher, trying to be helpful would get into school a few minutes early to put our allocation of milk on the classroom radiators to warm it through a little bit. Though well intentioned tepid milk without sugar did not taste very nice and the straws if we had any, would disintegrate in no time at all, so we had to drink it quickly. The tops were round cardboard lids, we had to poke a finger through the middle of the cardboard lid and then push our straw through. However, on one occasion, I could not get the cardboard top open with my tiny fingers. I lost my grip on the bottle and it fell to the floor spilling milk everywhere. I cannot remember if I got a second bottle, probably not. We loved to play on the field in the summer sunshine; however, if it was wet, we were not allowed to play on it. If it was covered snow, boys being boys would challenge each other to run around in the virgin snow just for the fun of it. However, when we were allowed on the field, the break time bell would ring three times instead of the usual one long ring and off we would go. As the year of 1945 progressed without air raids, blackouts, doodlebugs. With an end to getting up in the early hours to go to the shelter, all the fear of what might happen had long vanished. I remember granddad covering the front of the shelter with a piece of scrap wood from the mill to keep us out. I did not quite understand the significance of that piece of wood at the time as a simple act that signalled that the end of the war was just around the corner. We could play out as much as we wanted, so we made the most of it.

May 1945. Victory in Europe day. Being so young, I have just vague memories of that momentous day. Many streets had a V.E. party. Lake Street and Alldis Street were no exception . Terry, Ann and I were part of that momentous day. Not only Alldis Street, but Lake Street too, and anyone who wanted to join us. We had one or two pictures of me Ann and Terry having a little party of our own round at mill cottage, but as I said, not only are the pictures lost, but the memories too. Reading in dad's memoirs, he was on leave at the time of the German surrender, and had to return to his unit in Germany just the same. How heart breaking that must have been for mam and dad.

Even though the war was over we kids did not notice too much of a change, nevertheless some things must have begun to get a little better. As I said, no more air raids, no blackouts, no doodlebugs. If it was not for the fact that dad did not have any leave until the end of September, some 5 months after the end of the war, life must have felt much more settled. As you will have read, dad had quite an eventful time during his early days back in Germany ~~guarding,~~ sorry looking after the displaced persons and trying his best to keep out of trouble. His leave was marred by his Impetigo during his time at home. However, when he had to go back to Germany, he felt sure it was for the last time and hoped to be home for Christmas of 1945. As we now know dad wasn't home for a family Christmas until 1946 as he didn't get his demob until January of that year.

Throughout the war, our grandparents were more than just grandparents, they were our surrogate parents most of the time, our Cherrytree grandma and granddad living so close played quite important part in our upbringing. We could run out of the back gate, up the passage, across Coombs street up Lake Street towards Sandhurst road. On the right, there was a footpath and a gateway through the hedges and across the little wooden bridge over a stream then round to gramas' back door in only a few minutes. We would often go round just to see the ducks swimming around the boating lake that was part of the Blue Lagoon swimming pool complex. The pool was kept full as an 'Emergency water supply' for the cotton mill and the school, even though the mill had its own reservoir. As soon as the end of the war was in sight, the pool was drained and cleaned. It reopened Friday 12th May much to our disappointment. We spent many a happy time playing round the boating lake and sometimes the pool itself, only to be told to bugger off by spoilsport neighbours. Now we had a new adversary. A new manager of the pool. It was even more of a challenge than before and gave us hours of fun. The letters E.W.S. 'emergency water supply' were painted in two feet high white letters on the garden walls of the houses on the corner of the entrance to the pool. They were still visible for quite some time after the war. After school, we would sneak through the overgrown bamboo that formed the boundary between the mill and the 'Bluey' as we called it, and play around the picnic area until we were chased off by the new manager. Every morning about half a dozen ducks would waddle up the path and wait patiently by grandma's back door for a few scraps of bread. If grandma had not seen them, they would tap on the door with their bills until they got something to eat. I remember Terry picking up a frog by its back legs the offering it to the ducks thinking they would just sniff at each other, until one of them lunged at the poor little frog and swallowed it whole. When we told grandma, what Terry had just done (little snitches) she was very cross with him as she said they are all Gods little creatures and had to promise never to do it again, but I think he did. By the side of the path that ran from grandma's back door was a small iron pipe about an inch in diameter spouting hot water. It was some kind of safety valve from the mill. This trickle of hot water created a mini stream that ran along the side of the path and then it trickled into a slightly bigger stream about two or three inches deep and no more than twelve to eighteen inches wide. When it rained, we would love to stand on the little footbridge that dad built one time when he was home on leave and watch the long grass hanging onto the bank for dear life until the flow of water got the better of it. The stream ran from somewhere underneath some thick bushes and disappeared into a garden. I presume it is culverted by now. This short stretch of water was full of tiny little swimmy things, not fish but bugs of some kind. I was fascinated with them and often went round to grandmas during the summer months straight from school just to look at them. One day I spotted a curious looking bug in the water with bits of twigs and muck stuck on its back. Being curious as most little lads are, I just had to see what it was, and help it to shed all that rubbish off its back, little knowing I was not doing it any favours. On the contrary, I probably killed the poor thing. Years later, I discovered it was a Cadis fly and the detritus wrapped round it was its protection.

AT LAST, THE REAL END OF THE WAR.

Quite often, we would run an errand, or take a message from mam to grandmas. One message I do remember very distinctly was mam telling me to run round to grandmas to tell her that Japan had surrendered. I was so excited, but did not know why. When I blurted it out to grandma, she picked me up and squeezed me so tight to her bosoms I could hardly breathe. Mam still had to continue with her cleaning jobs as well as looking after four children. It was very handy for us to play round at Grandmas when we were not at school. I recall mam telling us that on one occasion as she was about to leave one of her cleaning jobs to come home, the lady of the house asked mam if she could just finish a few bits of laundry that was soaking in a bucket in the cellar. Mam, always one to oblige, said she would, and promptly took her coat off then went down to the cellar. As she stooped to collect the washing from a bucket, she realized that they were some very snotty slimy handkerchiefs. With gritted teeth, she washed them through and left, never to return. From all accounts, the best employer was a Mrs Heywood. She had a 'wine shop' on Buxton road but I doubt if she had much in the way of wine or any alcoholic drinks. She probably sold a few cigarettes and bottled beers.

Playing in grandma's garden, looking and playing in and around the stream, having a jam butty, and chasing the ducks we spent many happy times throughout the summer around mill cottages. At that time, Ann and I were a bit too young to visit Portwood grandma as she lived a bit too far away for us to travel on our own. As I told you earlier, Terry, Ann and I would love to play around the Rhododendron bushes, we would climb in and around the bendy branches and get dirty hands and knees. If one of us sustained the tiniest cut or graze, we would run into grandmas for a bit of sympathy and maybe a drink of pop. Sometimes we got a drink of Sarsaparilla to share between us. As kids we were so very curios simply because we had to entertain ourselves more often than not. Ann and I were fascinated with a flower called a Nasturtium. It was a mass of a hundred glorious shades of orange, in the late summer we were fascinated by the abundance of thousands of tiny green caterpillars nibbling away on the underside of the lovely delicate green leaves. The seeds formed into what we now know as a lookalike bunch of bananas. We didn't know what Bananas were at the time. Climbing amongst the bamboo canes growing by the boating lake, I slipped, impaling my knee on the world's biggest splinter. As I looked down, it was at least an inch long and as thick as a matchstick. Nevertheless, to me it was more like a telegraph pole. I ran to grandma crying all the way thinking my leg was about to fall off. Once again, to gentle tones of there there my little wounded soldier I will soon make it better. With a pathetic whimper for sympathy, I got my glass of pop and the biggest bandage ever and was soon on my way home, with a stiff leg of course to show mam. She too would call me her little wounded soldier as she looked at my bandage made from strips of old bedding wrapped round and round just to enhance the severity of the wound. We would muck about in the piles of dried up curly leaves that had gathered under the Rhododendrons and find suitable sizes to fit on our fingers to make us look like we had witches long fingernails. It was great fun, and free. Later in the year as autumn came upon us we were fascinated by the Lupins with their black seeds, we loved to pop open the seedpods and scatter them about in the hope that they might grow for dad when he came home. When we told grandma what we had done, we were made to wash our hands and not to touch them, as some of them are poisonous. Another poisonous plant I recall was Deadly Nightshade or Hemlock with its tiny purple berries. It even sounded poisonous so we kept well away from it. At the far end of grandma's garden, there were some upturned buckets with rusty holes in the bottom, now the top of course. We could just see little green crinkly shoots poking through. Granddad said it was rhubarb. They were covered with the buckets to force them to grow quicker to reach the sunlight so we would have enough to make stewed rhubarb and custard as a special treat. There was a patch of green stuff that looked like cabbage. If we fell and sprained an ankle or wrist, grandma would pick some 'cabbage', boil it in a pan for a few minutes until it went really soggy just like overdone cabbage then wrap the leaves round the offending area held in place with a bandage. After a day or two, the 'sprain' was all nice and better. It transpired that the cabbage was indeed Comfrey, or knit bone, a cure-all for strains and sprains. If we were to brush against stinging nettles, a spit upon Doc leaf would sooth the sting making it better within a few minutes. There was something special about Mill cottages; we loved playing on the grassed area at the front, and sometimes we would chase each other all the way round both houses and back again, it was great fun.

Whilst dad was away, me Ann and Terry would help mam as best we were able. On washdays, the very distinctive smell of Lanry would rise in the steam throughout the house. It was pale green/yellow coloured bleach with the consistency of water. It was stored in a glass bottle the shape of a whisky bottle, very dangerous. Mam used to soak some clothes overnight to help to get them clean. The following morning with a scrubbing brush and block of green washing soap she must have spent hours scrubbing away, rinsing them in the stone sink with a shake of 'dolly blue' in the final rinsing water for the whites, piling them into a bowl to wring out through the big wooden rollers of the mangle in the yard. Terry was by now growing big enough to help mam to wring out the wet washing. When the weather was very cold, I remember the washing would freeze solid as it hung on the line outside, and we were much amused to see the shirts or trousers standing up against a chair until they began to thaw with the warmth of the room. Mam would hang as much as she could on the rack, then haul it up and leave it overnight to dry. The smaller items were shunted round and round the fireguard top rail until they were dry. Ann and I would help in our own way by swishing the dolly blue in the water to make it bright blue being the only whitening agent at that time. The woollies were 'ponched' by hand in the sink in warm soapy water. Bedding, after an overnight soak in Lanry would be 'ponched' in a dolly tub with a 'posser'.

THE HUMBLE DONKEY STONE

Eli Whalley was the last mass producer of Donkey stones in the country till' 1979 at Donkey Stone Wharf. The ever popular 'donkey stone' originally used to put a non-slip surface on greasy stone staircases in the mills of Lancashire and Yorkshire. Later, proud housewives made stoning the front door step a form of decoration and a competition. The stones were produced in three colours, cream, brown and white. The cream was simply brown and white mixed in equal parts. The basic ingredients were finely ground stone mixed with bleach powder and cement. We loved to 'Donkey stone' the front steps. We splashed cold water on the steps and rubbed them over with the donkey stone until it was evenly coated with the sandy gritty powdered bleach stone, then wipe it with a wrung out cloth to make them nice and evenly clean. As it dried, it would look nice and clean and be a sure sign that our house was a clean house. No one actually bought a donkey stone they were given in exchange for a few rags. The rag and bone man in turn recycled the rags. He called every couple of weeks come rain or shine, he could be heard a long way off as he shouted "*bone*" followed by a pause and long "*boannne*". Sometimes it sounded like "Ra' Bone! When it rained, we sat on the back doorstep and watched the rain forming puddles near the back door. Now and again, a raindrop would make a big bubble for a few seconds, then we would wait to see how long it took another raindrop to pop the bubble made seconds earlier. When the sun came out, we played in the back yard and made mud pies using a piece of stick or an old spoon pinched from the table draw. We never played in our own Anderson shelter I think it was because it was often very damp, and one of us would end up getting hurt.

A TRIAN RIDE

If mam could scrape up two or three shillings, a special treat was a train ride from Woodsmoor station to Middlewood. Mam would leave Carol with Cherrytree grandma as three small children were enough to look after. Me and Ann sat in our twin trolley as Terry hung onto the handle as we walked down Moorland road with ever increasing excitement as we looked forward to our picnic. With our bread and scrape butties, a bottle of pop or watered down orange juice, we were full of excitement at the prospect of a ride on a train even if it was only about fifteen minutes duration. Bread and scrape was exactly that, spread margarine on the bread, then scrape it off leaving just a suggestion of margarine, the same with the jam or Marmite, scrape it on, and then scrape it off. Well, not all of it, but near enough. When the train arrived at Middlewood station, we couldn't wait to get off and run along the path to the woods. A tiny stream ran through the undergrowth, but it was not much good to play in. Mam would find our very own special place, and unpack our butties and pop. Off we went to collect some flowers and make daisy chains, look for squirrels and lions and tigers, play hide and seek and mess about for hours, it was great fun. We picked buttercups then ask mam if she liked butter, if she said yes we would test her by holding a buttercup under her chin to see if the golden yellow glow reflected under her chin. It always did. Every few weeks, mam would allow the fire to go out or cool down overnight so she could clean it out properly. We loved to watch mam cleaning out the ashes from under and around the grate so we could see how many 'Silverfish' we could catch and then throw them out of the back door. As a treat we were allowed to clean the upper part of the cast iron grate with black polish or 'Black lead' we would squabble over who put the polish on, and who polished it all nice and shiny, Ann always won.

As we grew a bit older and bigger, we got more adventurous. We, (the kids in Alldis street) were always looking for something to play on or in. The communal air-raid shelters on Coombes street and Lake Street were perfect. Some of us could just reach up to climb on the flat concrete roof. Those on the ground would make Ki! Ki! Ki! noises as if shooting up at the German planes. Those on the roof would make Da! Da! Da! noises as they shot back. We would push girls into the darkness just to hear them scream, and generally muck about in them not really appreciating what their significance had been. The Pennell's lived on the other side of the street at the end house, and were part of our gang. Freddy was about the same age as Terry, Raymond and Alan were about the same age as Ann and me and their younger sister pat was quite a bit younger. I cannot remember anything about their mam and dad but I suppose we must have known them.

THE FAMOUS TEN.

We could muster a gang of about ten when we played "Rolivo". I have absolutely no idea how the name or the game evolved. It was a sort of five-as-side hide and seek. We would separate into two gangs of four or five, run off in opposite directions for a while, and then try to find each other. Kids ah! On one of our 'hide and seek' games, I hid at the bottom of Lake Street behind some bushes across from the Congregational church. As I crouched down at the back of what was Webb's motorbike shop 'without motor bikes'. They used to sell Paraffin, ironmongery, firewood, coal, and a few tools if he could get any just to make ends meet. There, behind the bushes, I looked down where I had disturbed the dirt with my feet. There was a shillin' a sixpence, and a thrupenny bit, a grand total of 1/9d. A small fortune to little kids in such times. I can recall the find, but have no notion of what I did with the money. Ann said I gave it to mam. We had a rabbit at one time; I think it was name was Thumper. Mam fed it on dry porridge oats and left over tealeaves mixed in equal parts. I think we actually had two rabbits, one of which was a boy. In one of dads letters he tells mam to keep them well apart, it was easier said than done with obvious consequences'. I only remember them for a short while; we must have eaten them one Christmas.

A new experience was soon to be all consuming for our gang. Bonfire night! Ann, Terry, and me, with our gang would scavenge all manner of things to burn. Surprisingly we managed to gather quite a lot rubbish. Wood, paper, rags and hessian from granddads mill. We even chopped a tree down at one time. It was only a scraggy sapling about two inches in diameter; it took us a week to cut through it. We would borrow our mams bread knives in turn to have a go at it. Even a blunt axe could not overcome that determined sapling's effort to stay put, but we got the better of it eventually, not something I am proud of and would be very annoyed if I saw the like today. We really had little idea what Guy Fawkes was all about. Our villain of the piece was Hitler; we sang the very rude song. Hitler has only got one ball, Goering has none at all…. I do not recall any history lessons about Guy Fawkes or indeed any history lessons at all. Of course, no bonfires or fireworks were allowed during the war because of the blackout. However, after the war, a few fireworks appeared in the shops, and we were very excited when Cherrytree grandma managed to buy one or two bangers between the three of us, yes between us. We had the bonfire on the spare land on the right hand side of Sandhurst road. There was a similar plot of land opposite but for some reason we preferred the right hand side as we came round from Coombes street. The highlight of bonfire night was the treat of sitting in rows on the kerb along the bottom of Sandhurst road. With our own dish and spoon, we sat in eager anticipation and waited for our mams to come round and give all the kids a dollop of tatterash. Kids being kids would not hesitate expressing their preference for one or other tatterash much to the embarrassment of some of the neighbours. No one told the kids that meat was still on ration. When we all finished our tatterash, we let our fireworks off together so we could all share in the excitement that lasted all of ten minutes but we had a good time.

As soon as December arrived, we got a little more adventurous, and tried Carol singing. There were usually four or five of us, me, Ann, Terry, Freddy and Ray Pennell. We soon cottoned on that the best place to go was round Davenport Park where the posh houses were. Crossing Buxton road was never a danger, as there was no petrol; hence no traffic just the occasional tramcar. As we approached a likely looking house, there was always a scramble when we saw a red-lighted doorbell. One of us would call out 'red bell, red bell' and push each other out of the way to be first to press it. They were so dim and usually in a posh porch, they did not fall foul of the air raid warden. As we waited for the door to be answered, we jostled for position as none of us wanted to be at the front. Sometimes the householder would not answer to those horrible little urchins from Great Moor. Others were quite generous as none of us could carry a tune in a bucket; more often than not, the lady of the house would say to us, you sing a Christmas carol for us whilst I get you something. We were in too much of a state of expectation for our singing to justify whatever we were about to receive. Usually we got sixpence for our efforts made up of a farthing or two, a halfpenny and one or two pennies just to make it look more than it actually was. On one occasion, our singing was put to the test in a way we never ever thought of. As we waited for the lady to answer the door, we decided to sing 'Good King Wenceslas'. We had no idea what the words meant or how to sing it. The lady opened the door to five little urchins with red noses and frozen fingers. Trying to be polite we would say, "Please may we sing you a Christmas Carol?" We were gobsmacked as the woman "said yes, come in". There we were five scruffy little kids in a posh 'ouse on Davenport Park doing our best to sound angelic and as though we knew the words. # Good king Wensles last looked out on the feast of Stephen, as the snow lay round about, deep and crisp and eeeven. *BRIGHTLY* shone the moon that night, though the frost was crew---well, when a poor man came in sight, gathering winter few---ewe--wells. We sang few---ewe---ells, for effect! Away in a manger no 'crip' for a bed' was a favourite with the older ladies. The most memorable reward was for *not* singing. We knocked on the door of a posh 'ouse and waited in anticipation, when the lady answered the door, we said in our most polite little voices, please may we sing you a Christmas carol? The lady said not at the moment thank you, but wait a minute I'll get you something. A minute later she handed me a bar of chocolate, as I took it from her she said there is some money for you on the top. With the sweetest little voice ever, I said thank you and we all said 'Merry Christmas'. In the dark, I thought it was penny, how marvellous to discover it was a two bob bit, riches indeed. At Christmas we probably had the usual 'new jumpers', or a pair of 'newer' shoes from Mrs Miller's. A doll and skipping rope for Ann and maybe something like Draughts or a Ludo game for us all to share wrapped in lots of love and hope for the future. Grandmas and granddads did their best to make Christmas just that little bit more like Christmas for us, but all we really wanted was dad home for good.

Christmas 1945 must have been very disheartening for mam as she was hoping for a proper family Christmas with us all together. The best new year's present anyone could wish for was to learn that dad would be home in a few weeks' time at the end of January. I can remember dad being at home, but not the day of his homecoming, he wrote in his memoirs that we were all very excited.

He brought home some belated Christmas presents for us. Two pairs of pure white cotton socks for Ann and a German signal lamp for me.. It had two lights, a green one and a red one, we thought it was great. When we turned the thingamabob on the top, the lights would change colour, until the inevitable happened, the battery went flat. Being German, we had no way of charging it up again or finding another battery, but I played with it for ages using candles to light it up. Terry was very excited with his new tank aerial and could not wait to try it out on the following Saturday. Dad thought he had heard the last from the army, and had the shock of his life when a brown envelope dropped on the mat. The all too familiar markings "The war office" on the front was a shock indeed. Mam was almost in tears as dad opened it only to confirm there was no need to worry; it was a letter asking him to call in at the Armoury T.A. barracks on Greek Street with his army paybook to collect his service medals. He had forgotten all about his medals. He was entitled to three medals. The 1939/45 star: The France and Germany star: And a 39/45 war medal. Terry, Ann and me said those shiny medals were for the bravest dad in the whole world.

I took one to school to show my classmates but the teacher was either just being difficult or downright jealous; he took it off me saying I was disturbing the class and put it in his desk drawer saying I could have it back at the end of the week. When I asked for my medals back on Friday, the teacher claimed no knowledge of them. Such a thing would never happen today. I was too frightened to tell dad and kept quiet about what happened.

Remember when dad came home on leave and was able to celebrate V E day with all the family round the table, when Ann and I had to eat our tea stood twixt table and wall. One evening dad came home with four chairs, for a shillin'each from a Synagogue he was working on. I remember them well; they had a little box on the back for their Prayer Books and were very handy for hiding things in.

The winter of 1946 was the snowiest winter of the 20th century. Of course I don't remember it personally in any detail but I do remember lots of snowy winters as a little kid. When we got home from school, if the weather was not too cold, nor the snow to deep, Ann and I played together on a big red three-wheeler bike until mam called us in for our tea. Where the trike came from is anyone's guess. My guess is Mrs Miller. We had turns to peddle as one of us stood on the frame at the back. When we went out without on our bike, we loved to play with other kids on the field belonging to Tec' so long as the ground was not sodden with rain. We would be in a lot trouble with mam if we went playing in the wet grass in our school shoes. We could always play on the tarmac playground, and often did. The field stretched from Lake Street across to Mile End lane. The poor caretaker nicknamed 'appy arry' was plagued to distraction by the kids as he chased us round and round the bike sheds, but we meant no harm.

A NICE WARM BED

Soon after tea, mam and dad would get us all ready for bed then let us sit by the fire for a while as they listened to the wireless. Then it was off to the lavvy before we went up to bed so we did not need to go out in the cold or have to use the po during the night. I remember on extra cold nights mam would wrap the hot cast iron shelf from the oven in newspaper or a cotton sheet then place it in our bed for a few minutes to warm it up, then move it a bit further down to warm the lower part of the bed. As soon as mam called us, we ran up, jumped in, and snuggled up together. Then she would do the same for Terry. Sometimes we would all finish up in the same bed. On very cold nights dad would throw his army greatcoat over us all, only to deprive us of it when he went to work in the cold early morning. On very cold evenings, dad would light the fires up stairs to air the rooms out a bit. We were all very excited to watch as dad scooped up hot coals from the kitchen range onto the shovel then shout "stand clear" as he hurried up to the tiny fire places, throw the hot coals into the grate then throw some more coal on top. He would repeat this act of pyrotechnics to light the front room fire.

As the weather got a bit warmer, and the days longer we would play in what we called the swing park, or to give it its proper name, Great Moor Park. It was only round the corner from school by Norwood road and Ripley Avenue. As we got older, we went there straight from school. During the war, all the kids had to go home from school without any dilly-dallying in case there was an air raid. Now we ventured further afield. Quite often, with a bottle of water and a jam butty we walked along Woodsmoor lane, into Moorland road and down the steps by the railway station then along the gravel path, and follow a tiny stream and finish up at our very own secret place, a sort of overgrown sandy hollow at the far end of the golf course. We called it 'sand hills'. Sometimes we would make a slight detour down by the allotments and pinch a carrot to gnaw. Even though there was nothing in our secret place to climb on or in, we thought it was a great place to muck about and build dens. We went lots times during the school holidays. I recall a place called 'Happy Valley' off Bridge lane Bramhall. We only went if mam took us there. We would play in the stream that ran nearby, but I think it was a little too far to go very often.

On summer evenings, we searched the lawned areas round by the classroom windows of the Tec' because during hot weather, the teachers opened the classroom windows, resulting in bits of worn down blackboard chalk scattered all over the lawns. The teachers sometimes use the bits of chalk to throw at any misbehaving boys, who, in turn, threw at each other resulting in bits strewn over the lawns, much to our delight. The girls would draw squares for their particular games such as hopscotch and snakes and ladders. We boys would draw a goal area and touch line to play football. If only a few lads wanted a kick-about, or 'appy 'arry chased us off the playground we used a bald tennis ball to kick up and down the concrete passage (N° 1 passage) that ran at right angles between Lake Street and Alldis Street as I mentioned earlier. Another passage on the far side of

Alldis street, named by us as 'Stalton's Entry' after Mr Stalton the bread man who lived at number 18. It was no good for football as he often parked his bread van at the side of the end house. Plus the fact that it sloped quite a bit. One day, running down the back passage to join in a kick-about, I turned the corner, straight into the flight path of a tennis ball. It struck me smack square in my eye. I ran home to mam crying all the way. All kids make up rhymes to poke fun at people, places, and objects. We had one for Mr Stalton. "Don't eat Stalton's bread; it makes you shit like lead, no bloody wonder it makes you fart like thunder, don't eat Stalton's bread! It is a pity we didn't know at the time that his first name was Garrett; we could have made up even better rhymes. We had one for Mr Hampson, the Head Master at Southwood road school. 'Ampole 'Ampole stick it up your jumpole. Another one, Mrs Brown (teacher) went to town with her knickers upside down. An elderly lady on Coombes street we called 'mad Alice' did herself no favours by constantly shouting at us to clear off and play somewhere else. Being kids we would tease the poor woman until she came out of her front door and threw bits of dirt and small stones at us much to our delight. Back at school, every so often, we had a visit from the nit nurse, or dentist. Sometimes the doctor himself would call to give some children a Diphtheria immunisation. We heard stories that he would look at some of the older boy's willies.

THREE YEARS IS A LOT TO A LITTLE KID

I remember seeing Uncle Bert, dad's brother when he came round to our house to help dad to dismantle the air raid shelter so dad could make a kind of shed for his bike. The weather was quite warm, as I sat and watched him sawing a piece of wood; the beads of sweat all over his forehead and shoulders fascinated me. He lived in Sidcup with his wife Anna, but came to stay with grandma (his mam) for a few weeks as a sort a convalescence. I did not know at the time that he had had a very hard time in the Royal Navy as a boy sailor before the war and was very ill. A rheumatic heart left him in very poor health. I recall a time when grandma went in search of some ice cream for him one evening, as he was so hot. This, in the days long before supermarkets and late night opening. The only place she could think of was the Davenport cinema. The manager was very sympathetic and told her to call any time she needed any ice cream. The poor man died soon after. He was just 27 years old. Terry, being three years older than Ann and me did not want to play quite so much with the little kids, he preferred to play football with his newfound pals from his new big school Dialstone Lane Secondary Modern. He started there as part of the new intake for the spring term of 1945. Now we were growing up, our gang began to be a bit more adventurous particularly during the summer holidays. We thought it would be a good idea to go camping in our very own secret place. As I said, we ventured down there quite a number of times during the holidays but never actually camped out. The reason being, we did not have a tent, a must if we wanted to camp out. Nevertheless, we were quite happy to do without, as was our lot for most of us during our young lives. We would build a den of some kind, and pinch a few matches from home so we could light a fire. At the bottom of Alldis street was a kind of repair shop come garage, in the yard was a trailer with a tent shaped tarpaulin cover on it. The next day, with our bottles of water, dad's billycan and a few jam butties we set off on our big adventure. Ann by now was a real tomboy and joined us on most of our adventures. As usual, we walked along Woodsmoor lane, then down the steps by the station, along a path by the golf course, stopping off to 'borrow' a few spuds. When we got to our secret place, a tarpaulin was produced by one of the older lads and behold it was tent shaped, minus tent pegs, ropes and everything really. We hooked it over a tree branch, but it was not very good as it kept falling down, as we had no string we gave it up as a bad job. With spuds borrowed from one of the allotments, dad's billycan and a few bits and pieces like a penknife, a catapult, and a big stick to make us feel like real adventurers we were in our element. Of course, no one had a watch; I suppose we would go home when we were getting hungry. When we were settled in our secret place, we lit a fire to boil our spuds in dad's billycan. After about an hour of boiling over a fire that would not even boil an egg never mind potatoes, we decided that the time had come to try them. As we hacked at them with the penknife we all had a share of salt free hard-boiled potatoes, they were horrible. Even so, the sun was always shining and we had some great adventures. Terry's newfound hobby was fishing, but who introduced him to the delights of fishing I really do not know. I think it was the abundance of ex-Army Tank aerials that gave him the idea. Ann and me went with him to Poynton pool a few times, but we soon got fed up if he did not catch at least a small shark; we would have a wander round the ruins of a house at the top end of Towers road. It was overgrown with weeds and shrubs growing out of the top of the walls. It had scorch marks all over the walls and the windows and doors were gone. It must have burnt down at the beginning of the war and was waiting to be rebuilt. I could be wrong of course. As little kids, we made up all manner of more imaginative reasons for this "old house" as we called it. We pretended it was haunted and loved to play about in the ruins until Terry called us to go home. Ann and I can remember going fishing with Terry; we must have gone on a tram to the Rising Sun then walked the mile or so up Macclesfield road to Towers road. All through the summer, we did what kids had to do. With bikes beyond the budget of most families at that time, we made our own transport. We would scout around all over the place for those illusive pram wheels that were so necessary in the construction of a "dudder". Some kids call it a "bogey" or "trasher" (today, a go-cart) But we had the best name, dudder sounded tough, we could fasten a piece of cardboard or a strip of thin of wood to flick against the spokes making a great sound, and it really did go faster.

The bigger lads, if they were lucky enough to have a bike used the same go faster strips of card or wood. Throughout the summer, we were always looking for any planks of wood or sets of pram wheels for our next dudder in case ours got broken or pinched. We never had the luxury of proper brackets to fasten the wheel axle to the plank so a few bent over rusty nails had to suffice. The usual steering method was to place our feet on each side against the front axle. Some kids had two bits of string tied near the outer ends of the front axle; pull right to go right, simple. Freddy Pennell was a clever lad; he managed to fix a steering mechanism to his dudder complete with steering wheel. However, as usual, the brakes were our feet sliding along on the ground or against the wheels. Ann and I were happy in school at Southwood road though we did not see much of each other during the day. Dad and Uncle Charlie were managing to find more work; mam started work as a cleaner at Southwood road school when it reopened after the summer holidays. We all began to start a new life together. Ann and I started to attend the Congregational Church Sunday School at the bottom of Lake Street every Sunday afternoon. We were scrubbed and polished then packed off to school from about 2 o'clock until 4 o'clock so mam and dad could have a bit of a piece and quiet. It was quite some years later that the penny dropped why they wanted Sunday afternoon to themselves if you know what I mean. Terry would be off fishing somewhere. It seems odd to me but I must have attended more classes than Ann, because I received a book for good attendance. It was called Dick and his Donkey. It was light blue with a donkey and a little boy on the front cover, it was a children's story with a Christian message.

Sometimes mam and dad took us to Vernon Park, to attend a 'Drumhead Service' on Sunday afternoons. The name Drumhead at that time meant nothing to me but it sounded very exciting and brass band like. Drumhead referred to the arrangement of regimental flags draped on a number of drums arranged in a way to form a makeshift altar for use on the battlefield. It is still incorporated as part the services during armistice week and other military occasions. Lots of people would gather around the bandstand in Vernon Park, some of them in military uniform. The brass bands played, people sang, we ran about making a nuisance of ourselves and begging for an ice cream as kids do. We went quite a few times during the summer months and the Armistice Day service. Another special outing was the 'Dog Track' in Hazel Grove. It is now underneath a carpet shop. On nice summer evenings, me and Ann loved to collect as many discarded betting tickets as our little hands could hold. They were just like long tram tickets. We would take them to bed, count them, share them, then count them again. I was sent to the proper barbers on Buxton road one Saturday morning, I do not know why, but we were probably going to someone's wedding or something. As I sat waiting, the barber asked me to go into the back room. (That would never happen today) He said that he had a new boy learning how to cut hair and did I mind if he cut my hair for free. When I told mam, she was very pleased and gave me a penny for my honesty and said it looked very nice.

For the second time we had a 'Bonfire night.' I do not know why, or whose idea it was, but we kept all the bits of wood and stuff for the bonfire in our respective back yards until teatime on Saturday the 2nd of November because the 5th was on Tuesday. After 'appy 'arry had done his rounds and gone home, we all worked like little demons that would make any bin-man proud. Running back and forth with piles of rubbish we took it all to the middle of the tec' tarmac playground and lit it. We had the usual tatterash, made by some of our mams, only this time we all sat cross-legged in a big circle, a few more fireworks than last year and best of all, dad. The following morning we were up early in the hope we could rekindle the fire and muck about in the embers. When we saw what a mess the fire had made of the tarmac playground, we were horrified. There was a hole the size of our front room and about six inches deep where the heat of the fire had melted the tarmac. The surrounding area where the fire had spilled over was a real mess. We were frightened to death in case the police called at our school to find out who had caused the damage. We thought it best if we kept well away for a week or two. However, for some odd reason no one seemed to bother and we heard no more about it. The following year we went back to our usual plot of spare land on Sandhurst road where we could not do any damage. Speaking of fires, dad was cleaning out the ashes from under the grate one Sunday morning while mam was round at Cherrytree grandmas. As Carol looked on, dad scooped up some of the ashes to put in the dustbin. As he opened the back door to go to the bin, he heard such a scream. Carol now beginning to 'toddle' managed to cross the room, only to stumble against the bars of the grate slightly burning the top of her legs. Fortunately, the fire had cooled down somewhat as he was clearing it out. Fortunately, her injuries were only superficial scorch marks rather than actual tissue burns. Remember dad bringing home some army field dressings, well they came in very handy and no harm was done. In fact we had a funny moment when Carol was having her legs looked at, as dad lay her belly down on the table to see how she was getting on, she trumped out loud amid howls laughter.

NOTHING STAYS THE SAME

Once again, we went Christmas carol singing, but we were not quite as enthusiastic as we use to be. I think it was because we were a bit older and more embarrassed as we realized that we could not sing for toffee. We had to force ourselves to do just a little bit along Davenport Park road to get some money for Christmas. Money was the driving force behind our carol singing rather than any Christmas message. After the war, our Cherrytree grandma gave me Ann and Terry a thrupenny bit each week. We were supposed to save a penny or two if we could, but getting kids to save just a tiny part of their meagre allowance was nigh on impossible. Then she came up with a brilliant idea. She said, "If I save all these thrupenny bits and give them to you at Christmas, you would have all of your money in one big lump to by presents." As we waited in eager anticipation, the day came to receive our Christmas spends. Terry, Ann, and me, received the grand sum of half-a-crown each. I am not sure how many weeks spending money it represented, but I think we were short-changed somewhat as we managed to work out that it only took ten thrupenny bits to add up to half a crown. Now that we were old enough to appreciate the act of giving at Christmas, mam took us into Stockport to buy presents for grandmas and granddads. We walked around Woolworths with our half a crown tightly clutched in our tiny hand as we looked at tiepins and penny collar studs for granddads, and scented soap for our grandmas. If we were lucky, we might be able to hang on to a few coppers for ourselves. I am not sure if we got anything for mam and dad, but I remember making some cards and a calendar at school out pictures cut from magazines then we made a colourful pattern and pasted them on bits of card with flour paste. A tiny calendar stuck to the bottom edge looked great. When I think back, the only way we could make a bit of money was by our own efforts. Jam jars a penny, mineral bottles tuppence, run an errand and hope for a penny or two and that was it! Some cheeky kids tried to climb over the back gates of some shops to rescue a few empties then take them round the front again for the few extra coppers deposit money until the shopkeeper cottoned on and chased them off. Me Ann and Terry were little angels and would not do such a thing. However not all kids are honest all the time. I remember Ann and me saved some silver foil off dads tobacco wrapper and wrapped it round a ha'penny, then rub it in our hair to enhance the details of the coin to make it look like a two shillin' piece. We were so amazed at just how good it looked we went and bought some licorice with it. When we told mam what we had done, she made us go back to the shop and own up to our deception. We said to the shop lady we were very sorry, and that it was a mistake as we had been playing shop at home. The licorice sticks were taken off us until mam was sure we were sorry. The money for the licorice was worked off by running extra errands for mam and grandma', a sort of community service. The little sticks of licorice were separated in the box by using a layer of bay leaves between the rows so they would not stick together. We asked the shop lady if we could have some of the leaves but had no idea why we wanted them, I suppose it was because they were free. However, we soon put them to 'good' use. We found that if we rubbed a couple of the leaves between our hands it would soon resemble tobacco although it was a bit dry. Kids being kids just had to try to smoke it. If we managed to find some thin paper or even margarine paper that was close to cigarette paper and a few matches, we were in our element. We made quite a good likeness of a cigarette and the aroma was magic. From then on we would save and scrounge a few pennies so we could get more stocks of our secret 'mouldy lee' cigarette tobacco. We now know that smoking is bad for us, but I do not think we came to any harm with our 'mouldy lee' herbal cigarettes.

As you know, mam worked at Southwood road school, our school, and obviously had the same holidays as we did. When she finished at the end of term for Christmas, Mr Hampson asked mam asked if she would like the school's Christmas tree to take home for the children. Mam being mam literally dragged the seven or eight foot tree all the way home for us to enjoy over the Christmas holiday. Dad had to saw a three-foot length off it to get it through the front door to put it in the front room as there was no suitable corner in the back room, and besides we used the front room at Christmas as a special treat. All we had to do was decorate the tree and put up some of our homemade streamers, I am sure we all enjoyed the experience. 1946 was our first Christmas as a whole family, making it seven years since we had a proper peacetime Christmas. Ann and I were eight and a half years old; Terry would be eleven, pushing twelve. I am not sure what presents were available in at that time. But I can remember receiving two, yes two, diamond patterned sleeveless pullovers, one bright yellow, with grey and black diamonds. The other, grey with black/white diamonds. I thought they were wonderful never having had brand new jumpers in such abundance. We were soon into the new year and the weather was very cold, making the first three months of 1947 just about as bad as it gets. With millions of tons of vegetables frozen in the ground, four and a half million sheep perished, and cattle having a greater need to be under cover during the worst of the cold weather making the farmer's lot even worse. A shortage of coal, as stocks had not been fully replenished since the war prompting millions of people to buy electric fires to save their personal coal ration only to make things worse for the power stations. The winter of 1947 was long, and bitter cold for weeks on end. The snow was deep and fun for us to play in, but not all the time. We soon became fed-up with the cold and damp and having to go to school just the same. Mam and dad had to get to work too. Occasionally when the weather was particularly bad, mam would keep us off school for the day. Those days when we stayed home were like magic. The house seemed warmer, and with a special kind of atmosphere and the feeling of doing something we were not supposed to do made it even more exciting because mam said we could stay home. We would be as good as gold, and tried to help mam in the hope that we would be allowed to stay off again tomorrow, but it never worked. Dad being in the building trade was struggling to find any decent work, as very little house building was going on. Mam could not walk Ann and me to school, as she had to start at 7.30 am; too early to take us. We had to get ourselves ready most days. Sometimes dad would take us if he did not have any work. Terry would meet his pals on his way to Dialstone lane, so he was o.k. Buxton road froze solid because there was virtually no traffic as petrol was still on ration meaning fewer cars and Lorries to break up the ice, allowing it to build up until it was about four inches thick. Even the trams had difficulty getting up and down from Manchester to

Hazel Grove. They could just about get through as the council kept the tramlines clear. Moreover, the trams acted like bulldozers as they shaved the top layer of ice from the compacted roads. The binmen could not get around in the snow either, when they did try, the paths were so treacherous they could easily loose their footing on the icy cobblestones. I remember some binmen wrapping sacking or old socks round their feet in order to keep a grip on the icy footpaths. They did manage to empty a few bins from the schools. I remember clearly, bin day was a very noisy affair with the clatter of the heavy booted bin men. They let the lid crash to the ground then scoop up the bin and throw it on their upper arm and shoulder, often with rainwater running down their back from the rusty or damaged bin much to their annoyance because the lid had not been put on properly letting the rain or snow seep through. Then they had carry the bin down the garden path along the entry to the waiting cart with its three sliding up and over shutters on each side to stop the ash blowing all over the place. Ash and cinders made up about 90% of refuse for them to take away as there was virtually no wrapping paper or food scraps as everything was kept for further use, or put to good use feeding pets and quite often farm animals as well as keeping the home fires burning. One day when mam went out to get some coal, she stepped down the step and fell on her bottom into two feet of a snow and rolled over laughing. The green grocer used to call every week with his lorry (four-wheeled cart) piled up with the basic vegetables such as spuds carrots and cabbage. Fruit, a few apples, oranges, or lemons were hidden under a tarpaulin and kept for regular customers. Duke, the biggest Shire horse in the world was jet black with white 'feathers'. We all loved to stroke his nose being the only part we could reach. When too many of us tried to stroke him he would whinny and snort very loud, making us all step back with shrieks of laughter. If it had a poo, we would gather round the back and stand there fascinated, watching it perform, but if it had a wee, we had to jump well back before we got splashed. Another caller was the coal man. If mam was out, we had to either sit on the step or stand on a chair to watch through the window and count the number of sacks piled up by him to correspond with the number of sacks of coal to be paid for. If someone wanted five sacks of coal some unscrupulous coal men would hide an empty coal sack between the full sack they were carrying and their back. When they tipped the coal, with a bit of sleight of hand the empty sack would finish up on the pile of empty sacks making up the total delivered. Four bags on coal on the coal house floor looked very much the same as five bags if it was kicked about a bit. (Our coal man, Mr Bateson never short changed us) A householder could only store a maximum of 5 sacks at any one time (5 cwt costing 15-/7$^{1}/_{2d)}$ in case the inspectors called at random to check how much coal people had simply by weighing it. If you had more than you should, they would check when your last delivery was, and calculate if you had more than you should. If they thought you were trying to over stock with coal they would pay you for the excess then take it away. Fortunately, the authorities had more important things to deal with as we never saw anyone from the ministry of whatever. Besides, it was simple enough to hide a bit of coal under the stairs; another regular caller in the street was the knife man, sounds sinister doesn't it? As there was no such thing as stainless steel knives in those days unless you were posh, the knife man was a regular caller. He was a very tall man often wearing a long raincoat even when it was not raining. He sharpened knives or scissors on a contraption fixed to his bike. A grind stone mounted over the handle bars was driven by pedalling the back wheel with a long pulley that sent the grind stone whizzing round as the bike was supported on a stand lifting the back wheel off the ground. I seem to remember sixpence for a large carving knife and four pence for everything else. Mam did not use him very often, as she would sharpen our knife on the back stone step.

LOVELY WHITE SNOW, NOT REALLY

We, like all kids, loved to play in the snow, and make dangerous slides along the pavements much to the annoyance of passers-by. One day dad brought home a sledge for us to play with; it looked as though it had never been used for ages as the steel runners were quite rusty. It must have belonged to some posh kid who hardly ever used it. The real wooden seat was varnished and the rusting metal frame was red. It would have looked very smart when it was new. We soon got the runners clean by rubbing a piece of wet donkey stone along them for ages. When they were quite shiny we soon had it running down the Tec' playground and had lots of fun with it. From the minute we got home until teatime, we would play up and down the street and pester mam for something to cover our tiny frozen fingers. She went to Mrs Miller's down the street to see if she had anything for a few pennies that would keep us quiet for a while. If mam came back empty handed we were reduced to wearing old socks to keep our fingers just a little bit warm until they in turn got wet through. As winter prevented us playing out too much we began to learn to play 'tiddlywinks' and board games like 'Ludo' and 'Draughts' with Terry. Of course, the inevitable happened as with all children, we lost some of the draughts pieces and some tiddles or is it winks. Terry, ever the resourceful lad took mam's long sweeping brush and managed to saw off a few slices as if it were a cucumber, (whatever they were) making mam's long brush not so long, he said it was only a little bit shorter and mam was not very big so it would help her. The freshly cut draughts were a light wood colour that was o.k. if we needed white, but if we needed black, a rub with black lead or crayon would do the trick. However, our blackened fingers soon made the white ones black as well. Sometimes we used large buttons as markers but even buttons were in short supply and just as easy to lose. The loss of the dice was a bit more problematic but I suppose we got round it somehow, we just had to. After what must have been, a very long and difficult winter for everyone, the snow melted and the sun began to shine again. The ice was so thick and deeply frozen it took ages for it to thaw out completely. I remember the dirty icy water running down the gutters on Buxton road was so wide, we had to jump over it to get across the road. The granite cobles were very smooth and slippery even without the frost. A light shower was enough to make them like an ice rink.

The blossom, though late, began to appear and very welcome it must have been as spring began to spring. I remember my ninth birthday but not for the reason most nine year olds would expect to. Even though I played with the kids in Alldis street, I was a bit of a loner at school; I was often the little kid shivering in the corner of the playground. However, one day I plucked up the courage and asked some lads if I could play football with them. No, they said, you've got to be nine. I said I was nine as it was my birthday that day, so they let me join in. I cannot remember any birthday parties through my infant and junior days but we must have had some kind of party being twins. I remember going to a wedding once, I think it must have been Aunty Lena and Uncle Gordon's, but I could not be sure who's wedding it was. Terry would run a mile, or go fishing at the thought of getting dressed up for a soppy wedding, nevertheless, as you can see in some of the pictures of me Ann and Terry we were often in clothes that reflected the times we lived in.

ANOTHER TEN POUNDER

Summer brought better weather and a new edition to our family with the birth of our brother Anthony. Tuesday 15th of July 1947 was the day that made mam and dad's family complete. Me Ann and Terry were all at school on that day. Ann said Ray Pennell told her when he came back to school after dinner, "your mam has had a baby. Not believing him she kept it to herself, but as soon as the home time bell rang, she was off and ran all the way home to find a little brother in mam's arms. The midwife had gone by that time. As usual, Ann wanted to know where it came from and did daddy know. With her nursing and fussing about, she did not want to go to school for the rest of the week but of course she had to. We all played outdoors, but Ann just wanted to nurse her baby brother as often as she could. Anthony (Tony) weighed in at 10 lbs. The midwife called on mam a few times to see how she was getting on now that we had the benefit of a more generous National Health Scheme. *It is a pity that no photographs survive of Carol and Tony's infancy, so I have included a picture at the end of the book of Tony and Carol with farther Christmas. Circa 1953.*

After a while Ann was back being her usual tomboy self and wanting to play out more with the boys. By now, many boys began to realise that girls were different, as some girls would tuck their skirts into their knicker legs so they could skip better. One game the boys liked to play that did not involve too much running about of even skipping, was 'mother may we cross your golden water'. One of us, we tried to make sure it was a boy from our side of about six or seven would stand on one side of the street. The remainder on the opposite side would call out "mother may we cross your golden water" the one across the street would call out, not without a colour, the rest would shout, what colour, a colour would be called, if you were wearing that colour, you could cross. If you did not have the required colour, you had to run across without being tagged or given a Chinese burn. This was repeated several times until we ran out of obvious colours that could be seen. Boys being boys would think of a colour that the girl's knickers might be. They would call out pale green, pink, or white in the hope that at least one of the girls was willing to give the boys a treat by lifting their skirts very quickly to reveal the colour of her knickers, the boys would say they did not see them properly, but the girls were on to their tricks. We played knock and run as any kids do. Sapping for apples, searching for bits of wood, pram wheels, and still taking bottles back for a few coppers each.

PRESS BUTTON 'B'

In the early days of public telephone boxes, we discovered the sequence to make a 'phone call was as follows, put a penny in the slot; dial the number and wait for an answer. When the 'phone was answered, press button 'A' to be connected. If there was no answer, simply press button 'B' to get your penny back. Sometimes in frustration, the caller would forget to press button 'B' and leave the penny in the slot. As few people had private phones in those days, there were Telephone boxes on every other street corner or so it seemed. We would often nip in, press button 'B' in the hope of a penny dropping down into the cup then into our little grasping fingers.

We used to play knock and run quite often, I don't know why, as there was no money in it for us. One evening Ann and I decided to play knock and run by ourselves. After a couple of knocks and runs, we went a step too far. There was a shop on the main road in between Archer Street and Cherrytree lane; it had a very tempting red bell high up on the door frame. One of us pressed it then we ran as if the devil himself was after us. After we got about 100 yards down the road, we thought we were safe until two great hands grabbed us by the scruff of the neck. "*Come here you little buggers!*" We were frog-marched back to the shop, up the stairs into the living room and made to apologise to the woman of the house. We never rang *that* bell again. Someone in our gang found that if we pressed the back of a mature hawthorn leaf onto the back of our hands for a few minutes, the veins of the leaf would leave an imprint on our soft skin. Then if we gently rubbed a bit of dust from the gutter over the pattern then blow away the excess, our hands were marked with our very own secret sign. Even after our skin recovered its shape, the dirty mark was still clearly visible for quite some time. One day, dad brought home the rustiest bike you ever could imagine. It was a middle size bike for a ten to twelve year old. Granddad borrowed some oil from the mill for us to free up the chain and Terry and me soon set to and had the chain, and peddles turning in no time. Mam was not at all pleased when we bent spoon after spoon trying to get the tyres off to mend the punctures. Over the next few days, we spent every spare minute on it as we cleaned and painted it. The only colour we could find was some cream varnish paint left over after dad had painted the front room. The bike was intended for Terry, being bigger and older, but I can remember riding it from time to time as a reward for helping him to restore it. As I said, the only paint we could find was some that was left over from one of dad's decorating jobs.

NEW DÉCOR AND A POSH RADIOGRAM.

I remember quite clearly dad decorating our front room. He painted the ceiling and walls with some cream Walpamur Water Paint. When it was dry, he dipped a sponge in a saucer of the same paint with just a hint of green created by adding a tiny drop of undiluted dolly blue. Adding a little more 'dolly blue' to the mix of would make it a little darker and bluer. With the rinsed out sponge dipped in the new shade, he dabbed hither and thither between the previous dabs and very nice it looked too. With the ubiquitous three feet square of flowery varnish paper by the door, and cream varnish paint on the woodwork, mam was thrilled to bits. A new coconut matting looked a treat with the Rexene three-piece suite still looking good. A new polished real plywood radiogram adorned the corner of the front room by the middle door leading to the back room. It had a heavy steel turntable with a brown felt cover to place the records on and an equally heavy pick-up arm. There were two little Bakelite dishes, set into the top, one for new needles and one for the used needles. It had the CC41 "Civilian Clothing 1941" utility mark on the back. A mark to help standardise furniture and clothing quality. I am not sure what records they had, but remember finding some Victor Sylvester 78 rpm records in a cardboard box quite some years later and actually played some of them on my Dancette record player. Our new radiogram prompted Terry to start to listen to music and bits and pieces of comedy programs. However, Dick Barton special agent became a firm favourite with Terry. Dick Barton with his trusty friends Jock Anderson and Snowy White solved all sorts of crimes and escaped from dangerous situations and repeatedly saved the world from disaster. Terry encouraged me to listen to the wireless with him. We would settle down on the settee in the front room to make sure the radiogram had time to warm up so we could hear the theme tune; "The Devil's Gallop" It was the perfect tune being somewhere between a cowboy gallop, and the Flying Scott. I cannot remember any of their escapades, but it did help to open my ears to another world. Speaking of another world, we loved going to the pictures on Saturday afternoons. But first, we had some errands to do for mam. With a half-crown wrapped in a note, we were sent to Nelsons pork butchers on Heaviley every Saturday morning to get some pig's trotters and maybe the ham shank that mam had ordered and paid a deposit on during the week. Mam would make some pea soup and save some of the meat for dad's butties to take to work on Monday. Proper sliced ham was a rare treat. (Reserved for weddings and funerals I suspect)

When mam went to our regular ration book butcher on Buxton road, she had to be very selective in her rationed meat purchases. Things like ox tail, cows heart, or maybe a bit of brisket was the usual fare as meat was rationed by price. If you wanted some best steak, you could still only buy the monies worth. For instance, one lb of steak may cost 1/6, but two lbs of brisket would cost the same 1/6. Tripe and elder was a big favourite of mam's. The tripe was usually creamy white and the elder was yellow green both being part of a cow's udder lining. Sounds revolting, and it was. The elder was boiled slowly until tender, allowed to cool then sliced and eaten with bread and margarine. The tripe was simmered in half milk and half water with unions added. It looked and smelt equally revolting and none of us would go near it. Mam would relish the thought of eating it for tea or supper over two evenings. Sometimes she would go to U.C. P. United Cow Products in Stockport. Just to see if there was anything on offer that was not on ration. A rabbit for a pie or stew. There was a popular song at the time. # Run rabbit, run rabbit, run run run, don't give the farmer his fun fun fun, we'll get by without our rabbit pie, so run rabbit run rabbit run run run #. Cow's heart, was very good value for money as there was no bone or fat and it cooked and sliced very easily. Cow's tongue was something we never really liked, but we had to eat it or go without. Brawn was a part of the staple diet for a lot of people during the war as a cheap alternative to corned beef and other preserved meats for workers' butties. The treat we loved the best was a "savoury duck" it looked nothing like a duck; but it was a very savoury and spicy like a square meatball thingy. It is still available today. Occasionally mam brought home a chicken's claw, minus the chicken. When it dried out a little we would have great fun pulling the tendons to make its claws open and close. The most revolting meat on offer was a sheep's head. I can remember mam cleaning the snot out its nose and the blood from round its mouth and washing it under the cold tap, then boiling it for what seemed like hours. I don't know if anything was added other than a few spuds. I think we must have had our share but choose to forget it. The joke used to be "I'll leave the eyes in so it will see us through the week". Some chip shops sold tripe to earn a little extra as fish was in very short supply. A typical chippy would sell fish (when available) chips peas, or a bowl mix, for a shillin' bring you own bowl. Tripe is still a mystery to me.

Invalid 6ᵈ a lb.

Thick seam 7ᵈ a lb.

Elder 6ᵈ lb.

Slut 5ᵈ lb.

Trotters 7¹/₂ lb

Clean newspapers wanted.

'John Williams' grocery shop on the corner of Dysart Street was our ration book shop as for most of the area. Mrs Rogerson's shop was not big enough to cater for the wartime rationing. However, one thing that was not on ration was the good old stand by for many an ailment, Aspin, or 'Aspro' to give it its generic name. Many a time mam would send us to Mrs Rogerson's for a "tape of Aspros". It consisted of five Aspro tablets, pasted between the two strips of thin paper about five inches long and an inch wide with each of the five tablets in its own sealed pocket. Another cure-all was Beacham's cooling powders, the Calpol of the day in many ways. It was about half a teaspoon of powder folded in a square of paper. Stir it in a drop of warm water, and ha presto! A cure for everything. Fennings little healers was another good old standby for the "relief of coughs with colds and influenza". Doan's back and Kidney pills were a strange pill to take. It was for the relief of back pain and kidney infection. The strange phenomenon was the very green pee. Ann and I used to pinch one when mam was out, share it and wait for a while. Then we would pee in a jam jar to see the bright green pee.

MORE MISCHIEF AND A GREAT PLAYGROUND

Days and months blended into one another as we continued to play knock and run, sapping for apples, searching for wood and pram wheels, taking bottles back for a penny each, going to the pictures, playing cowboys and Indians round the boating lake at the back of the Blue Lagoon. We could have played pirates, were it not for the fact that all the rowing boats were under a tarpaulin and fastened together with a heavy chain throughout the war. One could have been forgiven if they thought the Germans were going to pinch them to cross the River Etherow one night. Even after the war they were chained up. One day thinking the caretaker could not count, we tried to pull one out of the water onto the bank so we could hide it and keep it as our very own pirate ship. He soon found out what we were up to and started to keep a close eye on the boats, 'and us'. We even tried to make our own pirate ship but the lack of even the basics to make anything proved too difficult even for scheming little kids like us. We were chased away from the swimming pool many a time during the war as it was kept full of water for emergencies with the mill and school being so close by. Speaking of water, Ann and I went to play on the edge of the golf course near Woodsmoor station after being told not to go anywhere near the wet field by the tec' or the swing park because the ground would be wet through after all the rain we have had over the past few days. We soon wished we had done as we were told. Ann tried to jump over a rather wide water filled bunker and promptly fell headlong into the cold dirty water. All the way home, we were expecting at least a telling off from mam and a good possibility of a smack bottom when dad gets home from work. However, luckily for us, the gutter at the far end of the passage was flooded more than usual and was the perfect answer to our dilemma. Mam was ready to give us a good telling off when she saw Ann in such a state. We said that Ann fell in the puddle at the bottom of the passage. That was the only time I can remember defying mam and getting away with it as we made up a very convincing tail of woe about Ann falling in the oversized puddle.

A TANNER FOR TARZAN

The Wellington pictures just up the road on the corner of Hillgate was the one we liked best for our Saturday treat. The program usually started with cartoons or a short film by Abbot and Costello, Laurel and Hardy, or Old mother Riley. Nevertheless, whatever was showing there was always a serial. Ming the merciless was a real baddy in "Flash Gordon conquers the universe". Always followed by a cowboy film, 'or cowy' as the main feature with the likes of Johnny Mack Brown, Hopalong Cassidy, Kit Carson, Roy Rodgers and Trigger. Roy Rodgers was a bit soppy for the boys, especially when he began to sing to a *girl*. All through the film, we loved to cheer the goodies "in white shirts and white hats" and boo the baddies "in black shirts and black hats" as they chased left to right across the screen then back again from right to left. The usherettes did not bother us too much, as most of them were not much older than we were and probably did the same. Mums and dads did not need to ask what film we saw, as all the boys, and quite often the girls too were making gun and galloping noises after a 'cowy', or jungle yelling noises, and mimicking Cheeta after a Tarzan film as they came out into the daylight. It was a great afternoon's fun for a few pennies. We found a way to make a very convincing horse galloping noise to make on our way home. We would slap our right hand on our right upper leg twice in quick succession, and then with the tiniest of a pause, we would give an in-between slap with our left hand on our left upper leg. As we all wore short trouser in those days the sound was very convincing. So it would be "slap slap....slap. Slap slap....slap Slap slap....slap" all the way home. Sometimes we got a present. Fruit was in very short supply even after the war, so an orange was a real treat especially as we could throw the peel at each other or bend it over and squeeze the juice at each other. If it went in our eyes, it would smart like anything. One treat I remember was a very crude set of water paints. A piece of cardboard about 8 inches by 4 inches had six or eight upturned milk bottle tops glued to face upwards and filled with some chalky pastel water paint with a little brush stuck through the cardboard. I was good at drawing as a kid and just wonder if that set of paints nudged me just a little. (When I was at Secondary School, one of my paintings I called "The tramp", was short listed for a children's exhibition at the War Memorial art gallery, but was not exhibited)

As you know, granddad was night watchman round at the cotton mill. We never went round the mill at any time during the war, as it could be a bit dangerous for little kids if there was an air raid warning. However, after the war when we were old enough realise the dangers of the mill's machinery we did have the occasional trip round with granddad when all the workers had gone home. I think the mill was a wool-combing mill, a process to make the raw wool ready for spinning into yarn. The lanolin in the wool gave off a distinctive fatty smell and made the wooden floors quite slippery. Ann and I loved the smell of that long gone 'cotton mill'. (Most of the original mill buildings and the cottages still survive.) We would run our fingers along some of the polished steel parts of the machinery to gather up the fine cotton fibres that had become stuck to the lightly lanolin oiled areas of the machines then squeeze it between our fingers to see the oil ouse out. The reservoir, from memory was about the size of a tennis court, thou' I suspect that we had never seen a tennis court at that time.

WHAT ARE HOLIDAYS MAM?

For most people, holidays were not something they gave much thought to, but a ride on a train was a wonder to behold. For a few coppers a week, and a contribution from the Congregational church. The Sunday school at the bottom of Lake Street would arrange a trip for the Sunday school pupils to Hayfield or Buxton so long as we could get there by train. About a dozen kids would set off mid-morning with some butties and pop, we had ours in dad's army respirator bag over my shoulder. It felt as though we were going a thousand miles away to the end of the world. When we arrived at our destination, usually a church hall or scout hut, if the weather was fine we would eat our butties outside and have a real picnic, and then we would play games in the fresh air, it was great fun. When the weather was not so nice, we played indoors at the Sunday school hall or scout hut. We would listen to a story from the bible and sing one or two children's hymns. The one I liked the best was, # All things bright and beautiful, all creatures great and small, all things wise and wonderful, the Lord God made them all. Each little flower that opens, each little bird that sings, He made their glowing colours, He made their tiny wings. #

Another favourite, # We plough the fields and scatter the good seed on the land; but it is fed and watered by Gods almighty hand: he sends the snow in winter, the warmth to swell the grain. The breezes and the sunshine, and soft refreshing rain. #. We would be back home just in time for tea, and have great fun telling mam and dad all about our day. We were soon off to bed and slept as sound as could be.

Ann and I were now responsible and old enough to go to our Portwood grandmas on our own. Most Sunday mornings, we caught the tram opposite the church on Buxton road. If we had to wait for the tram, we would knock on aunty Lena's door nearby at 250 Buxton road just to say hello. Of course, we did so in the hope we might get a penny as a treat. When mam got to know about this practice we were told to stop being so cheeky. We had to make sure that we caught the tram that was going to Reddish so we could get off at the bottom of Prince's street before the tram went up Lancashire hill. A short walk between Tiviot dale station and the river Mersey would take us past the massive Victorian railings on top of the stone wall towering what seemed like hundreds of feet above the river, we would press our faces against them to see if there was anything to see. Like a dead body, but there never was, just the occasional rat or two. We would walk through the back streets to the bottom of Marsland Street under the railway bridge to Grandma and granddads house. Thus avoiding the bombed out house just a few doors up Marsland Street. They were always pleased to see us and made such a fuss of us.

Granddad smoked a pipe using a very strong tobacco. The fumes hit us as soon as we went through the front door. We really loved the aromatic aroma wafting around the house. I have already described the terraces' in Marsland Street. However,

MILL COTTAGES A GREAT PLACE TO PLAY

OUR VERY OWN SECRET PLACE

Welcome
to the
MIDDLEWOOD
WAY

LIONS TIGERS BUTTERCUPS AND BLUEBELLS

the cosiness is impossible to convey to you but I will try. Imagine a house full of tangible warmth and love, then double it, and double it again. *(As I write this I can really feel and smell that little cosy home on Marsland Street)* Mam would give us tuppence each, for our tram fare being a penny each way. If Mrs Rogerson did not have any Oxo's, she gave us a penny for two Oxo cubes from the Herbalist on Great Portwood street. We had to make a detour from Tiviot dale up to the little shop but it was worth it. In cold weather, Grandma always had the kettle simmering by the fire. Before we could take our coats off grandma would be stirring boiling water into two little brown stoneware pots, *(Ramekins today)* over an Oxo in each. A piece of homemade bread made it extra special. Sometimes in the summer, if we had a penny to spare, we could have a penny drink from the same Herbalist shop. Two thick glass tumblers were produced from under the counter, a bright pink tablet about the size and taste of a dentures cleaner plinked into each glass. We waited as tepid water from the single tap ran cold, as each tumbler was held under the tap as the water poured over them to create a pink raspberry flavoured fizzy drink. Because the drink was in a glass tumbler, we had to drink it there and then. No wandering down the street then chucking the container in someone's garden. If we stayed at grandmas' for an early tea, we would have the luxury a soft-boiled egg each with little homemade bread soldiers to dip in the yoke. I remember asking grandma how she knew when they were just right to be lifted from the pan. She said put the eggs in plenty of cold water then bring to the boil very slowly, when they had been boiling for about two and a half minutes lift them out on a spoon, if the water on them evaporated right away they were done, if not leave them for a little while longer. 'They were always perfect.' I remember a kind of pewter dish about six inches in diameter. It was shaped like a squashed down pop bellied stove with a little handle on each side. An inner glass dish to hold the butter or margarine was placed into the dish held up by the rim round the glass. If the margarine was a bit hard, grandma poured warm water in the pewter dish then lower the inner glass dish down into the warm water

to keep the margarine soft enough to spread. I still had a fascination with the earwigs in the outside lavvy and had to pay a visit even if there was no need for me to go; I just wanted to see the earwigs scurrying about. I think by this time the steam driven lorry was no longer running, it was many years old and very noisy. "I wonder where it is now." On occasion, Ann and I were sent to the 'Electric shop' somewhere on Great Portwood street carrying between us an 'accumulator' to exchange for a fully charged up one. It was the only source of electricity in the house. The accumulator was for the wireless and lasted just a week. Most houses in areas like Portwood were without mains electricity and had to rely on such dangerous methods. As you can see in the picture, they were heavy portable lead acid battery in a thick glass housing with a wire carrying handle, a knob and two terminals on top. It was quite heavy so we carried it between us, can you imagine two little kiddies doing such a thing today.

When it was time for us to return home, we retraced our steps to the bottom of Lancashire hill to the tram stop. There were two pubs, next door to each other, the Tiviot Dale'; and the Railway. The Railway had very shiny painted stone windowsills at just at the right height for the tram users to sit on whilst waiting for the tram. The Railway pub has long since been demolished.

NAKED IN THE MIDDLE OF MERSEY SQUARE.

The words, the doctor is coming this morning struck fear into every one of us. I do not think we were told beforehand because some kids would 'wag off school' because more often than not, it meant some kind of needle. To my everlasting embarrassment, the doctor was checking some of the boy's genital development. (You may think I would be a bit too young at about 9 years old, but it really did happen.) We had no idea what it was all about. Boys only, lined up outside the assembly hall to wait in turn to see the doctor. We were all equally mystified by the boys' only examination. As I waited in line, I could see little of what was going on and as it turned out, I was glad I could not see. When my turn came the nurse said are you Kenneth Gibbons, yes miss. My height and weight were recorded; I was quite weedy for my age. I remember being called Belsen once, as I was so thin. I am sure it stopped as soon as people knew what it really meant. A listen to my chest and then the nurse said take your trousers down so the doctor can examine you. As I did not have any underpants on, and the fact that I was standing in front of a lady nurse, I was embarrassed beyond belief; The Doctor put his fingers at the side of my 'robin' as mam called it, and asked me to cough. Apparently, it was to assess the development of our genitals, but I felt as if I had been naked in the middle of Mersey square. The only comfort I could draw upon was the fact that I was not the only kid without underpants. We thought if a kid had underpants they were posh or a sissy. Some lads had underpants that were too long as they could be seen hanging about half in inch below their regular trousers. Some of the girls giggled with embarrassment when some of the braver boys told them about the doctor looking at their willies. Another trauma was a visit by the dentist, usually a woman, because many male dentists were still serving in the army. As usual, each class would line up inside the assembly hall or a classroom set aside for us and wait in turn. We could smell the Dettol before we got anywhere near the door for our very public oral examination. Afterwards we felt as if our mouths had been stretched much more than was needed for her have a good look round. Quite apart from the shortage of rubber or latex, cloves were rarely used; the dentist lady dipped her fingers in a bowl of milky white diluted Dettol after every child, then straight into the mouth of the next child. We could taste the Dettol for the rest of the day it was horrible. Most of us needed some kind of treatment, but I cannot recall too much about it. Ann said mam took her to a dentist at the bottom of Lancashire hill. She said she could remember the dentist placing a mask over her mouth and nose with the smell of a sweet sickly gas gently hissing from it. After a few minutes, she woke minus a number of teeth. She and mam were soon on their way home to a bowl of pobs (bread and milk) a sit on mam's knee, an Aspro, and early to bed. During the war, dentists had little time or inclination to offer treatment to families without the funds to 'go private'. Most people just had to grin and bear it. No pun intended. The wartime shortages included toothpaste, and toothbrushes, even if you had the means to buy them. Dental hygiene was sadly lacking in poorer households. Ours was no exception. Dad had a full set of false teeth by the time he was twenty-four. One home remedy to alleviate the agony of toothache would be for dad to roll a bit of his cigarette tobacco into a pea-sized ball and place it in or on the offending tooth, and then as if by magic, the pain would disappear in minutes. A trip to the dentist was not high on anyone's list of priorities; and often put off until deemed absolutely necessary. I can recall not only were we kids frightened to death, mam was too, and went only in a straitjacket and under general anaesthetic. (Just kidding) Terry, in later years used soot and salt to clean his teeth. One school visitor that was not in the least bit scary was the 'nit nurse'. As you may remember in the school log; the nurse inspected the children's heads quite often. It was great as we got a break from lessons for a while. The only down side was if you were found to have nits, the whole class got to know, and kids can be so cruel at times, as the child with nits was teased and called "nit head" and "bug head" for a while. We now know that nits are not too fussy if a head is clean or dirty. Ann and I would run lots of errands together; I remember going to the paper shop on Buxton road with a note from dad to buy half an ounce of 'GOLDEN VIRGINIA' cigarette tobacco, and a packet of RIZLA+ cigarette papers.

Every Friday mam would take me and Ann to Mrs Rogerson's for three 2ozs of dolly mixtures, wrapped in a paper cone made by twisting a square of paper round her tiny fingers. We would run home with them clutched tight to our chests to count them, pull them apart, swap them, squash them and see how long we could make them last. (More often than not, they had to last all week.) If one of us had more than the other, mam would have to share them out equally even if it meant cutting one in half. Sometimes she would eat the odd one herself just to teach us a lesson. Terry would count his and save them for his next fishing trip. Sometimes on Saturday morning, mam would take Ann and me to grandmas in Portwood. Before making our way back home, we were dragged round Woolworth's and British Home Stores. On a nice day, I remember being dragged up Bridge Street to Bennett's fishmongers to buy some fish or a rabbit for Sunday dinner. We could see the poor rabbits hanging upside down with dried blood round their mouths. Whale meat was offered for sale from time to time, but cannot remember if we ever had any. I suspect mam dare not tell us anyway. A visit to the market usually resulted in a visit to 'Sam's' stall for a few remnants to see what she could make for us or maybe a frock for herself. I remember on one occasion I went with mam to an office near the town hall. I think it was something to do with ration books or something. In front of the queue, a woman was being told she had to go to Hyde as she was in the wrong office. I could not help but overhear her being told to hide and wondered whom she had to hide from. I now know that the poor woman had to go to Hyde (in Tameside) but it did seem silly to me at the time. Once, on our way home on the tram I was dying for a poo. I told mam I would jump off the tram and run all the way home. As I ran up Lake Street holding my bottom I was on the verge of having a terrible accident but I made it. It's incredible how kids can remember such things.

The war was well behind us, and we were getting on in life. By now dad and uncle Charlie were becoming more established in their business as 'Gibbons bros'. So well in fact, he could afford the train fare to take us all to see his grandma and granddad in Sidcup Kent. You remember the one that sent him a shillin' postal order on his birthdays. The last time dad saw her was on the eve of his embarkation for France over three years ago. I can remember staying in someone's house and there were lots of people coming and going all the time. Terry discovered a little pond nearby; luckily, he took with him a small rod and a few bits and pieces and was as happy as Larry, as he sat there all day long in the summer warmth oblivious to the outside world and the cows watching him all day long. Ann and I had the use of two little bikes borrowed from a neighbour. We had a great time riding round the country lanes, now lost under the urban sprawl. It is a wonder we didn't get lost. I remember the weather was lovely and sunny all week, but of course, the weather is always great when you are a kid. It must have been a great time for mam and dad having nice walks round the country lanes with Carol and Tony in a borrowed pram. Some days, we all went on a picnic. Mam would watch Carol and Tony whilst dad took the rest of us paddling in a nearby stream just as we did with mam in Bramall Park. Dad said that one day as he lay on the grass, he looked up to the clear blue sky to see a skylark as a tiny dot whistling away. His mind went back to the days when that tiny dot could have been a Spitfire or a Hurricane or even a Messerschmitt 109. Dad's grandma looked after us in the evenings so mam and dad could go for a stroll down to the local pub for an hour.

To give you an idea how it was on that first idyllic holiday in the lovely warm Kent countryside in the summer of 1947 would be to liken it to the 'The darling buds of May' by H.E. Bates, later made into a T V series. We were only there for a week but we had a great time. We were growing as a family, with dad off to work, mam getting us all ready for school. Cherrytree grandma calling round to baby-sit Carol and Tony for an hour or two in the morning or afternoon so mam could go to work.

Tony was still a baby and Carol was not yet old enough for school but quite old enough in her own mind to help mam look after Tony. I expect she was just like Ann, when Carol was a little baby. As Carol, in turn wanted to look after her very new baby brother. Terry was in a different world with his new friends at Dial Stone School. He went fishing every weekend, but oddly enough always on his own. I have no idea how he got into fishing, maybe he just preferred his own company. Mam bought him a brown corduroy Windjammer to keep him warm during the coming winter. As you know, a Windjammer has an elasticated waistband and buttons (a zip today) down the front forming a very handy pouch to carry everything but the kitchen sink. Terry became quite an expert angler and usually caught Perch, Tench, or Bream only to throw them back. He often came home with wet feet, very tired and ravenously hungry. On some weekends, he persuaded dad to take him fishing so they could go a bit further afield as it meant a ride on the bus or even a train. On one of their trips, Terry was convinced that a particular river was just down this lane or that lane only to stop to peer over a parapet wall, and find they were looking at four rows of shinny railway lines. As Terry got a bit older and more independent, he would take off on his bike to Fog Brook in Offerton not very far from mam and dads first home. Poynton Pool and Wood Bank Park were equally popular with him. There was always the river Mersey and the Etherow to fall back for a change. I think there were different species of fish to be caught. With his fishing basket slung over his shoulder with a bottle of water and some Marmite butties, hooks, a tin of maggots, and reels, windjammer pockets full of frogs and snails and puppy dog's tails, his tank aerial fishing rod tied to his cross bar he was in his element. His tank aerial fishing rod did not come with any rod eyes to hold the line so he had to make his own. With help from dad's strong grip and a pair of pliers, he cut and bent some safety pins in such a way so he could fasten them to the rod with cotton bound tightly round and round, then smeared with a bit of glue or clear varnish on his finger. Often, a bent pin would have to do for a hook until he could afford to buy the proper hooks and a reel. He took heed of dad's philosophy of if you want something, go out and earn the money to buy it. He got himself a paper-round to help finance his new hobby. The only problem with it was the Sunday morning paper round. He would pester me to do his Sunday paper round along Woodsmoor and Moorland road so he could go fishing just that little bit sooner. How do I remember that there were 19 papers to deliver? It was worth it because I got a whole sixpence to myself. In school times, after tea he would sneak in the back of the Blue lagoon to try netting a few tiddlers from the boating lake.

By now bonfire night was becoming more of a challenge between rival gangs. Some kids from the Lowndes lane area just off Mile End lane would try to swipe some of our bonfire wood and stuff, but we soon put a stop to that by setting theirs on fire. We had our usual bonfire at the bottom of Sandhurst road. (not on the Tec' playground) With bigger and brighter fireworks, the older kids did some silly things. A banger in a bottle was stupid and dangerous, a rocket in a stelerized milk bottle could easily fall over and take someone's eye out, but it never happened. The tatterash was always wolfed down with alacrity and often an 'Oliver Twist' like voice saying can I have some more please. In between collecting Conkers, kicking piles of dried leaves about, scraping our knees, playing cowboys and Indians instead of fighting the Germans, the war seemed a long time ago and we were better off all round. After the inconvenience of going to school, we had our dens to play in and smoke our 'mouldy-lee'. The bay leaves for our 'mouldy lee' cigarettes were difficult to come by as a box of licorice sticks only used about eight or ten leaves and quite often the shop lady would throw them out once the box was empty so we could only try it now and again. We did not know it, but we had not a care in the world.

As the weather got colder, we played in front of the fire, me with a box of screws as make-believe soldiers. I would leapfrog them over and over in neat rows as if they were advancing on the enemy. Sometimes Terry and I would make a weird and wonderful contraption with what bits and pieces of the Meccano set dad found in a house he was renovating; it was in a dirty battered brown suitcase in the attic. Many bits were missing but we had fun washing it in the sink then finding that some bits were red and some were green. Then we tried to match the nuts with the bolts, it kept us occupied for hours. A lad at school, I think his name was Derick Jarvis asked me if I would like to go to his house at the bottom of the street to play with his Dinky cars, when I told mam she was pleased for me and said behave yourself. I thought he was dead posh because he had all these toy cars as well as real carpets. I think I only went two or three times, but I do remember it. Terry and I still listened to Dick Barton, Jock, and Snowy getting into all manner of scrapes. As soon as it finished, I would leave Terry to mess about with his fishing rods and bits and pieces on the kitchen table. If the weather was not too cold, we could always find someone play knock and run, or go Carol singing, just to earn a few pennies each so we could treat ourselves to a dead posh coffee in the Davenport café, we felt like millionaires. By now, Carol singing was a hit and miss affair, sometimes only two or three would want to go singing, making any semblance of a choir a non-starter as we sounded more like a cat's chorus. The expectation of presents and Father Christmas calling were always a time for giddiness. Ann was dancing on the kitchen table as she was putting up some streamers and stepped off as she was singing, "I'm dreaming of a white Christmas" pronounced "mismus" for comic effect. I am glad to say that she was not hurt. Me Ann and Terry were by now a bit too grown up for myth of father Christmas (not that I ever remember going to see him). Carol and Tony enjoyed the fantasy for a little while longer. It is a shame, but there are no photographs to be found of Carol or Tony when they were babies or infants. However I have placed a photo' at the end of the book showing them when they are a little older, as it seems a shame not to include them as they were a part of our lives more than we sometimes appreciate. Christmas gave us all something to look forward to as me Ann and Terry went with mam on our Christmas shopping spree to Woolworths. We were, in a way not too happy to spend our meagre savings, but had a lot of pleasure and a sneaking satisfaction as we went round to grandmas and granddads with yet more cuff links tie pin or collar studs, Cherrytree grandma would get bath crystals being the only one with a proper bath. We called on Portwood grandma with scented soap and maybe half an ounce of granddad's favourite pipe tobacco bought between the three of us. We went to Portwood grandmas' before Christmas because there would be few trams over the holidays.

Christmas gifts were still of a practical nature such as a new coat, shoes or jumper. Even three years after the end or the war, it was still a somewhat frugal affair for us after two hard winters. I remember Uncle Charlie, making me a yacht out of a piece of timber 4"x3"x two feet long. He had to hide it round at grandmas' whilst carving it into the shape of a ship's hull. The finished ship or yacht as I called it was painted dark brown with a lead weight nailed underneath as a keel, a piece of dowel as a mast, and a white cotton cloth try-angle for a sail. Dad must have saved some of Curly's tiny brass tacks when he was camp cobbler all those years ago, as Uncle Charlie tacked some round the edge of the deck, and then wrapped cotton round them to form a rail all the way around. It weighed a ton but it floated on the Blue lagoon boating lake and was great fun. I do not remember too many toys when we were little kids, not even the threadbare teddy on the back cover, but I never, even to this day, have any thoughts of being short of anything.

A NEW BEGINNIG

The New Year 1948 brought another new beginning. The boating lake at the Blue Lagoon was a real magnet to little kids like us. Being only about one and a half to two feet deep it was not particularly dangerous. I believe it had been there for well over a hundred years and gave rise to the name of Lake Street. There are stories that a length of chain and pieces of an iron frame were found thought to be part of a gibbet. I think it was called Black Lake many years ago. Every winter we threw stones on it to see how hard it was frozen. If we could not break it, we knew it would be safe to slide on. We threw bits of bread from grandma's just to watch the ducks sliding around, it was all very funny. The ducks became more and more adventurous. When they were hungry, they seemed to know grandma could not resist throwing something out for them. In fact, she would call upon one or two neighbours for some bread or scraps of vegetables, and was even kind enough boil up some greens and bread as a kind of stew from time to time.

Mam met a very soft-spoken Irish girl named Mary McGuire when they worked together at one of the myriad of mills in Portwood before mam got married. She was a lovely woman but very naïve and unworldly. For example when they first went to the pictures, mam wondered why she seemed so tall in the seat only to find that she did not know they were tip-up seats as she sat on the top edge until mam told her to fold it down. After mam got married, they lost touch. Then after the war, one Saturday, mam saw her in Stockport and struck up a renewed friendship. A friendship that must have been great for mam, giving her someone new to visit and to go shopping with around Stockport. She married a very nice, equally soft-spoken man by the name of Jim Sherain. We never knew them as aunty or uncle, just Mary McGuire and Jim Sherain. He was a gravedigger at Stockport Cemetery. As such, being in a reserved occupation he was exempt war service. Nevertheless, nobody could blame him; we still had to bury the dead. Mam and dad would call on them as they only lived on Dundonald Street in Heaviley. I remember mam and Margaret Cragg met up again after the war but it is all a bit vague. Now that Terry was around 14 he was quite capable looking after me Ann and Carol for an hour or so, mam and dad would take Tony with them in the pram. If dad and Jim fancied a pint in the Duke of York, Mam and Mary were quite happy to have a cup of tea and a natter. On some occasions, when mam and dad went to the pictures for the first house show. Terry had the chore of washing the pots. He would bribe Ann and me with the promise of a jam butty if we washed up for him, which we did willingly. One evening we were all playing up stairs jumping from mam and dad's bed head onto the mattress and having a great time, until one jump to many broke the bed in a way that it collapsed to the floor with a creaking, wood breaking sound. It was panic stations as Terry tried to nail together the very hard Mahogany base with a few bent nails and a tiny hammer without success. There was only one thing for it. We would have to confess what had happened. As if they would not notice. Terry ran all the way to Dundonald Street to tell mam and dad that the bed broke as we were just looking at it. Expecting a telling off, he got the surprise of his life, as they did not seem too bothered about it; in fact, we all had a good laugh. Mam and dad slept with the bed on the floor for a few nights. I think the posh new bed with an interior sprung mattress from Newday soon made things better.

As spring and the warmer weather approached, Ann and I with some of our gang would have great adventures playing around grandma's gardens, the Rhododendron bushes, and the Blue Lagoon boating lake. Tormenting 'appy arry' round the 'Tec' bike sheds. Knock and run, chasing each other round and round just for the sake of it, press button B in the hope of a penny, and just being kids while we could. Sometimes mam would take us picking black berries for Ann and mam to make blackberry and apple pie. Sometimes we went to Bramall Park to paddle in the brook until our legs were bright pink as we looked for Bullheads, Sticklebacks and Catfish in the icy cold water. In one of dad's letters, he says that mam was doing the right thing in letting us play out and get dirty. He would have loved to have been able to play about more when he was a kid and get dirty from time to time.

Throughout the summer, we went on great adventures down by the golf course to our secret place with our butties and bottle of water. The men from the council would cut the grass on the school playing field every two or three weeks much to our delight. Even though most of the grass cuttings were taken away, there was always enough left for us to play with. The boys would take great delight in stuffing handfuls down each other's necks including the girls and loved it when some of the girls began to fight back. Later in the year, we tormented each other particularly the girls by undoing the 'rosehip berries' to reveal the fibrous innards. We called them 'itchy backs' and chased the girls amid squeals of laughter, as we only needed to put just a tiny pinch of the fibres down their necks causing them to itch like mad.

SMACK BOTTOMS ALL ROUND.

Now that Ann and I were a bit bigger. On some Saturday mornings we didn't go to Nelsons butchers, instead, we had to take a bundle of laundry to a new washhouse opposite the Kings Arms on Andrew Square. We carried the laundry between us as we took the Reddish tram to the bottom of Lancashire hill, and then trundle over Union bridge round to the launderette. The laundry woman would help us to put the bundle of washing into the washer and then we gave her two shillin' for the wash and the special soap powder. I am not sure if we subconsciously wanted to get our money's worth, but we could not resist staying there for a few minutes to listen to the water rushing in and watch the magic the of such machines as our washing flopped around in the giant drum. When we felt satisfied the washer was actually washing, off we skipped round to grandmas for an hour or so, looking forward to a treat of an Oxo or a marmite and drippin' butty. After which time, we would collect the clean washing and take it home. Unfortunately, the laundry did not have drying facilities at that time and consequently, the laundry was still quite damp and weighed a lot more making our journey back home that bit more arduous. On one occasion as we trotted up Lake Street, we had the horrible realisation that we had left the laundry on the tram. To say panic set in would be an understatement. We were frightened to tell mam and pushed each other up to the back door. Mam knew something was wrong as soon as we set foot in the back door minus the washing. Before she could say anything, we were both in tears saying that we were sorry, and tried to explain what had happened. Truth was, we forgot it. When dad came home from County, we were expecting a smack bottom and a telling off, but he could see we were very sorry and said little. (County must have won) I suppose it was asking too much of two little kids. I am not sure what happened, I think dad went down to the tram depot and was lucky to find the bundle intact. Even though Rationing was coming to an end, lots of things were still in short supply. I cannot remember my first banana, but as we can see on the newsreels we were all very excited about them. You may remember reading in the school log, a collection of oranges was made to help someone in the Infirmary to get better. Thankfully, many items became more plentiful, such as a whole egg each, real milk instead of powdered milk, more jam and a few more toffees. Coal was still in short supply and everyone hoped for a warm summer and a mild winter to help build up our coal stocks. Portwood grandma was still able to gather some sweepings of coal as the waggons continued to spill some of their precious cargo of coal to help the people in Marsland Street.

As I told you earlier, dad was doing well in his plastering business with Uncle Charlie. So much so, he was able to take the whole family on our first proper holiday together. Remember mam and dad's favourite place during their courting days being Ainsdale near Southport. We had the treat of our lives when an enormous American car rolled up outside the front door one lovely sunny morning in the summer of 1948. We knew we were going on a proper holiday, but had no idea that we would be traveling in such style. Half the street came out to look at the big dark green American Buick. Being a little kid, I took quite an interest in such a magnificent car. Dad had booked it to take all of us to a little place called Crossens on the outskirts of Southport. I remember that great car ride as if it was yesterday as it glided along at fifty miles an hour. It was not a hire car, it belonged to someone dad knew from one of his business contacts. Quite a number of American cars were left over here after the war. He said he wanted to give us all a special treat, especially mam after the years of worry and doing without. When the driver dropped us off, mam and dad took our luggage into a large tin hut. We could not wait to run all round and explore the place. The accommodation was one of six former Nissen huts by the side of what I believe to be Crossens Recreational Park. Even though the hut was somewhat austere, it was very clean and divided into several areas using curtains. One end was divided into three bedrooms with appropriate beds and cupboards; the rest of the hut was a kitchen and dining area and the toilets were outside. The Gods must have been smiling on mam and dad, as the weather was warm and sunny all week. Can you imagine what it would have been like if the weather was cold and wet. Living in a Nissen hut, no transport and very little money. We may have had a wireless, but Television was something beyond our understanding at that time. Ann and I went to have a look round as soon as we arrived; through a little tatty gate in the fence, we found our very own 'swing park'. It had a row of four swings, a seesaw, and a roundabout. It was on the edge of a lovely big field to run about in all day long. Dad went to the local shop for a paper and his 'GOLDEN VIRGINIA' tobacco, and bought a nice new plastic football.(remember the letter) We played two-a-side football while mam sat with Carol and Tony on a nearby bench. We had one or two bus trips down to the beach, but the sea was so far out we could hardly see it but we were more than happy to play in the sand dunes. I remember finding some green lizards about five or six inches long in amongst the long sea grass on the dunes. They fascinated us; one lizard even bit its own tail off to escape our clutches. We took one to show mam, but she was not impressed. I think we went to Ainsdale beech itself as a sort of nostalgic trip back to their courting days of yesteryear. The week seemed to be the shortest ever as the time came for us to head back home. We were in tears as the big posh private car came to collect us. So ended our first proper holiday as a family. It was summer 1948.

Dad wanted to get cracking and earn more money and create a better standard of life for us all. Easier said than done. Our holiday seemed to be the catalyst that caused a certain amount of resentment between dad and uncle Charlie. I believe they had many disagreements about the work sharing and who did the driving. It seemed that dad was the one to get 'on the tools' whilst uncle Charlie wanted to act more like what he perceived to be a boss and swank about how well they were doing as he drove around in the car using precious petrol. Dad felt that things were not working out as well as he had hoped. After constant disagreements between dad and uncle Charlie, they agreed that as they could no longer work together, the best way to settle things was for each to go their separate ways. Cherrytree grandma and granddad were very upset that they could not get on together and make a go of things. At the toss of a coin, one would have the money in the bank and petty cash and one would have the vehicle, probably the tiny Austin seven van in the 'photo and half the jobs in hand, and some tools. Dad finished up with the money. Would you believe it was £90 give or take. The same amount as his Army gratuity he received three and a half years ago. Remember dad's philosophy, if you want something go out and earn it. I would add, "It's not how many times you get knocked down; it's the number of times you get up and start again that really separates the men from the boys.

ANOTHER NEW BEGINNING

After six years of wedded bliss, six years fighting for King and the wife and kids, demobbed in the depth of winter, no work, a spell in London trying to find a better future and the worst two winters for about a hundred years. Only to find disappointment in Charlie and his poor work ethic. Dad was just the man to get up and start all over again, again.

The rest of the summer, we played and mucked about as usual. I recall dad taking me to work with him from time to time during the summer holidays. One dinnertime I went to the chippy and got somewhat disorientated and took a wrong turn at a road junction. By the time I found my way back to the job, the chips were stone cold. My other duties were to pick any nails that were dropped and collect any bits of wood to take home for firewood. The worst job was to beat big clumps of horsehair on a mortarboard with two sticks about three feet long to get all the dirt, dust, and some kind of chalky lumps out of it ready to tease into thin strands to scatter into the plaster mix to help it to bind it all together. I can just imagine what social services would think of such a thing today. I remember having to drink strong tea out of dad's brew can lid, it was like Gorilla pea. (Though I have never tasted Gorilla pea) Nevertheless it did me no harm to drink some of dad's extra strong tea, and a lot of good with the fresh air and exercise, mam told me I looked as if I had put on quite a bit of weight during my time at work with dad. Some Saturdays if dad went to watch 'The County', and we went to the wellington pictures, but it was never quite the same. As autumn crept upon us we were up to our old pastimes collecting conkers, playing knock and run press button 'B'.

Some of the kids on reaching their eleventh birthday earlier in the year, sat their 'eleven plus' exams before the breakup of school for the summer holidays. Some went to Dialstone lane or the Tec' and made new friends as they began the second phase of their education. Our little gang began to break up during that autumn of 1948. Mam carried on cleaning; dad was getting to grips with his newfound motivation to do well and all seemed to be going along nicely. The clocks by now were back to the usual one hour on for summer and off again for winter. During the war, we had two hours on and two hours off. Bonfire night was upon us signalling the beginning of winter with the shorter days. We were now able to buy a few extra fireworks as many of the restrictions lifted. We had the usual scavenger forays for anything that was not tied down and could be burned. Once again we had our bonfire on the spare land at the top of Sandhurst road. For some reason we did not have any 'taterash' this time round, I think the camaraderie and the so called "wartime spirit" was not quite the same and suspect it never regained the same degree of meaning as it did during those very difficult times.

Christmas was not quite the same for Ann, me and Terry, as the focus of attention turned to Carol and Tony. Mam took them to Woollies' as she did with us but even those trips to woollies were never the same. I think if Carol or Tony were writing these last few pages you might read a very different story. Christmas presents were no longer of a strictly practical nature by now, as mam and dad could be just a little bit frivolous. We had things to play with rather than to wear. I probably had something like a toy car. Ann, a game or a doll, and Terry, well, guess what. Fishing tackle. We now felt that we were too grown up to look for a 'red bell' and pester people with our pathetic efforts at singing a Christmas Carol. However, we had a real treat just after Christmas when mam and dad took Terry,Ann and I to see a 'Pantomime' at the Davenport. Carol and Tony would be far too young to appreciate what it was all about and probably stayed round at Cherrytree grandmas'. I have no idea which pantomime we saw, but I think it was the one with a tree, a good fairy, a handsome prince and an evil baron. The winter weather was very cold as one would expect, but nowhere near as bad as the previous two winters.

In early 1949 with an ex-army Bedford 15 cwt truck similar to the ones he used during the war, complete with bullet holes and a contract to plaster the first phase of a new housing estate of Local Authority housing in Heaton Chapel, and ready to start again. We, as a family began to enjoy life a little more. Dad with his regular work, mam still cleaning at our school, thou' we never told anyone. We would have died of embarrassment. We still went to see grandma and granddad in Portwood about every other Saturday or Sunday. Sometimes we actually *paid* the sixpence to go in the Blue Lagoon and have a go on the rowing boats. We still played around at grandmas. At mill cottages, Granddad took us on little excursions round the mill Easter was a bit early that year at the end of March. Me and Ann continued to attend the Sunday school at the bottom of Lake Street. Terry was off fishing most Saturdays and Sundays. The National Insurance Scheme (N H S) was being rolled out evermore and everyone was looking forward to a better and brighter future.

I remember the 'eleven plus'. It was a test to ascertain junior school pupils best way forward, be it grammar school, a secondary modern or a technical school. The thinking behind this was that different abilities required different schooling. It may be a cliché, but the three 'R's, reading writing and arithmetic just about sums up our formal education to that date. Neither Ann me, or Terry passed our eleven plus. Homework was never an issue, as we were never set any homework. A good job too, as we had our own form of education as we preferred to play out, get dirty, discover things, do things, make things, improvise things, mend things, and make our own entertainment, and be children. After the test, the summer term came to an end and the holidays were upon us. I cannot remember any sad partings from Southwood Road Primary School or any rejoicing either. We must have had some kind of emotional feeling, but, as I have said before, it was a long time ago. Though I did not know or appreciate at the time, dad took me to work almost every day for something like six weeks. I fetched and carried as before but I did not get lost when I went to the chippy or with a 1/- wrapped up in a note for some Woodbines for one of dads workers. When dad left for work in the mornings, he would say "Good morning Mary" as he went through the door. I caused quite a laugh when I too called out "Good morning Mam".

During those six weeks, I increased my weight by about 10 lbs, and grew about one and a half inches taller. Even so, when I left School at fifteen I was still a skinny little kid at seven stone wet through and five feet six tall.

As the local council had to follow the guidelines on the separation of the sexes when children were nearing puberty, dad was very hopeful to rent one of the bigger four bedroomed houses he was working on. They had a proper bathroom, two toilets, and four bedrooms. The garden overlooked green fields complete with cows. Mam told us she was so excited to think how much more room we would all have. One teatime dad came through the back door at Alldis street, sat down as usual to take his boots off and then have a quick swill in the sink. As he did so he said, never mind Mary, as he put a brand new set of keys on the table, I can soon go up to the bathroom for a wash. As soon as mam realized what dad just said, she was overcome with tears of joy and could not wait to tell us all about it. We were all so excited. After the euphoria died down, we had second thoughts about actually leaving Alldis street and all the gang. Alldis street had been part of our lives for the past ten years, and remember we were only eleven. What we really wanted, would be to move the new house to Alldis street rather than leave all our pals and secret dens. No more playing round at mill cottages, no more grandma and granddad nearby, no sneaking round the blue lagoon to try out the frozen boating lake, or to throw bread for the ducks, no more happy valley, no more 'appy 'arry. But as I said, we all had to begin a new life and soon settled in at Dialstone Lane Secondary Modern School. Terry went to work for dad, me and Ann were part of the new intake at Dialstone school and the beginning of a new life in September 1949.

WHAT WAS SCHOOL LIKE DURING THE WAR?

The following 32 pages are transcripts of the hand-written Great Moor School Log. These pages cover the time from just before the outbreak of the war on 4th September 1939 until the end of hostilities in Europe on May 8th 1945.

 They have been reproduced and included in this book with the kind permission of Great Moor Council School.

Page 62

July 1939

13th The painters have been at work since Monday 10th July painting the outside of the school.

20th Exhibition of children's Handwork held in the Hall in the evening from 6.30 pm to 9,pm. Very well attended. Th Chairman and his wife, the Director and his wife, Alderman Shepherdson and several hundred parents and friends attended.

25th Gas mask drill taken throughout the school this morning.

27th Closed school this afternoon for the summer Holidays, Miss A Ridgway, ended her term as student teacher.

August

28th Re-opened school. 44 children admitted. Roll 434.

Present 392. Miss Jarrand, student teacher allocated to us.

Sept 4thScool to be closed all week owing to outbreak of war with Germany.

11th School closed for a further week. Teachers are taking First Aid and Gas lectures.

18th Re-opened school. Attendance 399. Roll 443. Children admitted 13. Infants are to attend only during morning session. Infants teachers employed making apparatus during the afternoon. Miss Garstang, student from Manchester University came for a fortnights school practice.

Page 63

Sept 19th

Children taken into cellars to-day to discover if all the children could be accommodated there in case of an air raid. We found they could.

20th Respirator drill taken to-day. Infants' teachers' teachers to take a section of junior classes each afternoon.

22nd Mr Lee and Mr Pullan H M I's called at school this morning. They took particulars of number on roll etc and of our anti- aircraft arrangements.

25th Children mustered in cellars this morning to show them their places.

26th Anti air-raid drill this morning. Children all assembled in the basement, juniors in 4 minutes, infants in 5 minutes

27th Anti air-raid drill again this morning. All children were in the basement in 4mins 5 secs.

Gas masks were then put on and worn for about half a minute.

29th Registers examined & found to be correct.

A small sub-committee together with the Technical Adviser from Manchester visited school this morning in connection with the construction of Air-raid shelters.

Page 65

Dec 8th

Attendance half-holiday this afternoon.

18th

Chairman visited school to inspect the air raid shelters .

Notified that Pauline Axon, age 5 1/2 yrs, class 9 was suffering from Diphtheria. All the material used by this child was burnt and the desk washed with disinfectant.

20th Nurse Smith visited school to examine the girls whose heads had been found dirty.

21st The Christmas concert was held in the Hall this afternoon.

22nd Registration checked & found correct. School closed for Christmas holidays.

1940

Jan 8th Re-opened school. Admissions 17 Roll 466 Present 377.

Alderman Patten called to view the air-raid shelter. Dr Rowell called with Dr…

and Dr …wished to view a modern school.

Miss Jarrand, student teacher, has been transferred to Adswood Cl' Sch' and Miss M C Jones has been transferred from Adswood to Great Moor.

An epidemic of mumps is responsible for the poor attendance.

Jan 15 th Miss Jones absent through illness.

Page 66

1940

Jan 15th Attendance still poor this morning 78.5 % owing to Mumps.

16th Miss Jones still absent.

17th Miss Jones returned to duty.

The fathers or brothers of children attending this school, who are in the army, navy or air force have now all received a Christmas present of a box of cigarettes and a large packet of chocolate subscribed for by teachers and scholars. Wool is being bought with the money in hand to knit mufflers, pullovers etc for members of the forces.

This week a collection is being held aid of our Stockport clog fund.

22nd Miss Ellis absent from duty with severe cold.

24th ~~Miss Elis returned to duty.~~ Mr Durose absent with cold on chest.

25th Miss Ellis returned to duty.

26th Mr Durose returned to duty. The weather this month has been very cold. Many children away with colds and mumps. Attendance has fallen as low as 62%

29th Attendance very poor to day owing to the severe snow storm. 42.9 %

Page 67

Jan 29th Miss Ellis absent again.

Feb 2nd Attendance for the week only 48%Conditions arctic.

Miss Ellis still absent with Influenza .

5th Miss Sheldon absent to day with cold. Attendance has improved to 71.2% no milk for the children all last week and none today.

6th Shrove Tuesday. School closed.

7th Miss Sheldon returned to duty.

8th Miss Ellis returned to duty.

9th Dental inspection this morning. Percentage attendance this week 71.

12th Miss Jackson absent this morning with cold and cough. Miss Barker absent this afternoon. She had received a telegram to say her brother had had a stroke and was not expected to recover.

13th Miss Barker returned to school this morning.

Dental inspection again this morning.

15th Alderman Patten visited school to see how the air raid shelters were progressing.

Miss Sheldon absent, Influenza.

19th Miss Jackson and Miss Sheldon still absent with influenza.

20th Mrs Grossman, supply teacher came this morning.

21st Mr Jones H.M.J. called this afternoon to see.....

Page 74

1940 Continued

June 28th Registers examined &found to be correct.

July 5th Miss Frost H.M.I. called this morning. She took particulars of children stating in our shelters etc and saw an air raid practice.

9th Nurse Smith called to examine the girls who had nits at the previous inspection.

11th Miss Plant who is entering Goldsmiths collage came for practice & obbs, today.

12th Attendance half-holiday today.

15th A collection of aluminium articles made today.

16th Nurse Smith called to examine girls seen on the 9th

19th Mr lee H.M.I. called this morning to congratulate Mr Ducrose on his appointment to the R W C S.

31st The chairman and director called at school this afternoon. They watched some of the items being taken in the hall as part of the 3 weeks' recreative and social activities instead of ordinary lessons during what would have been a holiday period but for the war.

August 1st Mr Lee H.M.I. and Miss Dewey H.M.I. visited school this afternoon and saw some of the social activities being carried on.

7th The director called at school this morning.

Page 75

1940 continued.

August 7th He discussed the choice of teacher to take the place of Ducrose.

15th Mr Lee H.M.I. called this afternoon to see Mr Ducrose.

16th Closed school this afternoon for summer holiday which is to be a fortnight this year. Attendance has been down this week because some parents who have been on holiday have kept their children from school.

September 2nd Reopened school. 33 children admitted. Roll 462 present 409

4th . Air raid warning this morning. Children assembled in shelters. Two warnings this afternoon. After the all clear for the second raid which was at 3.40 pm the children were taken to their classrooms and dismissed for the day.

5th Only 143 present at 9 am this morning owing to the extremely long air raid last night.

9th Alderman Patten visited school this pm and enquired about the air raid precautions.

12th Air raid alarm at 10 45 this morning.

16th Air raid alarm at 8.50 this morning. The few-

Page 76

-Children who had arrived at school went immediately into the school shelters.

17th Air raid alarm at 10 35 this morning. All clear about 11.20.

19th A cheque for £21-14/- was forwarded to the Mayor of Stockport for his fund to buy a Spitfire Aeroplane.

24th R   registration examined & found to be correct.

26th Exhibition of films by Cadbury Bros this morning in the Hall. 'A' life of a Gannet. 'B' West coast of Africa. 'C' Bourneville- work and recreation & Micky mouse. Closed school for Friday and Monday holiday.

October 1st Re-opened school. Miss Brown absent through illness.

2nd Miss brown still absent.

3rd Miss Brown returned to duty. A R P Practice assembly in cloakrooms and passages in case bombs fall near school before siren is sounded.

8th Air raid warning as we had assembled in the Hall at 9-0 am for the morning service. Children sent to shelters. All clear at 9.30 am. Air raid warning at 2.pm. All clear at 2.20 pm.

Page 77

1940 continued.

Oct' 11th The chairman of the Education Committee, Alderman Patten, and the Medical Officer of Health Dr Yule visited school and inspected the air raid shelters.

21st Enemy plane over this morning. Kept in shelters from 10.30 am until 12 am.

Another short alarm this afternoon. In the shelters about half an hour. Miss Cookson absent from duty with Lumbago.

23rd Miss Hindmarch absent from duty with cold.

24th Mrs Hoyle, supply teacher, commenced duties this morning. In the afternoon, we had a puppet show by Mr Bruno Tublin, an Austrian refugee from Vienna. Visitors present were the Chairman of the Education Committee, ALDERMAN Patten and Mrs Paten. The Director of Education, Mr Holgate, Alderman Shepherdson, Councillor Ellis, Mr Lee H.M.I. Miss Frost H.M.I.& Miss Wakefield H.M.I. The children were most interested in the performance.

28th Miss Cookson and Miss Hindmarch returned to duty. Miss Cowin absent with a sprained foot. Continued page 78

Page 78

Mrs Hoyle retained to take Miss Cowin's class.

OCT' 30th Short air raid alarm this afternoon.

Nov 1st Holiday

4th Holiday

5th Miss Cowin returns to duty.

8th Short air raid warning this morning.

Miss Hindmarch absent this morning with severe cold.

11th Armistice day. No service this year owing to the war. Flag flown half mast. Miss Hindmarch still absent.

15th Air raid alarm this afternoon lasting about half an hour.

18th Miss Hindmarch returned to duty.

25th Morning session begins at 9.30.am and ends 12. am. Afternoon session begins at 115pm and ends 3.15 infants and 3 30 juniors. This will continue until the end of February.

26th The head teacher absent this afternoon through illness.

28th The director visited school this morning and stayed till 10.45 am.

29th Beryl Powell a child in class 3 died this morning from diphtheria the staff and

Continued. On page 79.

Page 79

Children propose to show their sympathy by sending a wreath.

December 2nd Miss Barker absent owing to illness.

3rd Mrs Hoyle commenced duties as a supply teacher. The director of education visited school for a short time.

4th Short air raid warning 1.30 till 1. 45. The Director of education visited the school to arrange for the transfer of Mr (eligible) could be Jones and the consequent re' arrangement of classes.

5th Mr Jones transferred to Vernon Park school. Miss Barbara Ibbotson began duties here.

Miss Cook took over the class 1 boys.

5th Air raid warnings 1.10-1.40 All children used shelters 1 and 2. Register closed at 2 pm.

9th Miss Barker returned . Mrs Hoyle retained to assist during Medical Inspection.

10th Medical Inspection began

11th All day medical Inspection.

12th All day medical Inspection

Page 80

Dec 12th Air raid warning 2.45. -3.10. A number of parents who were here for the Medical Inspection were accommodated in the junior shelters.

13th Medical Inspection morning only.

16th Half day Medical Inspection. Air raid warning 2.10.-2.20.

17th Half day Medical Inspection Christmas concert in afternoon. This was unfortunately spoilt by air raid warning 2.15- 3.35.

18th Registration examined & found correct. Christmas concert continued from yesterday. Half day Medical Inspection.

19th The Director of education visited the school this morning. School closed for Christmas holidays.

1941

Jan 6th Re-opened school. Eight children admitted Headmaster returned to duty. Miss Cookson absent.

7th Miss Cookson returns to duty this morning.

Headmaster absent this afternoon owing to illness.

Page 87

1941

April 21st 13 children were admitted making a total 497 on the roll. This making 457 was present On the results of the Stockport Special Places examination 14 children have been awarded scholarships.

23rd Air raid alert 1.35-2.0 pm.

24th Mr A Sinclair who is a candidate for the position of H. M.I. IN Salford, visited the school this afternoon for observation of the method and apparatus in use in a junior school.

30th Alan Boak who has been a pupil at this school since 1934 has been awarded a Foundation Scholarship to the Manchester grammar school.

30th Three boys Alan Bleasby, Gordon Waterhouse and Barry Warrington have been awarded Singing Scholarships under the Kay Bequest.

30th 202 eggs and £3.16.6d in cash was sent to the Stockport Infirmary as the school contribution to the annual egg appeal.

May 1st The director of education visited the school this afternoon regarding the numbers of staff and the policy with regard to admissions.

Page 92

Sept' 16th The children went up to the main road at 10 o'clock this morning to see the tanks go by.

18th Miss Cookson absent 'bilious'

19th Miss Cookson returned to duty.

25th Register examined & found correct.

30th Dr Moir visited school in reference to the question of diphtheria immunisation.

Oct 7th Dr Kippen visited school for diphtheria immunisation. Twenty children were treated.

10th Mr Lee H.M.I. called at school this afternoon for a conversation with the Head.

14th Miss Cookson absent through illness

17th Miss Cookson returned to duty. Demonstrated gas rattle to whole school in the Hall.

28th Dr Kippen visited school to give the second diphtheria immunisation treatment.

30th Closed school for mid term holiday

Nov' 3rd Re-opened school. Miss Sheldon absent.

Page 95

Jan' 1942

15th 17 cwt 94 lbs waste paper to Cleansing Department. Dr Rowell visited school in connection with the supply of milk,

16th Address to children of the Bowater Paper mills. Mr A A Hughes finished his teaching practice.

19th Miss Cookson absent through illness.

20th Fall of snow last night reduced the attendance to-day. Miss cookson still absent.

26th £293-4-10d paid into school bank this month.

30th Miss Cookson absent this morning to visit the Infirmary. During the month 5 tons 8cwt. 16 lbs. of waste paper have been collected.

Feb 3 rd Inspector Williams visited school this afternoon to give a talk on Road Safety

5th Another 15 cwt waste paper for salvage.

8th Head teacher went out of school at 3.50p m to attend a meeting in the Town Hall re Warship week.

Page 96

Feb 9th Meeting at morning break to consider what further could be done for Warship week.

17th. Shrove Tuesday school closed.

20th Mr Lee H.M.I. called this afternoon. Yesterday the Cleansing Department collected

1 ton 18cwt 57lbs of waste paper and this morning 6cwt more.

23rd Warship week. Savings this morning.

24th Savings this morning.

25th "Stainless Stephen" comedian visited school this afternoon in connection with the salvage of paper. Alderman Patten was also present. It was also an open day for parents. Several hundred people visited school to see the exhibition of models of ships etc and to buy savings certificates. £1200 was taken during the day. There was also an exhibition of films in arts and crafts room on food production. Councillor Meredith and Mr Morgan, parks supervisor were present.

27th Close of sales for Warship Week. Receipts £2916-16/-

Page 98

1942.

MARCH 31ST Register examined & found to be correct.

April 1st Error in Reg 1 boys corrected. Closed school for Easter holiday.

13th Re-opened school with six children admitted Roll 458

15th Football match with banks lane Cl school on our ground. We lost 1-0.

16th Nurse Stanway examined the heads of 386 boys and girls. Sixteen had dirty heads.

21st Miss Early a student at Manchester Training Collage of domestic Economy attended this morning for general teaching practice. She will be here until 7th May '42

24th The B B C broadcast Service was taken this morning at the opening of school.

27th Dr Moir visited school to arrange for diphtheria immunisation.

May 1st Twenty three children received diphtheria immunisation treatment this morning. School windows cleaned this morning.

4th Workmen came to mow the lawns.

6th Respirator drill 1.45-2.0pm.

7th informed that Geoffrey Antrobus, Derek Seel con't 99Derek West of class 2 had won singing scholarships.

Continued page

Page 99

13th Nurse Stanway examined the children who had dirty heads at her last visit. Ten children still had dirty heads.

21st Empire Day Pageant held this afternoon in the Hall. There were about 100 visitors in addition to the children.

22nd Dr Moir came to school this morning to give the children who are having diphtheria immunisation treatment their second injection. Closed school for Whitsuntide Holiday.

June 2ND Re-opened school. Six children admitted.

3rd The Empire Day Pageant was given again at 7pm this evening. There were over 400 visitors. £2.17-6d was realised for the Red Cross. Miss Frost in school all day

4th the Siler cup for collecting most waste paper during Feb, March, April was again presented to the children this afternoon together with an illuminated certificate for

Continued page

Page 101

23rd Nurse Stanway came to examine the girl's heads Five are still not clear.

25th Workmen who came to mow the lawns and field taken away. Half of the field had not been mown. Error in Reg 4G made yesterday corrected.

29th Four cases of Scarlet Fever in class 7. Notified the Director and the School Medical Officer. Workmen came back to continue mowing the field.

30th Registers examined §found to be correct

July 1st Dr Powell and nurse Stanway examined all the infants but could find no further cases of scarlet fever.

8th The head teacher went to a meeting of head teachers with the director this afternoon at 2.o'clock to discuss the Summer Holiday arrangements under circular 1596.

10th Miss Cowin left school at 2.30 pm to attend a meeting to consider the school sports to be held during Wakes Week. Miss Sheldon left school at 4.50 pm to catch a train by the Directors, permission .....

Page 104

1942

September 3rd National day of prayers. The broadcast service was taken this morning from 11.amto 11.15 am.

7th Error in Reg 4B corrected.

11th Dr Rowell began the Medical Inspection. Was present morning only.

15th Dr Rowell continued the medical inspection this morning. Miss Ibbetson was ill this morning and had to go home at 11.0 am.

16th Dr Rowell continued the Medical Inspection all day. Miss Ibbetson still absent.

17th Error in register 5G corrected. Salvage collected today. The amount was 16cwt 105 lbs. The school has won the Silver cup presented to the school collecting most paper by the waste paper recovery Association for the third time in succession.

18th Miss Ibbetson returned to duty this morning. Dr Rowell continued the medical Inspection this morning only. Received the N.U.T. Cup won by the school at Sports held during Wakes Week.

22nd Dr Rowell in school this morning .

23rd Dr Rowell in school this afternoon.

Page 106

1942.

Oct'28th Miss Jones C T at the Infirmary till 11.o'clock. Leave of absence had been granted.

30th mid term holiday.

Nov 2nd " " "

4th Windows cleaned.

5th Received cheque for 11/2d from the English Sewing Cotton Co for cotton reels collected by the children. Mr Lee H.M.I. Miss Frost H.M.I. and Mr Charles H.M.I. called this afternoon.

6th Errors in Register 2B and 2G corrected.

10th Demonstration lecture in the Hall at 3.45.pm of music and movement, by Miss Holt to teachers attending the Froebel Lectures. Class 1 was the demonstration class. Junior children were dismissed at 4.50. pm so that the teachers could see the demonstration. Miss Frost H.M.I. was present.

11th Miss Jones C T. and Miss Lyon CT. absent today illness.

12th Miss Lyon C T returned to duty.

13th Attendance holiday this afternoon.

Page 109

1942

December 9th ....the Hall this afternoon. All the school was assembled to see the plays. A collection for the aid to China Fund realised £2 6.0d

17th Closed school for Christmas holiday at 3.30 pm.

1943

Jan 4th Re-opened school. Nine children admitted Roll 452 Present 354 There are many cases of whooping Cough and Chicken Pox amongst the infants. The dinner wagon for the school dinners was delivered during the school holidays.

7th Dr Moir visited school to give children the second injection against diphtherias.

12th £12 to the Blind fund subscribed by the children over the Christmas holiday.

14th Salvage Juniors 1 cwt 18 lbs Infants. 50 lbs Mr Holgate, Director, called just before noon. Class 1 raised £7 for the Aid to China fund by a "bring and Buy sale".

21st Salvage, Juniors 3cwt 10 lbs, Infants 100lbs. Miss Sheldon absent with a hurt toe.

22nd Miss Sheldon still absent.

Page 111

1943

Feb 11th Salvage. Juniors 5cwt 98lbs Infants 5cwt 65lbs

16th Richard Shore a pupil in class 7 died rather suddenly. He was an evacuee from Guernsey. The children subscribed for a wreath and there was £3 over which was given to Mrs Shore who is in poor circumstances.

18th Salvage ,. Juniors 3cwt 70 lbs. Infants 1cwt 3 lbs

22nd Miss Lyon still absent.

25th Salvage Juniors 4cwt 30lbs. Infants 1cwt 7lbs

March 4th Salvage Juniors 2cwt 45lbs Infants 1 cwt 7lbs. Miss Lyon C T. returned to duty. Miss Brown U.C.T. absent because of her brother's death in the Forces in Madagascar. Mrs Boyle, supply teacher retained to take Miss Browns class. Alan Michael Clark, 5 years, class 10 died today of diphtheria. A wreath is being sent to the funeral.

8th Miss Ellis, C T absent through death of her father Mrs Boyle, supply teacher retained.

9th Shrove Tuesday. School closed.

10th Mrs Boyle supply teacher absent with a cold.

11th Salvage Juniors 2cwt 46lbs. Infants 100lbs.

12th Mrs Boyle returned to duty.

Page 113

1943

April 1st Salvage. Juniors 7cwt 3 lbs Infants 2cwt 36lbs.

5th Miss Lyon C T absent this morning. Having Tonsil operation.

7th Mrs E V Raw, supply teacher, came this morning at 10.50 to take Miss Lyon's place.

12th twenty benches received this morning for school dinner use.

14th Three men came to mow the field.

15th Salvage. Infants 2cwt 26lbs Juniors 5cwt 57lbs.

16thChildren went on the field to play.

20th Miss Lyon C.T. returned to duty.

21st Received notice that 9 girls and 6 boys have been successful in the Free Place Examination. School closed for the Easter Holiday.

May 3rd Re-opened school. Eleven children admitted. Roll 464 present 436. Mr Yates called at school again re' school dinners.

10th Began the school dinners to-day. 118 children paid for dinners and there were 4 children on the free list.

Page 114

continued from page 113.

Six rails broken in the fence facing Westwood Rd by the cleaning department lorry.

14th The dinners have been good all week. The children have enjoyed them and nine more children have paid for next week's dinners. Error in Reg3 corrected for may 13thNo 7was present. Attendance holiday this afternoon.

17th "Wings for Victory" week. The Hall will be decorated in readiness for our open day on Wednesday.

19th Open day. Saving Certificates sold in the school to parents. A bring and by sale was also held which realised £20. The Mayor & Mayoress, Alderman Randles and Mrs Richmond were present. The Director of Education called later.

20th Alderman Paten called this morning.

21st Our "Wings for Victory" realised £4,676-18 -8d Free gift to Mayoress's effort £32-18-3d

25th Miss Sheldon absent all day. Nurse Stanway examined all the children. Seven children had dirty heads.

26th Miss Sheldon returned to duty today.

28th Class 1 attended the swimming baths this…..

Page 128

1944

July 26th Concert in the hall this afternoon by children of Class 1 to remainder of the school.

27th School closed for the summer holiday at 4pm.

August 28th Reopened school. 69 children were admitted. Of these 69 children, 27 were from the London area. There are now 36 evacuees London. The Roll is 494. A temporary caretaker. Mr Cotton was present this morning, the old caretaker having given in his notice to leave.

Miss Mary Hoyle attended for duty as Student Teacher. She is at present with the infant's class.

September 8th Half Holiday this afternoon for attendance.

11th Mr J Platt took over caretaker's duties this morning.

14th Mrs Purves absent all day, ear trouble. Miss Sheldon absent this afternoon, cold Mr Holgate called in the afternoon

15th Mrs Purves returned to duty Miss Sheldon absent all day.

18th Miss Sheldon returned to duty.

20th 100 children visited the road Safety film at the town Hall this afternoon.

Page 131

1944

December 13th Miss Sheldon, Mrs Purves absent to-day with leave of absence to visit Leigh St Council School Hyde.

14th Headmaster absent all day with leave of absence

18th Miss Sheldon & Mrs Purves visited north Reddish Infant School this morning.

20th Children assembled in the Hall for the Christmas concert this afternoon.

21st Register examined & found correct. Christmas parties in the classrooms this afternoon. Miss Sheldon terminated her duties here this afternoon. She takes up her post as Head Mistress at St Georges C.of E. School after the holidays. Miss Barker also finished her duties today. She is retiring. She would be aged 65years next April. A presentation of a handbag was made to Miss Barker this morning after the service. Miss Sheldon's present had not arrived so it will be presented to her at later date. School was closed for the Christmas holiday this afternoon.

Page 132

1945

Jan 8th Reopened school. Fifteen admitted. Roll 479. Mrs Vickers, C.T. and Miss Kitt, M.C.T. came to take the places of Miss Sheldon and Miss Barker.

9th Received notice this afternoon that Miss Kitt was being transferred to Hollywood Park Cl School temporarily.

10th Miss Sheldon C T absent this morning. Miss Pearson is taking class 5 while the head master takes class 3.

11th Miss Clarkson still absent. Miss Moss also absent today. Miss Barker, retired teacher came in school today to give a hand.

12th Miss Moss returned to duty but Miss Ibbetson C T is absent. Miss Barker again helped us out. Medical certificate received from Miss Clarkson.

15th Miss Clarkson still absent. Miss Ibbetson back again.

17th Nurse Smith called in school to see three children about spectacles.

18th Error in Reg 2 corrected. No 23 was present. Miss Clarkson C T returned to duty this afternoon.

22nd Dental Inspection by Miss Sellers all day.

23rd Dental inspection continued all day. Weather very cold and snowy. 112 children absent. Dental inspection finished.

Page 133

1945

Jan 25th Mrs Vickers, supply teacher, absent al day.

26th Mrs Vickers still absent.

29th Mrs Vickers returned to duty. School dinners did not arrive until 1.5 pm.School afternoon session began at 1.50 pm.

31st Mrs Barker C T absent through illness

Feb' 2nd The attendance for the week was only 63.9% due to the snow and cold and cases of Measles and Mumps Mrs Barker C T is still absent

5th Mrs Barker returned to duty

13th Shrove Tuesday, school closed all day.

18th Visited Stockport Theatre Royal for presentation of Salvage Cup. 100 children and two teachers and head teacher went from the school.

21st Mrs Purves left school at 3.15 pm to get the 3.30 pm bus to meet her husband who is coming on leave from Holland. She has been given nine days leave of absence.

22nd Captain Purves did not arrive home so Mrs Purves is at school again today.

23rd Mrs Purves absent today her husband now having reached home.

March 1st Mrs Purves been absent all week with leave of absence.

Page 135

1945

April 10th Miss Ibbertson C T absent with leave of absence. Miss Pearson, student teacher, absent this afternoon through illness.

13th President Roosevelt died last night at 10.30pm. The flag was flown at half-mast all day and a talk was given to the children after the morning service on President Roosevelt and his great friendship for this country.

16th Received word that this school has again won the Salvage cup and two guineas. The Mayor is to present the trophy on Wednesday morning 18 th Error in register 10 girls corrected. Error in register 7 boys corrected no 18 present.

18th 10 am. The Mayor and members of the Waste Paper Recovery Association visited school to present the Salvage cup and the first prize of two guineas. Mrs Hutton C T absent , leave of absence. Brian Mellor class 1 has won a foundation scholarship to Manchester Grammar school. Miss Ibbetson returned to duty.

20th School dinners taken out of doors today. Dinner were delivered half an hour late.

23rd Dinners were not delivered until 1.25 pm Began school at 2pm.

25th Mrs Sutton returned to duty.

Page 136

1945

May 2nd Mrs Purves absent through illness.

3rd Mrs Purves C T returned to duty.

8th Victory in Europe day. The Germans surrendered unconditionally.

A thanksgiving service held in school at 9.0 am this morning and then school was dismissed for the two days national holiday.

11th Attendance half-holiday this afternoon Workmen have been engaged mowing the field and lawns since 30th April.

15th Miss Ibbetson absent this morning due to mother's illness She returned to duty in the afternoon.

17th. The Director of Education and town clerk called at school this morning.

18th School closed this afternoon for Whitsuntide Holiday. Miss Jackson, Infant teacher left at 3.5 pm to catch a train.

29th Miss Clarkson absent through dental trouble. 30th Miss Clarkson returned to duty.

June 1st Keith Swindles, a boy in class 2 aged 10 years was killed whilst boarding a tramcar. He ran back to the pavement and was caught by a motor lorry.

Page 137

1945

June 4th Mrs Hutton C T absent today through illness

5th Mrs Hutton returned to duty

8th Attendance half holiday this afternoon.

13th David Whitehead, a scholar in class 6, fell on way home this afternoon. He was conveyed home by the headmaster.

15th Mrs Purves C T absent this afternoon with leave of absence.

28th Mrs Hutton C T absent all day with leave of absence. Nurse Smith examined the children's hair this afternoon. Twelve children had dirty heads.

29th Register examined round to be correct.

July 2nd Miss Sheldon C T absent all day through illness

4th Mrs Hutton C T absent all day through illness. Miss Ibbetson returned to duty this morning.

5th School closed all day it being used as a polling station for the General Election.

Mam and dads special song. Sing it to yourself as a waltz

One day when we were young, one wonderful morning in May,

you told me you love me, when we were young one day.

Sweet songs of spring were sung and music was never so gay.

You told me you love me, when we were young one day. #

STOCKPORT - Mk.Ia R7215 at Eastleigh in March 1941 has the name under a crest with the motto ANIMO ET FIDE. It was lost on 7 December 1942 when the ship in which it was being carried to Port Sudan was torpedoed by a U-boat. [HU3253]

These penny tickets were sold on Stockport's trams. It was just one of many Lord Mayor Initiatives to raise money for the war effort. In this case, £5.200 was raised towards the cost of a Spitfire.

The Stockport Spitfire fund, Cheshire donated £5,200 in October 1940 for Mk. Ia R7215, which carried only the Stockport coat of arms on its cowling with the motto *Animo et fide* (By courage and faith). The aircraft was taken on charge at No. 8 MU Little Rissington on 18 March 1941, being allocated on 9 July to No132 (City of Bombay) A squadron just re-forming at Peterhead and coded FF-E. On 10 August, the aircraft ran off the runway and tipped on its nose without injury to Flt Lt G S R Haywood, repairs being carried out on site. On 11 September the undercarriage collapsed after the aircraft swung off the runway into soft ground. Sgt A.G.Russell was unhurt and the category Ac damage was repaired on site by October 11. On 3 November, the aircraft was sent to No. 52 O T U at Aston Down, being Category B damaged in a flying accident on 25 April 1942, collected by No 50 MU Faygate and taken to No1 Civilian Repair Unit at Cowley on 4 May. Awaiting collection on 27 June, R7215 was flown to No 9 MU Cosford on 30 June, and transferred to No 215 Mu Dumfries on 25 September to be shipped aboard SS *Peter Mearsk* bound for port Sudan on 8 November. However, the ship was torpedoed by U-158 on 7 December 1942 west of the Azores with the loss of all 67 lives.

Even though it lies in a watery grave the Stockport spitfire helped to train many pilots. O T U means Officer Training Unit.

DECEMBER 1940

PORTWOOD. Night raid.
Combined H.E. and Oil Bomb.

This bomb on Marsland street was far too close for comfort for grandma and granddad. (The snowy look on the photograph really is snow.) Mam said they could stay with us, but granddad said, "I would not budge for the Keizer, and I am not moving for bloody Hitler either." As I said, a real old contemptible.

Early in the 1950ˢ Carol and Tony had the treat of their young lives with a visit to see 'Father Christmas' at Woolworths. I remember Carol saying that the fairy had a dirty frock. I have included this picture simply because there are few images of either of them.

As I said near the beginning of this book, a Harry Jenkins played for "The County" sometime in 1946. Below is an extract from the County archives. He was in the R A F stationed at Woodford. At the end of the war, he married mam's sister Ruth and moved to south Wales soon after.

The image here is of the crowds jostling to get near the tank. It could have been one of those passing along Buxton road as mentioned in the school log Sept 16th 1941. It was part of a war weapons week. The Mayor is accompanied by council dignitaries as he addresses the crowd of onlookers. The Tank is thought to be a "Matilda" the same tanks we waved at as they roared along the main road on September 16 1941 as you can see in the reference of teacher's daily log page 220.

THE TANKS COME TO STOCKPORT.
To Stimulate The National Savings Campaign.

Stockport Express Photo.

THE MAYOR—accompanied by Alderman Bowler and Councillor Randles—addressing the crowd from the top of a Covenanter behind the Town Hall. Pressure upon the people of Stock- | The "Matilda" was the type of tank

Manchester League

Stockport County 3 (Beamsley, Stallard, Lewis.)

Bury 0.

County: Daniels, Stafford Jenkins, Stones, Robinson, Swindells, Ken Shawcross, Postings, Beamsley, Jack Stallard, Lewis.

FINALLY FOLKS

As dad was by now well established with his own plastering firm, one summer evening he and mam were reminiscing about the time when dad and Curly were in France and Germany. Why don't you try to get in touch with him mam said? This came as quite a surprise as dad had put that time of his life well and truly behind him. After a little thought, he wrote to Crown Wallpapers in Darwen to see if they could help him trace Mrs Tomlinson as she used to work there during the war. He had the shock of his life when a letter dropped on the mat with a Darwen postmark on it. After a few letters mam and dad went to visit them in Darwen and rekindled their friendship. Ann and I went with mam and dad on a number of occasions and agreed that Curly really was the best friend one could have had in times of war. He and dad remained friends forever.

I would like to end by saying that after all is said and done, we did ok.

Kenneth Gibbons.

Lightning Source UK Ltd.
Milton Keynes UK
UKOW07f1217131115

262643UK00002B/8/P

9 781481 769686